Marx, Engels, and Marxisms

The Marx renaissance is underway on a global scale. Wherever the critique of capitalism re-emerges, there is an intellectual and political demand for new, critical engagements with Marxism. The peer-reviewed series Marx, Engels and Marxisms (edited by Marcello Musto & Terrell Carver, with Babak Amini, Francesca Antonini, Paula Rauhala & Kohei Saito as Assistant Editors) publishes monographs, edited volumes, critical editions, reprints of old texts, as well as translations of books already published in other languages. Our volumes come from a wide range of political perspectives, subject matters, academic disciplines and geographical areas, producing an eclectic and informative collection that appeals to a diverse and international audience. Our main areas of focus include: the oeuvre of Marx and Engels, Marxist authors and traditions of the 19th and 20th centuries, labour and social movements, Marxist analyses of contemporary issues, and reception of Marxism in the world.

More information about this series at
http://www.palgrave.com/gp/series/14812

James Steinhoff

Automation and Autonomy

Labour, Capital and Machines in the Artificial Intelligence Industry

palgrave
macmillan

James Steinhoff
University of Toronto
Toronto, Ontario, Canada

ISSN 2524-7123 ISSN 2524-7131 (electronic)
Marx, Engels, and Marxisms
ISBN 978-3-030-71688-2 ISBN 978-3-030-71689-9 (eBook)
https://doi.org/10.1007/978-3-030-71689-9

This Palgrave Macmillan imprint is published by the registered company Springer Nature Switzerland AG
The registered company address is: Gewerbestrasse 11, 6330 Cham, Switzerland

A.M.S.G.

Series Editors' Foreword

Titles Published

1. Terrell Carver & Daniel Blank, *A Political History of the Editions of Marx and Engels's "German Ideology" Manuscripts*, 2014.
2. Terrell Carver & Daniel Blank, *Marx and Engels's "German Ideology" Manuscripts: Presentation and Analysis of the "Feuerbach chapter,"* 2014.
3. Alfonso Maurizio Iacono, *The History and Theory of Fetishism*, 2015.
4. Paresh Chattopadhyay, *Marx's Associated Mode of Production: A Critique of Marxism*, 2016.
5. Domenico Losurdo, *Class Struggle: A Political and Philosophical History*, 2016.
6. Frederick Harry Pitts, *Critiquing Capitalism Today: New Ways to Read Marx*, 2017.
7. Ranabir Samaddar, *Karl Marx and the Postcolonial Age*, 2017.
8. George Comninel, *Alienation and Emancipation in the Work of Karl Marx*, 2018.
9. Jean-Numa Ducange & Razmig Keucheyan (Eds.), *The End of the Democratic State: Nicos Poulantzas, a Marxism for the 21st Century*, 2018.
10. Robert X. Ware, *Marx on Emancipation and Socialist Goals: Retrieving Marx for the Future*, 2018.

11. Xavier LaFrance & Charles Post (Eds.), *Case Studies in the Origins of Capitalism*, 2018.
12. John Gregson, *Marxism, Ethics, and Politics: The Work of Alasdair MacIntyre*, 2018.
13. Vladimir Puzone & Luis Felipe Miguel (Eds.), *The Brazilian Left in the 21st Century: Conflict and Conciliation in Peripheral Capitalism*, 2019.
14. James Muldoon & Gaard Kets (Eds.), *The German Revolution and Political Theory*, 2019.
15. Michael Brie, *Rediscovering Lenin: Dialectics of Revolution and Metaphysics of Domination*, 2019.
16. August H. Nimtz, *Marxism versus Liberalism: Comparative Real-Time Political Analysis*, 2019.
17. Gustavo Moura de Cavalcanti Mello and Mauricio de Souza Sabadini (Eds.), *Financial Speculation and Fictitious Profits: A Marxist Analysis*, 2019.
18. Shaibal Gupta, Marcello Musto & Babak Amini (Eds), *Karl Marx's Life, Ideas, and Influences: A Critical Examination on the Bicentenary*, 2019.
19. Igor Shoikhedbrod, *Revisiting Marx's Critique of Liberalism: Rethinking Justice, Legality, and Rights*, 2019.
20. Juan Pablo Rodríguez, *Resisting Neoliberal Capitalism in Chile: The Possibility of Social Critique*, 2019.
21. Kaan Kangal, *Friedrich Engels and the Dialectics of Nature*, 2020.
22. Victor Wallis, *Socialist Practice: Histories and Theories*, 2020.
23. Alfonso Maurizio Iacono, *The Bourgeois and the Savage: A Marxian Critique of the Image of the Isolated Individual in Defoe, Turgot and Smith*, 2020.
24. Terrell Carver, *Engels before Marx*, 2020.
25. Jean-Numa Ducange, *Jules Guesde: The Birth of Socialism and Marxism in France*, 2020.
26. Antonio Oliva, Ivan Novara & Angel Oliva (Eds.), *Marx and Contemporary Critical Theory: The Philosophy of Real Abstraction*.
27. Francesco Biagi, *Henri Lefebvre's Critical Theory of Space*.
28. Stefano Petrucciani, *The Ideas of Karl Marx: A Critical Introduction*.
29. Terrell Carver, *The Life and Thought of Friedrich Engels, 30th Anniversary Edition*.

30. Giuseppe Vacca, *Alternative Modernities: Antonio Gramsci's Twentieth Century.*
31. Kevin B. Anderson, Kieran Durkin & Heather Brown (Eds.), *Raya Dunayevskaya's Intersectional Marxism: Race, Gender, and the Dialectics of Liberation.*
32. Marco Di Maggio, *The Rise and Fall of Communist Parties in France and Italy.*
33. Ryuji Sasaki, *A New Introduction to Karl Marx: New Materialism, Critique of Political Economy, and the Concept of Metabolism.*
34. Kohei Saito (Ed.), *Reexamining Engels's Legacy in the 21st Century.*
35. Paresh Chattopadhyay, *Socialism in Marx's Capital: Towards a De-alienated World.*
36. Marcello Musto, *Karl Marx's Writings on Alienation.*
37. Michael Brie & Jörn Schütrumpf, *Rosa Luxemburg: A Revolutionary Marxist at the Limits of Marxism.*

Titles Forthcoming

Miguel Vedda, *Siegfried Kracauer, or, The Allegories of Improvisations*

Gianfranco Ragona & Monica Quirico, *Frontier Socialism: Self-organisation and Anti-capitalism*

Vesa Oittinen, *Marx's Russian Moment*

Kolja Lindner, *Marx, Marxism and the Question of Eurocentrism*

Jean-Numa Ducange & Elisa Marcobelli (Eds.), *Selected Writings of Jean Jaures: On Socialism, Pacifism and Marxism*

Adriana Petra, *Intellectuals and Communist Culture: Itineraries, Problems and Debates in Post-war Argentina*

George C. Comninel, *The Feudal Foundations of Modern Europe*

James Steinhoff, *Automation and Autonomy: Labour, Capital and Machines in the Artificial Intelligence Industry*

Spencer A. Leonard, *Marx, the India Question, and the Crisis of Cosmopolitanism*

Joe Collins, *Applying Marx's Capital to the 21st century*

Levy del Aguila Marchena, *Communism, Political Power and Personal Freedom in Marx*

Jeong Seongjin, *Korean Capitalism in the 21st Century: Marxist Analysis and Alternatives*

Marcello Mustè, *Marxism and Philosophy of Praxis: An Italian Perspective from Labriola to Gramsci*

Satoshi Matsui, *Normative Theories of Liberalism and Socialism: Marxist Analysis of Values*

Shannon Brincat, *Dialectical Dialogues in Contemporary World Politics: A Meeting of Traditions in Global Comparative Philosophy*

Stefano Petrucciani, *Theodor W. Adorno's Philosophy, Society, and Aesthetics*

Francesca Antonini, *Reassessing Marx's Eighteenth Brumaire: Dictatorship, State, and Revolution*

Thomas Kemple, *Capital after Classical Sociology: The Faustian Lives of Social Theory*

Tsuyoshi Yuki, *Socialism, Markets and the Critique of Money: The Theory of "Labour Note"*

V Geetha, *Bhimrao Ramji Ambedkar and the Question of Socialism in India*

Xavier Vigna, *A Political History of Factories in France: The Workers' Insubordination of 1968*

Attila Melegh, *Anti-Migrant Populism in Eastern Europe and Hungary: A Marxist Analysis*

Marie-Cecile Bouju, *A Political History of the Publishing Houses of the French Communist Party*

Gustavo Moura de Cavalcanti Mello & Henrique Pereira Braga (Eds.), *Wealth and Poverty in Contemporary Brazilian Capitalism*

Peter McMylor, Graeme Kirkpatrick & Simin Fadaee (Eds.), *Marxism, Religion, and Emancipatory Politics*

Mauro Buccheri, *Radical Humanism for the Left: The Quest for Meaning in Late Capitalism*

Rémy Herrera, *Confronting Mainstream Economics to Overcome Capitalism*

Tamás Krausz, Eszter Bartha (Eds.), *Socialist Experiences in Eastern Europe: A Hungarian Perspective*

Martin Cortés, *Marxism, Time and Politics: On the Autonomy of the Political*

João Antonio de Paula, Huga da Gama Cerqueira, Eduardo da Motta e Albuquer & Leonardo de Deus, *Marxian Economics for the 21st Century: Revaluating Marx's Critique of Political Economy*

Zhi Li, *The Concept of the Individual in the Thought of Karl Marx*

Lelio Demichelis, *Marx, Alienation and Techno-capitalism*

Dong-Min Rieu, *A Mathematical Approach to Marxian Value Theory: Time, Money, and Labor Productivity*

Salvatore Prinzi, *Representation, Expression, and Institution: The Philosophy of Merleau-Ponty and Castoriadis*
Agon Hamza, *Slavoj Žižek and the Reconstruction of Marxism*
Kei Ehara (Ed.), *Japanese Discourse on the Marxian Theory of Finance*
Éric Aunoble, *French Views on the Russian Revolution*
Elisa Marcobelli, *Internationalism Toward Diplomatic Crisis: The Second International and French, German and Italian Socialists*
Paolo Favilli, *Historiography and Marxism: Innovations in Mid-Century Italy*
Terrell Carver, Smail Rapic (Eds.), *Friedrich Engels for the 21st Century: Perspectives and Problems*
Juan Dal Maso, *Hegemony and Class: Three Essays on Trotsky, Gramsci and Marxism*
Patrizia Dogliani, *A Political History of the International Union of Socialist Youth*
Alexandros Chrysis, *The Marx of Communism: Setting Limits in the Realm of Communism*
Stephen Maher, *Corporate Capitalism and the Integral State: General Electric and a Century of American Power*
Paul Raekstad, *Karl Marx's Realist Critique of Capitalism: Freedom, Alienation, and Socialism*
Alexis Cukier, *Democratic Work: Radical Democracy and the Future of Labour*
Christoph Henning, *Theories of Alienation: From Rousseau to the Present*
Daniel Egan, *Capitalism, War, and Revolution: A Marxist Analysis*
Genevieve Ritchie, Sara Carpenter & Shahrzad Mojab (Eds.), *Marxism and Migration*
Emanuela Conversano, *Capital from Afar: Anthropology and Critique of Political Economy in the Late Marx*
Marcello Musto, *Rethinking Alternatives with Marx*
Vincenzo Mele, *City and Modernity in George Simmel and Walter Benjamin: Fragments of Metropolis*
David Norman Smith, *Self-Emancipation: Marx's Unfinished Theory of the Working Class*
Ronaldo Munck, *Rethinking Development: Marxist Perspectives*

Preface

2020–2021 was a weird time to transform a dissertation into a book. The uprising of Black Lives Matter and the COVID-19 pandemic are only two factors that made the intentionally narrow focus of this project, on artificial intelligence and Marxism, sometimes feel divorced from matters of immediate social concern. Yet, one book can only be about so many things and, I suspect, the capitalist use of machines will continue to be a determining factor in most people's lives for a while to come.

Toronto, Canada James Steinhoff

Acknowledgements

Before this text was a book it was a dissertation. For the writing of that dissertation I was fortunate enough to be supervised by Nick Dyer-Witheford. This book would never have come to be without his guidance. I'd also like to thank Marcello Guarini and Jeff Noonan for formative experiences studying the philosophy of AI and Marx, respectively. Special thanks go to my FIMS friends and colleagues Victoria O'Meara, Ryan Mack, Tyler Wagner, Chandell Gosse, Daniel Goyette, Vincent Manzerolle, Atle Mikkola Kjøsen and Indranil Chakraborty as well as my postdoctoral supervisor Anissa Tanweer.

I also want to express my gratitude to an old circle of friends. In subtle ways, this book came to be on the basis of years of bizarre discussions and artistic endeavours with Bohdan Pidskalny, Kyle Lefaive, Joshua Olsen, Nicholas Manuel, Trevor Pepper, Martin Schiller, Caleb Farrugia, Colin Wysman, Nate Gelinas and James Oltean-Lepp.

I'm grateful to Rob Simone, who produced some fine diagrams for this book, and to Sean Landis, whose stellar editorial work improved the quality of what you are about to read by several orders of magnitude. Of course, any errors or inadequacies remain my own.

This book draws on research kindly supported by the Social Sciences and Humanities Research Council of Canada and the Harry Bridges Center for Labor Studies at the University of Washington.

Contents

List of Figures

CHAPTER 1

Introduction: Automation, Autonomy and Artificial Intelligence

Your Means of Production

A friend sent me a meme in 2016.[1] "You have been visited by the Time Travelling Terminator of Full Automation" read bold text above a legion of skeletal anthropoid robots assembled in front of the red banner of the USSR. The Terminator's statement was captioned: "Your means of production… give them to me now! And capitalism will collapse under the weight of its own contradictions". This utterance puns on Arnold Schwarzenegger's famed line, delivered nude in the 1991 James Cameron film *Terminator 2: Judgment Day*: "I need your clothes, your boots and your motorcycle". While the T-800 model Terminator played by Schwarzenegger merely wants garments so it can blend into human society, the Time Travelling Terminator of Full Automation has a slightly larger demand: the totality of machines, tools and facilities for producing goods and services. This is the very same demand made historically by Marxists and communists who would seize the means of production from their capitalist owners. In the Terminator mythos, the eponymous android is a creation of Skynet; an artificial intelligence produced by the technology corporation Cyberdyne Systems. In *Terminator 2*, a captured Terminator is reprogrammed against Skynet, and sent back in time from a

[1] The original meme cannot be included here due to the indeterminate copyright status of memes.

J. Steinhoff, *Automation and Autonomy*, Marx, Engels, and Marxisms, https://doi.org/10.1007/978-3-030-71689-9_1

dystopian future in which machines are exterminating the last remnants of humanity, to 1995 Los Angeles to defend the pre-teen delinquent John Connor, the future leader of the human resistance. In the meme, automation, a technique by which capitalists aim to increase the productivity of labour, is turned against capital and threatens to destroy it.

How did Marxism and a pop culture android end up in one meme? In a roundabout way, this book aims to answer that question. Marxist thought has a long and complicated relationship with technology. Yet, it has engaged relatively little with artificial intelligence (AI), especially in its contemporary form called machine learning (ML). The first goal of this book is to contribute to a Marxist understanding of AI. AI, as it exists in the world today is, I argue, best understood as an automation technology. The primary context for understanding AI is not academia nor science fiction, but industry—specifically, the emergent AI industry, a small but influential subset of the broader tech industry. Since its inception, AI has been implicated in the capitalist mode of production that now covers the world.

The second goal of this book is, to borrow from Raniero Panzieri (1965), to "defy all kinds of mystical ideas" about labour. Marxist thinkers have extended and adapted Marx's work to the increasingly computational capitalism that has evolved since his time. One particularly influential line of thought has been the theory of "immaterial labour" (Hardt and Negri 2000). On the basis of a study of the AI industry and labour therein, we will assess the adequacy of immaterial labour theory for explaining the nature of contemporary high-technology work. This introductory chapter outlines the central argument in the pages to come. But first, we should answer a suite of more general questions. Why draw on Marx to think about AI? Why look at the AI industry to think about Marxist theory? What can writings from one hundred and fifty years ago tell us about purportedly intelligent machines? Simply put, two central and deeply integrated elements of Marx's analysis continue to hold sway over our lives today: capital and machines.

Revolutions

Marx conducted his analysis of capital in the wake of what is commonly known as the industrial revolution, in which steam-powered, machine-based manufacturing became the predominant form of industry in Europe and parts of North America, somewhere between 1760 and 1840

(Toynbee 2011 [1887]).[2] Marx published the first volume of *Capital* in 1867. A second industrial revolution, characterized primarily by the proliferation of electricity, took place from around 1870 to the First World War in 1914 (Landes 2003 [1969]). This was followed by a third, characterized by the proliferation of digital networks and information technologies, after the Second World War (Rifkin 2011). Since the mid-2010s, we have purportedly been living amid a fourth industrial revolution. According to Klaus Schwab (2017), founder and executive chairman of the World Economic Forum, the fourth industrial revolution is defined by a "confluence of emerging technology breakthroughs, covering wide-ranging fields such as artificial intelligence (AI), robotics, the internet of things (IoT), autonomous vehicles, 3D printing, nanotechnology, biotechnology, materials science, energy storage and quantum computing" (7). The economists Erik Brynjolfsson and Andrew McAfee (2014) argue that after a long first machine age following the first industrial revolution, we are now entering a "second machine age" defined by the same array of technologies referred to by Schwab. Brynjolfsson and McAfee (2017) suggest that of these technologies, AI will be the most significant because, like electricity or the combustion engine, it is a general-purpose technology with nearly limitless applications (3–4). Perhaps unsurprisingly, AI luminaries agree.

Professor, entrepreneur and venture capitalist Andrew Ng has called AI the new electricity. He asserts that AI is going to remake the world "[j]ust as electricity transformed almost everything 100 years ago" (Lynch 2017). This sentiment is widespread. The consulting firm Accenture proclaims that AI is "the future of growth" (Purdy and Daugherty 2016). However, it is important to note that the history of AI is characterized by waves of excessive hype, followed by troughs of disappointment. Whatever its future may be, since 2015 AI has been riding high on a wave of enthusiasm. The consulting firm Gartner (2018) put the approach to AI known as deep learning at the apex of its hype cycle—the "peak of inflated expectations"—but AI ebullience continues unabated.

[2] The notion of the industrial revolution has been justly criticized for oversimplifying complex social processes, attributing deterministic power to technology and overlooking the gradual nature of historical change (De Vries 1994; Žmolek 2013). I use the concept here only as a means for summarizing technological milieus and to produce an overview of the technological evolution of capital.

AI in the Real World

A degree of this enthusiasm is warranted. AI is having real effects on the world. AI is now an integral component of all kinds of digital technologies. So-called smart speakers, like Amazon Echo and Google Home, use AI to recognize human speech. Police use facial recognition AI from companies like Clearview AI and iOmniscient to automatically scan surveillance video for persons of interest. AI is being used to automate all kinds of business processes, from advertising to logistics to human resources. Autonomous freight trucks, powered by AI from companies like Waymo and TuSimple, now operate in limited areas (with human overseers) and automated retail stores, such as Amazon Go, use AI to dispense with (some) retail employees. While it is not yet replacing human workers *en masse*, AI is widely used to conduct sophisticated analytics and make predictions anywhere large quantities of digital data are available.

A distinct industry is emerging around AI within the broader technology industry. In 2016, for the first time the top five largest companies in the world by market value all came from the same country and industry: US big tech (Mosco 2017, 65). The same five were still on top in 2019: Apple ($961.3 B), Microsoft ($946.5 B), Amazon ($916.1 B), Alphabet/Google ($863.2 B) and Facebook ($512 B), with the Chinese technology corporation Alibaba in sixth place ($480.8 B) (Murphy et al. 2019).[3] All of these companies are now deeply involved in the production of AI.

Beyond industry, in the virtual worlds of games, AI systems have won a series of unexpected victories over human experts. In 2015, DeepMind's AI system AlphaGo, trained on massive amounts of data from expert human gameplay, defeated the world champion of the ancient strategy game Go. Two years later, AlphaGo was defeated by its successor, AlphaGo Zero, which drew on no human gameplay data and instead learned the game by playing itself repeatedly in simulations (Silver et al. 2017). Such tales of the increasing power and autonomy of AI systems have led public figures including Bill Gates, Elon Musk and the late Stephen Hawking to describe AI as an existential threat to humanity. In less eschatological terms, concerns have been widely voiced over the possibility of widespread technological unemployment driven by a new wave of

[3] All quantities of money are in United States dollars (USD) unless otherwise noted.

AI-powered automation. Concerns about automation have been amplified by the COVID-19 pandemic (ongoing at the time of writing in 2021), which is compelling many businesses to seek new ways to minimize labour costs (The Economist 2020).

Predictions vary widely in terms of what the social and economic effects of AI will be and when they will happen. However, across the political spectrum, and from a variety of sectors ranging from academia to government to industry, a vague consensus is emerging that, sooner or later, capitalist economies are going to have to address the question of what to do when machines are able to perform much of society's necessary labour. For this reason, among others, the analyses conducted by Marx in the late 1800s remain relevant. It is true that Marx's work is historically specific; he was writing about the particularly new industrializing capital of his time and place. However, at the same time his analysis is concerned with the persistent features and "structures that lay at the heart of every particular capitalism" (Heinrich 2007, 4). One of these features, since even before industrialization, is machinery.

Machinery and Marxists

Marx argued that capitalism is distinguished from previous modes of production by its systemic production and reincorporation of surplus-value. Machines are capital's primary means of controlling and enhancing the productivity of the labour on which it relies to produce surplus-value. Marx showed how capital is inherently driven, by competition and class struggle, to ceaseless technological revolution founded on the capture of skills and knowledge from workers and their emulation in machines. Capital tends towards an increasingly machinic state. Marx thus described machinery as a "most powerful weapon" for capital (1990, 562). Today we typically refer to the process by which capital becomes more machinic as automation.

The term automation was not coined until after the Second World War. In an account of production at Ford Motor Company for the magazine *American Machinist*, Le Grand (1948) defined automation as "the art of applying mechanical devices to manipulate work pieces into and out of equipment, turn parts between operations ... and to perform these tasks in timed sequence with the production equipment so that the line can be wholly or partially under push-button control at strategic stations".[4] Four years later, management theorist John Diebold (1952) popularized the notion of automation as "denoting both automatic operation and the process of making things automatic. In the latter sense it includes several areas of industrial activity such as product and process re-design, the theory of communication and control, and the design of machinery" (ix). An adequate history of automation would require its own volume(s), but the interested reader can refer to the excellent and neglected work of Ramin Ramtin (1991), which I draw on throughout this book.

Ramtin distinguishes automation from mechanization. Mechanization involves the introduction of thermodynamic machines into (primarily manual) labour processes, which Marx witnessed in his time. Automation involves the implementation of manual or cognitive labour processes with information technology. For Ramtin (1991) automation is defined by the "systemic application of the principle of feedback" or the use by a system of its output as input (60). While simple forms of feedback have been utilized since antiquity, according to Ramtin, automation proper did not exist until the advent of software computing technology which "can be programmed to perform an unlimited number of tasks" (Ramtin 1991, 50). Automation is distinguished from mechanization by this flexibility. By harnessing feedback, computing technology can perform many tasks. Capital, which is continually driven towards an increasingly machinic state, has a complementary relationship with the computer's capacity to harness feedback.

Thinkers since Marx have developed and revised his framework to analyse the evolution of capital throughout the subsequent industrial and technological revolutions. Marxist thinkers call the era around the second industrial revolution Fordism, which finds its most famous expression in the assembly line and its deskilled "mass worker" (Wright 2002). The digital third industrial revolution has been described by Marxists and others as a transition to post-Fordism, which refers to how capital sought to overcome the organized power of the mass worker through the deployment of information technologies (Amin 1994, 1–34).

[4] According to Yost (2017, 293) the term "automation" was first uttered by Ford Motor Company vice president for manufacturing Delmar S. Harder, but Le Grand was the first to publish the term.

The school of thought called ***post-operaismo*** (post-workerism) has been highly influential in the analysis of post-Fordism, but it disputes the complementary relationship between capital and computers suggested above. *Post-operaismo* thinkers argue that the proliferation of computers upsets the technological balance of power, in favour of labour. Previous kinds of work are transformed into what they call "immaterial labour" (Lazzarato 1996) which possesses new powers which "cannot be contained by the capitalist modes of control" (Hardt and Negri 2009, 143). In the early days of the internet, Antonio Negri (1996), a prominent figure in *post-operaismo*, asked: "[i]s this the third industrial revolution or the time of transition to communism?" (156).

While information technology has yet to catapult the world into communism, *post-operaismo* continues to advance its immaterial labour theory with little revision. In this respect, Hardt and Negri's *Assembly* (2017) differs little from *Empire* (2000).[5] Immaterial labour theory was conceived around the birth of the public internet, but is it still useful in the era of capitalist machine learning? Is it possible that information technology is increasing the power of labour against capital, even as new streams of capital coagulate around an artificially intelligent attractor and big technology firms achieve previously unheard of power and wealth?

The Central Argument

Post-operaismo thinkers celebrate the proliferation of information technologies because they see them as increasing the capacities of the labouring class for self-organized immaterial labour. Empowered by technology, immaterial labourers, the argument goes, can obtain an increasing autonomy from capital. Eventually, they can throw off capital completely and transition to a new autonomous mode of production. The claim for a new sense of autonomy is the central focus of this book. I will assess

[5] The past decade has seen the rise of techno-optimist left accelerationist thinkers, influenced by immaterial labour theory (Williams and Srnicek 2014; Mason 2016; Bastani 2019). These thinkers attribute similar revolutionary significance to fourth industrial revolution technologies as *post-operaismo* did to those of the third. Their calls for full automation and the end of work have been extolled by no less than Negri (2014) himself. I focus primarily on *post-operaismo* throughout the book, but consider left accelerationism briefly in the conclusion.

it via a case study of the AI industry. According to *post-operaismo*, high-tech workers, such as the data scientists and machine-learning engineers in the AI industry, should be immaterial labourers *par excellence*. However, if we examine the work they do, we find little evidence that these labourers possess the attributes accorded to them by *post-operaismo*—especially autonomy from capital. On the contrary, AI work presents us with yet another example of the fragmentation, deskilling and automation of labour processes long familiar to Marxist labour process studies. I argue that the AI industry demonstrates the increasing autonomy *of capital from labour* and not the other way around.

Central to my argument is an empirical study of work in the AI industry based on interviews that I conducted in 2017–2018 with workers (labour) and management (representatives of capital) in the AI industry. I interviewed a variety of technical workers, including data scientists and machine-learning engineers, as well as several CEOs.[6] For anonymized profiles of the interviewees, see the Appendix. *Post-operaismo* tends to make sweeping claims about the economy as a whole so it is useful to test its claims by drilling down into a specific sector.

The empirical study is interpreted through a reading of Marx which draws on labour process theory (LPT) and value-form analysis or the New Reading of Marx (NRM). The crux of the study is an analysis of the machine learning labour process, or the concrete series of actions that go into producing AI commodities (Chapter 6). Labour and capital encounter one another in the labour process and their encounters are mediated by technology. How labour processes are structured and how they change can tell us about relations between labour and capital. The labour process is where the new autonomy of immaterial labour posited by *post-operaismo* theorists should be evident.

Analysis of the labour process alone is, however, not enough. Labour processes are structured according to the broader dynamics of an industry, from class struggle to inter-capitalist competition, and must therefore be situated in that context. To get such a higher order perspective I also conduct a political economy analysis of the AI industry (Chapter 5).

[6] There are two unfortunate lacunae in my interviews. Women are entirely unrepresented. The difficulty I had recruiting women reflects the gender imbalance in the industry discussed in Chapter 5. Ghost workers, whose essential contributions to AI production are discussed also in Chapter 5, are also unrepresented. This is simply because, at the time I conducted interviews, I was unaware of the significance of their work.

Further, since any given industry is a product of the social and material conditions that came before it, an attempt at historicizing is also necessary. This book therefore also includes a rough history of how AI became an industry (Chapter 4). A complete chapter breakdown is provided at the end of this chapter. But first we need to determine exactly what kind of machine AI is.

Computing Machinery

Artificial intelligence is so infused with hype that it is important to begin discussing it from the most mundane level. AI is software, intended to model some aspect(s) of intelligence (loosely defined), which runs on the hardware of a digital computer. AI is not equivalent to robotics. Robots may incorporate AI, but this is not necessarily the case. Robots have bodies of some type while AI systems are software programs. A precise definition of AI is hard to come by because there is no consensus on how to define intelligence nor on how it should be implemented in machines (Legg and Hutter 2007; Wang 2008). One early AI researcher defined AI as "making a machine behave in ways that would be called intelligent if a human were so behaving" (McCarthy et al. 1955). Another defines AI as "making machines intelligent, and intelligence is that quality that enables an entity to function appropriately and with foresight in its environment" (Nilsson 2010, xiii). The problem of definition has been further complicated by a phenomenon, often called the AI effect, whereby once a problem in AI is solved, it is no longer regarded as requiring intelligence. AI pioneer and first AI historian Pamela McCorduck (2004 [1979]) notes that "every time somebody figured out how to make a computer do something—play good checkers, solve simple but relatively informal problems—there was a chorus of critics to say, 'that's not thinking'" (204).

There is one famous way of defining AI which requires mention. The mathematician, computer scientist and cryptographer Alan Turing (1950) proposed it first in his now famous thought experiment "the Imitation Game". Often called the Turing Test today, this game involved a subject engaging in textual dialogue with a machine and a human, both of which were hidden from view. The subject would attempt to determine which was human and which was machine, and if he/she could not, the machine would win the game. The Turing Test posits that when an interlocutor cannot distinguish between machine and human, the question of machine intelligence becomes moot. Turing's test is thus not concerned with what the inner workings of the machine are, nor how (or if) they produce intelligence at all. Turing's approach, which centres on the appearance of intelligence, rather than its technical definition, is philosophically interesting, but it is not very useful when talking about AI that exists in the world today, most of which we do not engage with linguistically.

Instead, let us assemble a working definition of AI that applies to all its possible applications. For Wang (2008), intelligence is "adaptation with insufficient knowledge and resources" which means that an intelligent system "is finite, works in real-time, is open to novel tasks, and learns from experience" (371). Kaplan (2016) defines the "the essence of intelligence" as the "ability to make appropriate generalizations in a timely fashion based on limited data. The broader the domain of application, the quicker conclusions are drawn with minimal information, the more intelligent the behavior" (5–6). By positing criteria of temporal finitude, finite data and generality of application, the definitions offered by Kaplan and Wang aim to distinguish AI from mere computation. Their definitions usefully highlight the fact that human intelligence functions with limited data all the time, except in formal situations with "perfect information" like Chess (Mycielski 1992, 42). They also draw on the intuition that a program which could theoretically solve a difficult problem if it were given 4,000,000 years to conduct an exhaustive search through every possible solution does not possess intelligence in the same sense that we attribute to humans.

These definitions also usefully raise the issue of generality. True intelligence, they suggest, has general applicability, while mere programs have a single function. Artificial general intelligence (AGI) is the name given to hypothetical AI with human-like capacities "to transfer learning from one domain to other domains" (Muehlhauser 2013).[7] While AGI research remains highly speculative, there are at least 45 active AGI research projects across academia and industry (Baum 2017). Actually existing AI is, by contrast, called "narrow" because each system is designed to accomplish a particular task (Johnson et al. 2016, 4246). Just as a word processor is not useful for generating 3D models, facial recognition AI

[7] Yann LeCun, the deep learning expert, makes the compelling point that human intelligence is "nowhere near general" because there are many operations it is very poor at or incapable of (quoted in Macaulay 2020). Regardless, we can consider human intelligence *relatively* general.

is not going to make stock market predictions or interpret speech. All references to AI in this book, unless otherwise noted, refer to actually existing narrow AI.

I suggest a working definition of AI as the array of computational techniques intended to model some aspect(s) of intelligence (loosely defined) which are capable of overcoming barriers of finite time, data and resources and are possibly capable of transferring learning from one domain to others. As a heuristic, the more domains a program can function in, and the less time, data and resources it requires, the more "intelligence" it exhibits. This is an imperfect formulation, but it will suffice for the purposes of this book. As we will see, the divide between AI and computation is not a hard and fast one.[8] Even the most advanced AI involves, to a large degree, computing techniques which require much more resources, such as data, than human intelligence. On this heuristic continuum of intelligence, there is no existing AI that is anywhere near the human. Actually existing AI does not, in any widely accepted sense, think. It is worth spending some time elaborating this. Even if we attempt to distinguish AI from mere computation, as a program, what AI does is compute. Computation is the execution of a process which "proceed[s] from initially given objects, called inputs, according to a fixed set of rules, called a program, procedure, or algorithm, through series of steps and arrive[s] at the end of these steps with a final result, the output" (Soare 1996, 286). Computation can only proceed if the algorithm governing it is "precise and definite, with each successive step clearly determined" (Soare 1996, 286). As anyone who has tried coding will know, the slightest error can render a program useless, because a computer follows all instructions precisely, lacking anything like common sense or reflection. Computation occurs "without any understanding of the significance or meaning of the task" (Carter 2007, 55).[9]

[8] One hard boundary we should establish is between actually existing and fictional AI. While we will not spend time on the philosophical aspects of AI, it is important that AI not be conceived as sentient or conscious machinery. For the purposes of this book, it is irrelevant whether AI ever could be truly intelligent, conscious, moral or anything else. We are interested in what sorts of uses actually existing AI is being put to in the absence of such qualities.

[9] Unfortunately this is not the place to explore whether or not the human mind–brain is a computational system. For more on computationalism, see Piccinini (2015) and Negarestani (2018).

Computation might seem like an innovation of the digital era, but it has existed for thousands of years. Around 800 B.C.E. in the Hindu *Shulba Sutras*, an even more ancient oral tradition was captured in writing, describing precise step-by-step instructions for building geometric altars from thousands of variously sized and shaped bricks (Pasquinelli 2019). And around 330 B.C.E. the Greek mathematician Euclid of Alexandria discussed an algorithm for computing the greatest common divisor of two positive integers (Kleene 1988, 19, cited in Soare 1996, 287–288). Euclid's algorithm is precisely defined: first, the larger integer is divided by the smaller, then the resulting denominator is divided by the remainder. This stage is repeated until there is no remainder. The resulting denominator is the greatest common divisor. This algorithm can be implemented with hand, pencil and paper. The digital computer is but one possible way to implement algorithms.

Indeed, from the mid-eighteenth century until after the Second World War, "computer" referred to people who did calculations by hand, following sets of rules to process an input into an output (Grier 2013). Early non-human computers were electromechanical; there was no such thing as software and each new program was physically assembled from an array of electrical switches driven by mechanical relays. The earliest programming thus consisted of "rerouting cables and setting switches" (Copeland 2004, 23). The vacuum tube later replaced mechanical relays, speeding up computing considerably. It was not until 1947 that an algorithm was stored in electronic memory rather than mechanical apparatus. Only then did the technology we call software appear (Chun 2005, 28). This early software was called a stored program and one of its first implementations was in the University of Pennsylvania's ENIAC, the first general purpose digital computer. General purpose here implies simply that programs were not fixed in the architecture of the machine, but that various programs could be stored there depending on need. With the stored program it became "for the first time … a practical and attractive proposition to use a computer to assist with the preparation of its own programs" (Randell 1974, 12). Since a stored program exists within the computer, it can be modified by another program, or even by itself. Software cannot modify hardware, but software can modify software. With software, "commands, data and addresses are all represented internally by binary numbers. The classic distinction between functions and arguments, operators and numerical values has become permeable … [This] permits operations to be applied to operations, and ramifications to be automated" (Kittler 1996). Software thus enables a feedback circuit within the computer which was not possible when each program was rigidly specified by a particular hardware configuration.

The notion of software was anticipated by Turing (1937), decades before ENIAC, in another thought experiment concerning a hypothetical device, now called a Turing Machine. This was a deceptively simple machine consisting of an infinitely long tape on which symbols are written, a mechanism which can read and write these symbols, a register of the machine's current state and a set of rules that prescribe how the machine can move from one state to another on the basis of symbols read on the tape. Turing demonstrated that any algorithm that could be precisely formulated could be simulated by (or we might say, run as a program on) a Turing Machine. His intention was to show that a vexing mathematical problem called the *Entscheidungsproblem*, which cannot be simulated by a Turing Machine, is therefore unsolvable (Leavitt 2006, 98). More relevant to the purposes of this book is that the Turing Machine "foresaw the concept of software" (Dyson 2012, 460). Turing, in turn, was preceded by Ada Lovelace (1842) who adumbrated the computer program nearly a century before Turing's Machine, with an algorithm for computing Bernoulli numbers using Charles Babbage's hypothetical mechanical computer, the Analytical Engine (Aurora 2015).

The Turing Machine is hypothetical. In practice it would be an immensely slow way of implementing computation. But because it is able to write as well as read, the Turing Machine achieves, in theory, the feedback loop that software would later enable in practice. According to media theorist Friedrich Kittler (1996), Turing thereby stated in advance the "principle of all digital technology". The possibility of simulating all existing algorithms with the mechanisms of one relatively simple machine contains the notion of a universal computer—a machine with one physical configuration that can run other machines as programs.

Recursion

The historical significance of a universal computer is hard for us to grasp today, accustomed to such machines as we are. But Turing was quite aware of the revolutionary nature of his hypothetical machine. He mused that with it one no longer needs: "to have an infinity of different machines doing different jobs ... A single one will suffice" (Turing 2004, 414). We can grasp the property of universality presented by the Turing

Machine, and software generally, with the concept of recursion. Recursion has a dense mathematical and computational history which goes beyond the scope of this study (Hofstadter 1979; Totaro and Ninno 2020). I draw primarily on Tim Jordan's (2015) understanding of recursion as the "application of information to itself" (31). For Jordan, recursion describes the property of computational technologies to allow "a particular process to use either itself or products or elements of itself back within that same process" (2015, 33). The output of an algorithm, or that algorithm itself, can be fed back into that same algorithm as input, forming a loop or "self-recursive stream of numbers" (Kittler 1999, xl). Recursive loops are not, however, simply the repetition of the same:

> Recursion is ... the reapplication of a processing instruction to a variable that is itself already the result, or interim result, of that processing instruction. The variable changes with every iteration, and the effect of the repetition is not the production of identity but a predefined variation. Recursion is thus not simple but expanded reproduction; it brings together repetition and variation with the goal of producing something new that cannot be executed in advance (Winkler 1999, 235, quoted in Winthrop-Young 2015, 74).

Through the reinsertion of output into an algorithm, recursion allows "infinite results from finite means" (Jordan 2015, 33). Recursion thus allows algorithms, which are rigidly specified mechanistic procedures, to produce output which is adaptive, unexpected or novel. Turing would go on to explore the notion that even human thought processes could be translated into a series of recursively linked discrete states, and thus be subject to algorithmic implementation (Edwards 1996, 16). Turing thus proposed the conditions by which a machine might obtain the capacity for the "self-reflexivity of thought" (Caffentzis 1997, 49). Recursion describes the basic function of the digital computer, and serves as the conceptual bridge between computation and human cognition. But that is not all. Recursion will reappear throughout this book.

In Chapter 2, we will see that Marx described capital as fundamentally recursive; it is defined by a circuit or loop of amplification which Marx called valorization. Jordan (2015) suggests that loops are the locus of recursion's "politico-technological" power (37). I will argue that this is true of capital, which integrates its output (both in terms of value and concrete technologies) back into new production processes, producing new technological milieus which enable new techniques of surplus-value extraction. Jordan (2015) points out that for recursive loops to form, an operation of homogenization must occur: "recursions must in some way create or modulate information so that information can be applied to itself ... any recursive process must in some sense make the information it is using self-consistent" (38). For instance, operating systems can only use appropriately formatted programs. An iOS app will not function on an Android device; a specific Android version must be produced. Marx also noticed this function of rendering homogenous in capital's circuits, which reduce the heterogeneity of the world to value. In sum, recursion is a conceptual core around which the argument of this book gathers. In the chapters that follow, I suggest that the history of the AI industry can be read as the saga of capital's attempts to appropriate the computer's capacity for recursion for the augmentation of its recursive circuits of valorization.

What This Book Is Not

There is a lot of valuable research being done on AI. This book tackles a very particular angle and leaves out many others. This section surveys related works which cover topics beyond the scope of this book. The interested reader may find them useful. At the least, it should be helpful to know what this book is not about.

This book does not delve into the vast philosophical literature on AI (Boden 1990; Copeland 1993; Carter 2007). Neither does this book engage with the discussions around posthumanism (Haraway 1990; Hayles 2008; Braidotti 2013; Roden 2014), transhumanism (Moravec 1988; Kurzweil 2005; Ranisch and Sorgner 2014), nor the technological singularity and superintelligent AGI (Good 1966; Vinge 1993; Bostrom 2014). This book also does not engage much with issues of race and gender in relation to algorithmic technologies (O'Neil 2017; Eubanks 2018; Noble 2018; Benjamin 2019; Criado Perez 2019) and robotics and AI (Adam 2006; Larson et al. 2016; Broussard 2018; Rhee 2018; Atanasoski and Vora 2019).

Nor does this book engage with the debate on the precise future effects of wide-scale automation. However, since automation is a central topic of interest here, it is worth outlining the contemporary discussion. The term "technological unemployment" was coined before Turing began writing about intelligent machines (Keynes 1972 [1930]), but it experiences regular revivals. Its latest resurgence began when economists Frey and Osborne (2013) claimed that 47% of all US jobs were potentially automatable through the application of "computerization" over the next ten to twenty years (1). Since then, a spate of studies have followed (Arntz et al. 2016; Manyika et al. 2017; Hawksworth et al. 2018; Muro et al. 2019; Gartner 2020). No consensus can be derived from these reports. As Acemoglu and Restrepo (2018) note, "we are far from a satisfactory understanding of how automation in general, and AI and robotics in particular, impact the labor market and productivity" (1). Some analyses believe job losses to automation will be counterbalanced by employment gains due to overall economic growth and the emergence of new types of AI-related work (Lee 2018b; Hawksworth et al. 2018) while others predict wide-scale technological unemployment.

Jerry Kaplan (2015) asserts that widespread AI-powered automation will reveal that Marx was right that capitalism "is a losing proposition for workers" (11). Kaplan (2015) proposes a framework of "free-market solutions to address the underlying structural problems we are creating" but even on his own terms these seem inadequate to deal with the revolutionary changes he expects (13). While Kaplan recognizes that AI presents a heightening of the labour–capital conflict, he does not recognize this conflict as irreducible under capitalism. Martin Ford (2015) does not think the problems posed by AI can be addressed without modifying the capitalist mode of production itself. Ford is skeptical of free market fixes like Kaplan's because he recognizes that automation is not a choice made by individual managers, but results from the competition inherent in capitalism. Stopping the tide of AI automation "would require modifying the basic incentives built into the market economy" (Ford 2015, 256). This book does not engage with these large-scale debates, focusing instead on the AI industry, and automation therein, in particular. Having surveyed what this book is not about, this introductory chapter now concludes with an overview of what it *is* about.

Chapter Outline

Following this introduction, Chapter 2 surveys several different schools of Marxist theory through the lens of a conceptual triad: labour, capital and machine. We will see that these three concepts, although always connected in Marxist thought, have been configured in very different ways. We will also see that despite their interest in technology, only a few Marxists have discussed AI. The chapter begins by briefly discussing one of the conceptual milieus from which Marx's work emerged—classical political economy. Then it moves on to elaborate Marx's critique of political economy and his theorization of capital's tendency towards an increasingly machinic state. I show that, for Marx, machines are capital's favoured weapon in its ongoing struggle with the human labour it relies on. I survey Soviet Marxism, Western Marxism and the earliest Marxist engagements with AI and robotics. This is followed by a discussion of labour process theory, which focuses on concrete labour practices, and value-form Marxism, specifically the New Reading of Marx (NRM), which focuses on the ontological transformations of value in capitalism. Finally, I explain my own theoretical perspective, which draws on both LPT and NRM.

The third chapter continues the survey of Marxist theory begun in the second. Here we encounter *operaismo* and the object of critique for this book—*post-operaismo*. I outline *post-operaismo*'s fascination with information technology and its reconfiguration of the concepts of labour, capital and machine. I devote special attention to *post-operaismo*'s theory of immaterial labour and, in particular, the claim that the proliferation of information technologies is driving a new sense of autonomy for immaterial labourers from the domination of capital. I reconstruct the logic of *post-operaismo*'s argument in support of this thesis as made up of three cyclically occurring stages: human–machine hybridization, abstract cooperation and new autonomy. With the object of critique set out, the book moves on from theory to study the AI industry.

The fourth chapter consists of a political economic history of the AI industry. It begins by situating the emergence of AI in a broader context of labour, automation and computing technologies. In the wake of the Second World War, capital fielded novel automation technologies against an empowered industrial labour. At the same time a new type of labour emerged around computing technologies. I trace how AI research was connected to the US military in its earliest days, how it persevered through the first "AI winter" and first formed a distinct industry around GOFAI expert systems in the 1980s. Next I look at how states engaged in competing strategic computing programs which involved AI and chart the decline of expert systems as a different AI paradigm, called machine learning (ML), arose in the late 1980s. I also consider the paradigm shift wrought by ML, which aims to extract solutions to problems from data automatically. The chapter closes by tracing how the tech industry came to embrace machine learning in the wake of the 2009 economic crash, forming a second era of the AI industry.

The fifth chapter takes up where the previous one left off and analyses the political economy of the contemporary AI industry. I consider the capital side of the AI industry, including its scale and scope and the various types of companies that make it up, from the oligopolistic tech giants to ethereal startups. I discuss the types of products produced and the peculiar dynamics that distinguish the AI industry from others, including the proliferation of open-source AI tools, the centrality of cloud-based platforms and emerging proprietary AI hardware. We then consider the labour side of the industry, including the hierarchy of AI labour, from the massive salaries earned by data scientists and engineers to the mere pennies paid to platformized ghost workers. I discuss the composition of AI industry labour, its predominant white maleness and widespread sexism as well as the recent emergence of labour organization and activism in AI and other high-tech labour, which has been historically characterized by its apoliticism.

The sixth chapter switches from macro-scale analysis to focus on the labour process in the contemporary AI industry. Drawing on interview data, I sketch a picture of how machine learning AI is produced. I delve into the different types of ML and how they variously confront the problem of the data/labour bottleneck. First, I conduct a walkthrough of the three stages of the ML labour process: data processing, model building and deployment. Next, I present four key themes drawn from my interviews which show how the ML labour process is structured by the exigencies of capitalist production. The four themes are: the commodity form of AI, empirical control of the ML labour process, AI as an automation technology and the automation of AI work. The chapter concludes with a discussion of the automation of AI work with the technology of automated machine learning (AutoML), which is being applied in all stages of the ML labour process. In conclusion, I argue that ML and AutoML might represent a new type of "synthetic" automation which could enable capital to overcome its reliance on living labour.

The seventh chapter mounts a critique of *post-operaismo*'s purported new autonomy of immaterial labour. I argue that based on the analysis of the AI industry presented in the previous chapters, AI work—which is immaterial labour *par excellence*—does not exhibit in any sense the new autonomy described by *post-operaismo*. On the contrary, AI work, especially in light of the emerging technology of AutoML, seems to indicate a trajectory for the increasing autonomy of capital, rather than labour. The chapter closes by elaborating on the significance of synthetic automation, as a potential countervailing tendency to readings of immaterial labour theory which understand it as describing a tendency.

The eighth, and final, chapter elaborates on the intentions behind this book. I assert that the goal is not to defeat one school while championing another, but to contribute to the sophistication of the analysis of life under capitalism by working towards a synthesis of NRM, LPT and *post-operaismo*, all of which possess useful attributes. I also argue that whatever else it entails, AI's function as an automation technology should be recognized. As such, the study of AI indicates the continued relevance of the Marxist class antagonism, mediated by machines. Finally, I hold that while this book may seem pessimistic, it offers a practical stance for grasping the contemporary configuration of labour, capital and purportedly intelligent machines.

Appendix 1: List of Interviewees

Name	*Age*	*Position*	*Education*	*Company type*
Juan	33	CEO	Did not complete university	Startup
Mahir	36	CEO	M.Sc. Medical Science	Startup
Arvin	29	Research and Design Programmer	M.Sc. Computer Science	Startup
Chris	32	CEO	M.Sc. Operations Research	Startup
Laslo	28	CEO	B.A. Marketing/Finance, Data Science Certificate	Startup
Albert	43	Senior Software Engineer	M.Sc. Computer Science	Startup bought by larger firm
Nikolas	33	Data Scientist	M.Sc. Industrial Engineering, M.Sc. Computer Science	International firm
Yimin	34	Data Scientist	Ph.D. Atmospheric Science	Startup within larger firm
Carlo	27	Inference Engineer	M.Sc. Machine Learning	Startup
Dinesh	39	Senior Software Engineer	Ph.D. Quantum Computing	International firm

(continued)

(continued)

Name	*Age*	*Position*	*Education*	*Company type*
Tolu	38	CEO	Ph.D. Machine Learning	Small established company
Edward	30	Graduate Student	M.Sc. Machine Learning	Research institute
David	34	Lead Scientist	Ph.D. Mathematics	Startup within larger firm
Martin	30	Machine Learning Scientist	Ph.D. Cognitive Science	Startup
Chafic	31	Research Intern	Ph.D. Cognitive Science	Startup

Bibliography

Acemoglu, Daron, and Pascual Restrepo. 2018. Artificial Intelligence, Automation and Work. National Bureau of Economic Research Working Paper #24196.

Adam, Alison. 2006. *Artificial Knowing: Gender and the Thinking Machine*. New York: Routledge.

Agrawal, Ajay, Joshua Gans, and Avi Goldfarb. 2016. The Simple Economics of Machine Intelligence. *Harvard Business Review* 17.

Amin, Ash. 1994. Post-Fordism: Models, Fantasies and Phantoms of Transition. In *Post-Fordism: A Reader*, ed. Ash Amin. Oxford: Blackwell.

Arntz, Melanie, Terry Gregory, and Ulrich Zierahn. 2016. The Risk of Automation for Jobs in OECD Countries: A Comparative Analysis. OECD Social, Employment, and Migration Working Papers 189.

Atanasoski, Neda, and Kalindi Vora. 2019. *Surrogate Humanity: Race, Robots and the Politics of Technological Futures*. Durham: Duke University Press.

Aurora, Valerie. 2015. Rebooting the Ada Lovelace Mythos. In *Ada's Legacy: Cultures of Computing from the Victorian to the Digital Age*, ed. Robin Hammerman and Andrew L. Russel. New York: Morgan and Claypool.

Bastani, Aaron. 2019. *Fully Automated Luxury Communism*. London: Verso.

Baum, Seth. 2017. A Survey of Artificial General Intelligence Projects for Ethics, Risk, and Policy. Global Catastrophic Risk Institute Working Paper 17–1. https://papers.ssrn.com/sol3/papers.cfm?abstract_id=3070741.

Benjamin, Ruha. 2019. *Race After Technology: Abolitionist Tools for the New Jim Code*. New York: Wiley.

Boden, Margaret A. (ed.). 1990. *The Philosophy of Artificial Intelligence*. Oxford: Oxford University Press.

Bostrom, Nick. 2014. *Superintelligence: Paths, Dangers, Strategies*. Oxford: Oxford University Press.

Braidotti, Rosi. 2013. *The Posthuman*. Cambridge: Polity.

Broussard, Meredith. 2018. *Artificial Unintelligence: How Computers Misunderstand the World*. Cambridge, MA: MIT Press.

Brynjolfsson, Erik, and Andrew McAfee. 2014. *The Second Machine Age: Work, Progress, and Prosperity in a Time of Brilliant Technologies*. New York and London: W. W. Norton & Company.

Brynjolfsson, Erik, and Andrew McAfee. 2017. The Business of Artificial Intelligence: What it Can–and Cannot–Do for Your Organization. *Harvard Business Review Digital Articles* 7: 3–11.

Caffentzis, George. 1997. Why Machines Cannot Create Value; or, Marx's Theory of Machines. In *Cutting Edge: Technology, Information, Capitalism and Social Revolution*, ed. Jim Davis, Thomas Hirschl, and Michael Stack. London: Verso.

Carter, Matt. 2007. *Minds and Computers: An Introduction to the Philosophy of Artificial Intelligence*. Edinburgh: Edinburgh University Press.

Chun, Wendy Hui Kyong. 2005. On Software, or the Persistence of Visual Knowledge. *Grey Room* 18: 26–51.

Copeland, Jack. 1993. *Artificial Intelligence: A Philosophical Introduction*. Oxford/Malden, MA: Blackwell.

Copeland, Jack. 2004. Computable Numbers: A Guide. In *The Essential Turing*, ed. Jack Copeland. Oxford: Oxford University Press.

Criado Perez, Caroline. 2019. *Invisible Women: Data Bias in a World Designed for Men*. New York: Harry N. Abrams.

De Vries, Jan. 1994. The Industrial Revolution and the Industrious Revolution. *The Journal of Economic History* 54 (2): 249–270.

Diebold, John. 1952. *Automation: The Advent of the Automatic Factory*. Princeton, NJ: D. Van Nostrand Company.

Dyson, George. 2012. Turing Centenary: The Dawn of Computing. *Nature* 482 (7386): 459.

Economist, The. 2020. The Fear of Robots Displacing Workers Has Returned. *The Economist*, July 30.

Edwards, Paul N. 1996. *The Closed World: Computers and the Politics of Discourse in Cold War America*. Cambridge: MIT Press.

Eubanks, Virgina. 2018. *Automating Inequality: How High-Tech Tools Profile, Police, and Punish the Poor*. New York: St. Martin's Press.

Ford, Martin. 2015. *Rise of the Robots: Technology and the Threat of a Jobless Future*. New York: Basic Books.

Frey, Carl Benedikt, and Michael A. Osborne. 2013. The Future of Employment: How Susceptible Are Jobs to Computerisation? *Technological Forecasting and Social Change* 114: 254–280. https://www.oxfordmartin.ox.ac.uk/downloads/academic/The_Future_of_Employment.pdf.

Gartner. 2018. Hype Cycle for Emerging Technologies, 2018. August. https://blogs.gartner.com/smarterwithgartner/files/2018/08/PR_490866_5_Trends_in_the_Emerging_Tech_Hype_Cycle_2018_Hype_Cycle.png.

Gartner. 2020. Gartner Predicts 69% of Routine Work Currently Done by Managers Will Be Fully Automated by 2024. https://www.gartner.com/en/newsroom/press-releases/2020-01-23-gartner-predicts-69–of-routine-work-currently-done-b.

Good, Irving John. 1966. Speculations Concerning the First Ultraintelligent Machine. In *Advances in Computers* 6: 31–88. Elsevier. https://www.stat.vt.edu/content/dam/stat_vt_edu/research/Technical_Reports/TechReport05-3.pdf.

Grier, David Alan. 2013. *When Computers Were Human*. Princeton: Princeton University Press.

Hardt, Michael, and Antonio Negri. 2000. *Empire*. Cambridge, MA: Harvard University Press.

Hardt, Michael, and Antonio Negri. 2009. *Commonwealth*. Cambridge, MA: Harvard University Press.

Hardt, Michael, and Antonio Negri. 2017. *Assembly*. Oxford: Oxford University Press.

Haraway, Donna. 1990. A Manifesto for Cyborgs: Science, Technology, and Socialist Feminism in the 1980s. In *Feminism/Postmodernism*, ed. Linda Nicholson, 190–233. New York: Routledge.

Hawksworth, John, Richard Berriman, and Saloni Goel. 2018. Will Robots Really Steal Our Jobs? An International Analysis of the Potential Long Term Impact of Automation. *Pricewaterhousecoopers*. https://www.pwc.co.uk/economic-services/assets/international-impact-of-automation-feb-2018.pdf.

Hayles, N. Katherine. 2008. *How We Became Posthuman: Virtual Bodies in Cybernetics, Literature, and Informatics*. Chicago: University of Chicago Press.

Heinrich, Michael. 2007. Invaders from Marx: On the Uses of Marxian Theory, & the Difficulties of a Contemporary Reading. *Left Curve* 31.

Hofstadter, Douglas. 1979. *Gödel, Escher, Bach: An Eternal Golden Braid*. New York: Basic Books.

Johnson, Matthew, Katja Hofmann, Tim Hutton, and David Bignell. 2016. The Malmo Platform for Artificial Intelligence Experimentation. In *Proceedings of the Twenty-Fifth International Joint Conference on Artificial Intelligence* (IJCAI-16), 4246–4247. https://www.ijcai.org/Proceedings/16/Papers/643.pdf.

Jordan, Tim. 2015. *Information Politics: Liberation and Exploitation in the Digital Society*. London: Pluto Press.

Kaplan, Jerry. 2015. *Humans Need Not Apply: A Guide to Wealth and Work in the Age of Artificial Intelligence*. New Haven, CT: Yale University Press.

Kaplan, Jerry. 2016. *Artificial Intelligence: What Everyone Needs to Know*. Oxford: Oxford University Press.

Keynes, John Maynard. 1972 [1930]. Economic Possibilities for Our Grandchildren. In *The Collected Writings, Vol. IX: Essays in Persuasion*. London: Macmillan.

Kittler, Friedrich. 1996. The History of Communication Media. *Ctheory*. http://www.ctheory.net/articles.aspx?id=45. Accessed 16 June 2020.

Kittler, Friedrich. 1999. *Gramophone, Film, Typewriter*. Stanford, CA: Stanford University Press.

Kleene, Stephen C. 1988. Turing's Analysis of Computability and Major Applications of It. In *The Universal Turing Machine: A Half-Century Survey*, ed. Rolf Herken. Oxford: Oxford University Press.

Kurzweil, Ray. 2005. *The Singularity Is Near: When Humans Transcend Biology*. New York: Penguin.

Landes, David S. 2003 [1969]. *The Unbound Prometheus: Technological Change and Industrial Development in Western Europe from 1750 to the Present*. Cambridge: Cambridge University Press.

Larson, Jeff, Julia Angwin, and Terry Parris Jr. 2016. Breaking the Black Box: How Machines Learn to be Racist. *ProPublica*, October 19. https://www.propublica.org/article/breaking-the-black-box-how-machines-learn-to-be-racist?word=Trump.

Lazzarato, Maurizio. 1996. Immaterial Labor. In *Radical Thought in Italy: A Potential Politics*, ed. Paulo Virno and Michael Hardt, 133–147. Minneapolis: University of Minnesota Press.

Leavitt, David. 2006. *The Man Who Knew Too Much: Alan Turing and the Invention of the Computer*. New York and London: W. W. Norton & Company.

Lee, Kai-Fu. 2018a. *AI Superpowers: China, Silicon Valley, and the New World Order*. New York: Houghton Mifflin Harcourt.

Lee, Timothy. 2018b. Waymo Jobs: Self-driving Cars Will Destroy a Lot of Jobs—They'll Also Create a Lot. *Ars Technica*, August 24. https://arstechnica.com/tech-policy/2018/08/self-driving-cars-will-destroy-a-lot-of-jobs-theyll-alsocreate-a-lot.

Legg, Shane, and Marcus Hutter. 2007. A Collection of Definitions of Intelligence. *Frontiers in Artificial Intelligence and Applications* 157: 17.

Le Grand, Rupert. 1948. Ford Handles with Automation. *American Machinist* 92: 107–109.

Lovelace, Ada Augusta. 1842. Sketch of the Analytical Engine Invented by Charles Babbage, by LF Menabrea, Officer of the Military Engineers, with Notes upon the Memoir by the Translator. *Taylor's Scientific Memoirs* 3: 666–731.

Lynch, Shana. 2017. Andrew Ng: Why AI Is the New Electricity. Insights by Stanford Business, March 11. https://www.gsb.stanford.edu/insights/andrew-ng-why-ai-new-electricity.

Macaulay, Thomas. 2020. How Facebook's Yann LeCun Is Charting a Path to Human-Level Artificial Intelligence. *The Next Web*, September 8. https://thenextweb.com/neural/2020/08/14/how-facebooks-yann-lecun-is-charting-a-path-to-human-level-intelligence/.

Manyika, James, Michael Chui, Mehdi Miremadi, Jacques Bughin, Katy George, Paul Willmott, and Martin Dewhurst. 2017. A Future that Works: AI, Automation, Employment, and Productivity. *McKinsey Global Institute*. https://www.mckinsey.com/~/media/mckinsey/featured%20insights/Digital%20Disruption/Harnessing%20automation%20for%20a%20future%20that%20works/MGI-A-future-that-works-Executive-summary.ashx.

Marx, Karl. 1990. *Capital*, vol. 1. New York: Penguin.

Mason, Paul. 2016. *Postcapitalism: A Guide to Our Future*. London: Macmillan.

McCarthy, John, Martin Minsky, N. Rochester, and Claude Shannon. 1955. A Proposal for the Dartmouth Summer Research Project on Artificial Intelligence. http://www-formal.stanford.edu/jmc/history/dartmouth/dartmouth.html.

McCorduck, Pamela. 2004 [1979]. *Machines Who Think*. Natick, MA: A. K. Peters.

Mittelstadt, Brent Daniel, Patrick Allo, Mariarosaria Taddeo, Sandra Wachter, and Luciano Floridi. 2016. The Ethics of Algorithms: Mapping the Debate. *Big Data & Society* 3 (2).

Moravec, Hans. 1988. *Mind Children: The Future of Robot and Human Intelligence*. Cambridge, MA: Harvard University Press.

Mosco, Vincent. 2017. *Becoming Digital: Toward a Post-Internet Society*. Bingley: Emerald Publishing Limited.

Muehlhauser, Luke. 2013. What Is AGI? *Machine Intelligence Research Institute*, August 11. https://intelligence.org/2013/08/11/what-is-agi/.

Murphy, Andrea, Jonathan Ponciano, Sarah Hansen, and Halah Touryalai. 2019. Global 2000: The World's Largest Public Companies: 2019 Ranking. *Forbes*, May 15.

Muro, Mark, Robert Maxim, and Jacon Whiton. 2019. Automation and Artificial Intelligence: How Machines Are Affecting People and Places. *Brookings*, January 24. https://www.brookings.edu/research/automation-and-artificial-intelligence-how-machines-affect-people-and-places/.

Mycielski, Jan. 1992. Games with Perfect Information. In *Handbook of Game Theory with Economic Applications*, vol. 2, ed. Robert J. Aumann and Sergiu Hart. Amsterdam: North Holland.

Negarestani, Reza. 2018. *Intelligence and Spirit*. Falmouth: Urbanomic.

Negri, Antonio. 1996. Twenty Theses on Marx: Interpretation of the Class Situation Today. In *Marxism Beyond Marxism*, ed. Saree Makdisi, Cesarae Casarino, and Rebecca Karl, 149–180. Hoboken: Taylor & Francis.

Negri, Antonio. 2014. Some Reflections on the #accelerate Manifesto. In *#accelerate: The Accelerationist Reader*, ed. Robin Mackay and Arven Avanessian. Falmouth: Urbanomic.

Nilsson, Nils. 2010. *The Quest for Artificial Intelligence*. Cambridge: Cambridge University Press.

Noble, Safiya Umoja. 2018. *Algorithms of Oppression: How Search Engines Reinforce Racism*. New York: NYU Press.

O'Neil, Cathy. 2017. *Weapons of Math Destruction: How Big Data Increases Inequality and Threatens Democracy*. New York: Broadway Books.

Panzieri, Raniero. 1965. Socialist Uses of Workers' Inquiry, trans. Arianna Bove. Originally published in *Spontaneita' e organizzazione. Gli anni dei "Quaderni Rossi"* 1959–1964, ed. S. Merli for BFS Edizioni, Pisa 1994. English translation published in *Transform*. http://www.generation-online.org/t/tpanzieri.htm.

Pasquinelli, Matteo. 2019. Three Thousand Years of Algorithmic Rituals: The Emergence of AI from the Computation of Space. *e-flux* 101. https://www.e-flux.com/journal/101/273221/three-thousand-years-of-algorithmic-rituals-the-emergence-of-ai-from-the-computation-of-space/.

Piccinini, Gualtiero. 2015. *Physical Computation: A Mechanistic Account*. Oxford: Oxford University Press.

Purdy, Mark, and Paul Daugherty. 2016. Why Artificial Intelligence Is the Future of Growth. *Accenture*. https://www.accenture.com/us-en/insight-artificial-intelligence-future-growth.

Ramtin, Ramin. 1991. *Capitalism and Automation: Revolution in Technology and Capitalist Breakdown*. London: Pluto Press.

Randell, Brian. 1974. The History of Digital Computers. Computing Laboratory, University of Newcastle Upon Tyne. https://citeseerx.ist.psu.edu/viewdoc/download?doi=10.1.1.444.5949&rep=rep1&type=pdf.

Ranisch, Robert, and Stefan Lorenz Sorgner (eds.). 2014. *Post-and Transhumanism: An Introduction*. New York: Peter Lang.

Rhee, Jennifer. 2018. *The Robotic Imaginary: The Human and the Price of Dehumanized Labor*. Minneapolis: University of Minnesota Press.

Rifkin, Jeremy. 2011. *The Third Industrial Revolution: How Lateral Power Is Transforming Energy, the Economy, and the World*. London: Macmillan.

Roden, David. 2014. *Posthuman Life: Philosophy at the Edge of the Human*. New York: Routledge.

Schwab, Klaus. 2017. *The Fourth Industrial Revolution*. New York: Crown Business.

Silver, David, Julian Schrittwieser, Karen Simonyan, Ioannis Antonoglou, Aja Huang, Arthur Guez, Thomas Hubert, Lucas Baker, Matthew Lai, Adrian Bolton, Yutian Chen, Timothy Lillicrap, Fan Hui, Laurent Sifre, George van den Driessche, Thore Graepel, and Demis Hassabis. 2017. Mastering the Game of Go Without Human Knowledge. *Nature* 550 (7676): 354.

Soare, Robert I. 1996. Computability and Recursion. *Bulletin of Symbolic Logic* 2 (3): 284–321.

Susskind, Richard E., and Daniel Susskind. 2015. *The Future of the Professions: How Technology Will Transform the Work of Human Experts*. Oxford: Oxford University Press.

Totaro, Paolo, and Domenico Ninno. 2020. Biological Recursion and Digital Systems: Conceptual Tools for Analysing Man-Machine Interaction. *Theory, Culture & Society* 37 (5): 27–49.

Toynbee, Arnold. 2011 [1887]. *Lectures on the Industrial Revolution in England: Popular Addresses, Notes and Other Fragments*. Cambridge: Cambridge University.

Turing, Alan. 1937. On Computable Numbers, with an Application to the Entscheidungsproblem. *Proceedings of the London Mathematical Society* 2 (42): 230–265.

Turing, Alan. 1950. Computing Machinery and Intelligence. *Mind* 59 (236): 433.

Turing, Alan. 2004. *The Essential Turing: Seminal Writings in Computing, Logic, Philosophy*, ed. Jack Copeland. Oxford: Oxford University Press.

Vinge, Vernor. 2013 [1993]. Technological Singularity. In *The Transhumanist Reader: Classical and Contemporary Essays on the Science, Technology, and Philosophy of the Human Future*, ed. Max More and Natasha Vita-More, 365–375. New York: Wiley.

Wang, Pei. 2008. What Do You Mean by 'AI'? In *Artificial General Intelligence*, ed. Ben Goertzel and Cassio Pennachin, 362–373. Berlin: Springer.

Williams, Alex, and Nick Srnicek. 2014. #accelerate: Manifesto for an Accelerationist Politics. In *#accelerate: the Accelerationist Reader*, ed. Robin Mackay and Arven Avanessian. Falmouth: Urbanomic.

Winkler, Hartmut. 1999. Rekursion: Über Programmierbarkeit, Wiederholung, Verdichtung und Schema. *c't Magazin* 9: 234–240.

Winthrop-Young, Geoffrey. 2015. Siren Recursions. In *Kittler Now: Current Perspectives in Kittler Studies*, ed. Stephen Sale and Laura Salisbury. Cambridge: Polity.

Wright, Steve. 2002. The Historiography of the Mass Worker. *The Commoner* 5. https://libcom.org/library/historiography-mass-worker-steve-wright.
Yost, Jeffrey R. 2017. *Making IT Work: A History of the Computer Services Industry*. Cambridge: MIT Press.
Žmolek, Michael Andrew. 2013. *Rethinking the Industrial Revolution: Five Centuries of Transition from Agrarian to Industrial Capitalism in England*. Leiden: Brill.

CHAPTER 2

Labour, Capital, Machine: Marxist Theory and Technology

Introduction

One might think it uncommon to encounter both Marx and artificial intelligence in a single text, this book and perhaps a few other academic tomes being an exception. Yet, since around 2017 it has been possible to find that very combination in such venues as tech industry community website Hacker Noon (Del Corro 2017), specialized journalism such as *MIT Technology Review* (Avent 2018) and even mass media like *The Washington Post* (Xiang 2018). This chapter explores how Marx's ideas can be useful for thinking about contemporary AI. The matter is complicated by the fact there is not just one Marxism. Marx's ideas have been reworked in dozens of different ways in various contexts over the past century and a half.

While an exhaustive survey is not possible in one book, this chapter examines several strands of Marxist thought to compare how they configure three essential concepts: labour, capital and machine. A fundamental Marxist tenet is that there exists an antagonistic relation between capital and labour, or the capitalist and working classes. This conflict is fought out in a number of domains, but one of the most important is machines. Marxist thinkers have devoted relatively little attention to AI, but by looking at how they have variously understood machines, this chapter takes a step towards a Marxist perspective on AI.

J. Steinhoff, *Automation and Autonomy*, Marx, Engels, and Marxisms,
https://doi.org/10.1007/978-3-030-71689-9_2

I follow the conceptual triad labour, capital and machine from its primordial manifestations in the classical political economy of Adam Smith and David Ricardo, through Marx's critique of political economy, and on to its diverse permutations in various Marxisms, including Soviet Marxism, Western Marxism, labour process theory (LPT) and the New Reading of Marx (NRM). I also discuss various other Marxist authors who have grappled with information technologies and the increasingly cybernetic nature of capital. The next chapter covers *operaismo*, and *post-operaismo*, the object of critique of this book. By mapping the Marxist theoretical landscape, these two chapters provide conceptual tools for the study of the AI industry in Chapters 4, 5 and 6. The chapter closes with an explanation of my own theoretical perspective, which is influenced by both LPT and NRM.[1]

Political Economy

The diverse Marxisms have roots in the work of the eighteenth- and nineteenth-century political economists who sought to understand the capitalist system. While the young Marx focused his critique on philosophers such as Hegel and Feuerbach, the mature Marx shifted attention to the political economy of Adam Smith and David Ricardo, among others; Marx's *Capital* is subtitled "a critique of political economy". While Marx severely critiqued the political economists, his work built upon the foundation they established. Along with the centrality of value and labour, the political economists recognized the fundamental importance of machines to capital. They also discerned an antagonism between labour and capitalist machinery—an antagonism inherently connected to the production of value.

The eighteenth-century philosopher and political economist Adam Smith recognized the integral link between technology and labour in capitalism. Labour was the basis of capitalist economies because it was the labour expended in production that determined the value of a commodity: "The value of any commodity … to the person who possesses it, and who means not to use or consume it himself, but to exchange it for other commodities, is equal to the quantity of labour which it enables him

[1] A note on an unavoidable issue of circularity. My interpretation of Marx is inflected by LPT and NRM and my exposition of his work necessarily reflects that.

to purchase or command. Labour … is the real measure of the exchangeable value of all commodities" (Smith 1991 [1776], 36). This is quite different from today's mainstream economics which holds that the value of a commodity is determined solely in exchange, or by what a buyer is willing to pay for it. By positing labour as the source of value, Smith developed the intuitive idea that the amount of work something requires to produce should impinge on its value. For example, a riding lawn mower is worth more than a teaspoon. Smith thus initiated an investigation of what lies behind the act of exchange, gesturing towards value as labour's social form in a society founded on exchange (Pitts 2018, 28). Smith supposed that value derived not only from the work of workers but also from the "work" of the other two classes: landowners, who generate rent and capitalists, who generate interest. Marx would later deny the comparison of labour to rent and capital, but he would elaborate on Smith's notion that value is connected to production and not only exchange.

Smith is also notable for acknowledging that capital and labour possess inherently opposed interests. While Smith is hallowed by apologists of capital, who purport that the increase of capital benefits all sectors of society, he adumbrated a theory of class conflict in *The Wealth of Nations*:

> The workmen desire to get as much, the masters to give as little as possible. The former are disposed to combine in order to raise, the latter in order to lower the wages of labour. It is not, however, difficult to foresee which of the two parties must, upon all ordinary occasions, have the advantage in the dispute, and force the other into a compliance with their terms. (Smith 1991 [1776], 98)

The clash of class interests, Smith noted, was asymmetric since law and resources tended to be on the side of capital. One such resource was machinery. Already in the late eighteenth century, capital was driven, by competition between capitalists and revolt by labour, towards the application of technology in production. Smith famously detailed and extolled the division of labour in manufacturing for its enhancement of the productivity of labour through specialization, and his respect for machines ran along similar lines. Machines are valuable because they "facilitate and abridge labour, and enable one man to do the work of many" (Smith 1991 [1776], 21–22). Therefore, a "much smaller quantity of labour becomes requisite for executing any particular piece of work" (Smith 1991 [1776], 338). While overall Smith was optimistic about the prospects of capitalist machinery, by situating it within an admittedly asymmetric class conflict he planted the seeds of a more critical view.

Generally positive evaluations of technology were widely held in the early nineteenth century, which saw the invention of the Jacquard loom, steam-powered locomotion and machine tools, to take only a few examples. A sense of the technological enthusiasm of the times is palpable in the works of Charles Babbage, a Cambridge mathematician, and Andrew Ure, an industrial chemist, who both wrote books on the emerging use of industrial machinery. Babbage extolled machinery for its ability to "supersede the skill and power of the human arm" (2003 [1832], 9). He described three advantages derived from the use of machines: "The addition which they make to human power. The economy they produce of human time. The conversion of substances apparently common and worthless into valuable products" (2003 [1832], 10). Ure went so far as to assert that: "The constant aim and effect of scientific improvement in manufactures are philanthropic, as they tend to relieve the workmen either from niceties of adjustment which exhaust his mind and fatigue his eyes, or from painful repetition of effort which distort or wear out his frame" (1835, 8). Both Babbage and Ure were also quite enamoured with the use of machines to control refractory workers (Zimmerman 1997, 9). They pointed out that capital and machines have an affinity, although they were not interested in the perspective of labour.

The political economist David Ricardo introduced a critical class dimension to political economy. Like Smith, Ricardo advocated a labour theory of value. He held that the "value of a commodity, or the quantity of any other commodity for which it will exchange, depends on the relative quantity of labour which is necessary for its production, and not on the greater or less compensation which is paid for that labour" (Ricardo 2001 [1821], 8). Ricardo's conception of labour was, however, narrower than that of Smith's broad social conception and focused on the concrete act of labour at the point of production (Pitts 2018, 29–30).

In the 1817 first edition of his *On the Principles of Political Economy and Taxation,* Ricardo saw machines as benefiting both capital and labour. However, by the third edition of 1821, Ricardo revised the text to argue that while the introduction of machines into production certainly benefits the capitalist because it increases output and decreases labour costs, the "substitution of machinery for human labour, is often very injurious to the interests of the class of labourers" (Ricardo 2001 [1821], 283; see also Kurz 2010, 1197–1198). Ricardo thus affirms what Smith noted, that different classes in society may have differing and contrary interests, and he placed machinery squarely in the middle of the class antagonism. He reasons that the "same cause which may increase the net revenue of the country, may at the same time render the population redundant, and deteriorate the condition of the labourer" (Ricardo 2001 [1821], 284). Under capital, the products of labour may be turned against their creators. This essential point would later be elaborated by Marx.

Ricardo even speculated on the possibility of a fully automated mode of production, in what we might call Ricardo's Fragment on Machines: "If machinery could do all the work that labour now does, there would be no demand for labour. Nobody would be entitled to consume any thing who was not a capitalist, and who could not buy or hire a machine" (Ricardo 1951–1973, VIII: 399–400, cited in Kurz 2010, 1195). Ricardo envisioned a capitalism in which machines are functionally identical to human workers and wholly replace them, while their capitalist owners continue to profit. The asymmetry of capitalist machinic mediation is illustrated vividly by this speculative extrapolation. What exactly happens to the former workers is unknown.

Classical political economy set the scene for Marxist theory by triangulating labour, capital and machines. As a whole, however, political economy only managed to describe the functioning of capitalism on its surface. In the words of Pitts (2018), while Ricardo attempted to dive below surface appearances of capital to unearth the truth of labour, "he did not pose the question as to why and how products of labour become value-bearing commodities on this basis [of labour]" (30). While political economy asked about how capitalism works, Marx would ask why it is that capitalism works the way it does.

Marx on Value and Labour

Marx's critique of political economy is elaborated throughout the three volumes of *Capital* (Marx 1990, 1991, 1992) and the notes made during its composition, *Grundrisse* (Marx 1993). Marx deepened the contradiction that Ricardo noted between labour and machines under capital. But Marx also seems to suggest that machines might ultimately betray capital to the benefit of labour. Different interpretations of the properties of machinery in Marx are one reason for theoretical divergence among different strands of Marxism.

To grasp the significance of Marx's critique of political economy one has to see how his use of the categories of political economy (such as labour) differs from that of the political economists. As indicated above, Marx's goal was to get past the surface appearances of capital. However, this does not mean that reading Marx's gospel will dispel the false preconceptions of the reader and somehow give her an undistorted access to reality. This is because the surface appearances of capital are nonetheless real things with real effects. As Smith (2009) puts it: "Marx's main theoretical task is to explain how the social relations of capitalism necessarily generate appearances that distort what capital essentially is (appearances that none the less have material effects)" (125). To grasp this odd situation we will begin by looking at Marx's concept of labour.

Like Smith and Ricardo, Marx held a labour theory of value. Labour is first of all a generic term for workers and the working class. However, labour also refers to an activity performed by humans in which they process their environment in ways useful to themselves. In this sense, labour is a "condition of human existence which is independent of all forms of society; it is an eternal human necessity which mediates the metabolism between man and nature" (Marx 1990, 132). Under capitalism, however, labour takes the particular form of wage labour, in which a capitalist pays a worker a wage for control over the worker's capacity to labour for a period of time. Labour thus exists in two forms: concrete and abstract. Concrete labour is the universal human capacity to process the environment into useful products or services, creating use-values. In the capitalist mode of production, however, most concrete labour simultaneously exists as abstract labour or "an expenditure of human labour-power" (Marx 1990, 137). Labour-power is simply the capacity to labour (Marx 1990, 270). It might seem banal to hold that each concrete labour is also an expression of a general human capacity to do work, but for Marx, abstract labour is a necessary condition for capitalism. Abstract labour enables capitalist exchange by allowing dissimilar commodities to be brought into relation with one another through a shared attribute, value. Abstract labour "takes on a physical form in the equal objectivity of the products of labour as values" (Marx 1990, 164). Abstract labour translates into value through the measure of the duration of labour time. Since duration is a pure quantity, value is defined as "congealed quantities of homogenous [abstract] human labour" (Marx 1990, 128). The homogenous metric provided by value allows one commodity to be compared, and exchanged, with another.

Yet the actual quantity of hours worked cannot determine value alone, or merely working slowly would increase the value of products. Therefore, Marx reasoned, the value of a commodity is determined by the average socially necessary labour time for its production. This refers to the "labour-time required to produce any use-value under the conditions of production normal for a given society and with the average degree of skill and intensity of labour prevalent in that society" (Marx 1990, 129). The value of a commodity is thus not equivalent to the amount of time spent working on it by its immediate producer, but rather the average time that it takes to produce such a commodity in that particular time and place. Socially necessary labour time thus reveals value, which appears as a thing or property of things, as a social relation. Value's "objective character … is … purely social" (Marx 1990, 138–139). It is not, contra Ricardo, imparted to the commodity by the concrete labour of producing it, nor is it some substance that inheres in commodities after their production: "[n]ot an atom of matter enters into the objectivity of commodities as values" (Marx 1990, 138). Value arises from the social form of commodity production and exists as a social relation.

Value is central to Marx's analysis, and like labour, it manifests in two ways. Marx distinguishes exchange value (which is expressed as price) from value, which is determined by socially necessary labour time. The two do not necessarily coincide. In fact, Marx argues that capital is not primarily driven to maximize exchange value. Instead, the aim of capital is to produce "surplus-value" (Marx 1990, 293). Surplus-value is a quantity of value which capital appropriates from labour without recompense. This appropriation is the goal which immanently configures the capitalist mode of production. How does capital appropriate surplus-value from labour? Against today's common sense, Marx holds that surplus-value does not arise from selling commodities for more than they were produced for (this generates profit, which is not the same) but rather, surplus-value arises from the unequal exchange between capital and labour.

The labour-power of the worker is a commodity which the worker sells to the capitalist. The quantity of capital invested in labour-power is called "variable capital" and is differentiated from "constant capital" or capital invested in means of production or "raw materials, auxiliary material and the instruments of labour" (Marx 1990, 317). The value of constant capital, such as a machine, does not vary in magnitude during production; it is simply transferred from the machine to the products produced. The value invested into wages for purchasing labour-power, on the other hand, may change in magnitude, because labour-power can produce more value than is paid for it. From this special property of labour-power, the possibility of surplus-value arises.

The value of labour-power depends on the average socially necessary cost for the ongoing survival of the worker (Marx 1990, 274). The labour time it takes a worker to earn enough money to obtain the means to stay alive and thus reproduce her labour-power for another day is defined by Marx as "necessary labour" (1990, 325). The capitalist aims to pay the worker as little as possible without impinging on the reproduction of labour-power while also maximizing the time the worker works beyond necessary labour. Labour time beyond necessary labour is "surplus labour" in which the worker produces value for which the capitalist has not paid an equivalent—surplus-value (Marx 1990, 325). The wage paid to the worker is worth less than the value produced by the worker. This unequal exchange defines Marx's concept of exploitation and forms the basis of the inherent antagonism between labour and capital (Marx 1990, 418–421).[2]

What then is capital? Marx defines the "general form of capital" as M-C-M' where "M' = … the original sum advanced plus an increment … This increment or excess over the original value I call surplus-value" (Marx 1990, 251). This formula represents the process by which money (M) is invested in the production of commodities (C) which are sold and turned into more money than was initially invested (M'). While surplus-value is appropriated during production, it does not contribute to the valorization of capital until the commodities produced are exchanged for money worth more value than was invested in their production. Capital "only becomes real capital" when it creates more capital (Marx 1990, 1061). Thus, to say that surplus-value is extracted by capital in the exploitation of labour in production is only part of the story. Only if capital successfully realizes the value of the commodities produced by exploited labour and reinvests it as capital, has capital been "valorized" (Marx 1990, 252). Noting this circuitous process, Marx asserts that "capital is not a thing" (1990, 932). Capital, and value, are processes made

[2] Not all labour is productive of value. Productive labour is only "that which is directly consumed in the course of production for the valorization of capital" (Marx 1990, 1038) or in other words, that which "directly creates surplus-value" (Marx 1990, 1039). The same concrete labour can thus be either productive or unproductive, depending on its context.

up of social relations, or ensembles of human social interactions occurring over time. This means that valorization is "not simply an economic process but involves the creation and maintenance of a social relation" (Mackenzie 1984, 483). Capital depends on people continuing to behave in a particular way. I will elaborate on that central point below, but first I want to consider the deeper significance of capital's circuitous nature.

Not only is capital not a thing, it is not in itself finite. Since valorization is an "end in itself ... The movement of capital is therefore limitless" (Marx 1990, 253). For capital to exist as capital, valorization must be perpetually repeated. This is why new markets must continually be opened up and new spheres of life commoditized. All other considerations, be they ethical, aesthetic or ecological, are, under capital, subjugated to the valorization imperative. This conception of capital as a potentially infinite, self-referential process which supervenes on the exploitation of labour is perhaps Marx's greatest innovation. It reveals capital as a blind, recursive mechanism. As Land (2017) puts it, capital "appeals to nothing beyond itself, it is inherently nihilistic. It has no conceivable meaning beside self-amplification. It grows in order to grow". Recall that Jordan (2015) describes recursion as the ability of a process "to use either itself or products or elements of itself back within that same process" (33). Capital is defined precisely by the output of a process being reintroduced as input. Value is both the output and input of valorization. Jordan (2015) also notes that for outputs to be reintroduced as inputs, they must be made "self-consistent in some way or other" (38). Capital achieves self-consistency via its nihilistic reduction of the heterogeneity of the world to value. Concretely different things and services are brought into relation via their shared existence as commodities, which are bearers of value.

The primacy of the recursive augmentation of value means that under capital, humans, capitalist and worker alike, have predefined roles to play in the program for capital's prime directive. The "characters who appear on the economic stage are merely personifications of economic relations" (Marx 1990, 179). Individual possibilities for action are delimited by the exigencies of valorization. Marx (1990) describes even the capitalist as a puppet of capital, or "nothing but the personification of objectified labour which cedes a part of itself to the worker in the form of the means of subsistence in order to annex the living labour-power for the benefit of the remaining portion, so as to keep itself intact and even to grow beyond its original size by virtue of this annexation" (1003–1004). Marx also sometimes attributes subjectivity to capital, calling it the "automatic subject" and the "subject of a process in which, constantly assuming the form in turn of money and commodities, it changes its own magnitude, throws off surplus value from itself … and valorizes itself independently" (Marx 1990, 255). Such formulations might seem to erase labour, and to contradict the claim, discussed earlier, that capital is made up of the social relations of humans. In fact, both capital's autonomy and its existence as social relations of humans obtain at once. To elaborate how this is the case, we can unpack Marx's concept of fetishism. Marx suggests that to grasp how the commodity functions we must make a comparison to the "misty realm of religion" where:

> the products of the human brain appear as autonomous figures endowed with a life of their own, which enter into relations both with each other and the human race. So it is in the world of commodities and the products of men's hands. I call this the fetishism which attaches itself to the products of labour as soon as they are produced as commodities, and is therefore inseparable from the production of commodities. (Marx 1990, 165)

Within the capitalist system, commodities appear to possess economic properties, like value, in themselves. However, because value is a social relation, the properties of the commodity are also social. The commodity "reflects the social characteristics of men's own labour as objective characteristics of the products of labour themselves … Hence it also reflects the social relation of the producers to the sum total of labour as a social relation between objects, a relation which exists apart from and outside the producers" (Marx 1990, 164–165). The social relations which make up capital, as well as the commodity, appear to people as objective properties. Fetishism refers to this quality of capital, by which social relations are congealed into things.

It is important to note how exactly Marx phrases the relation of fetishism. The "products of the human brain *appear* as autonomous figures" and assume "*for them*, [humans] the fantastic form of…" (Marx 1990, 165, emphasis added). Appearance denotes an illusory character. But within the capitalist system, such illusions are efficacious. Individual capitals are compelled to pursue valorization or face bankruptcy (thereby ceasing to exist as capital) while workers are obliged to sell their labour-power or starve. Fetishism describes how commodities (along with value and capital) are simultaneously illusory and efficacious, non-physical but having real effects on the physical world. Marxists have dubbed this dual nature "real illusion" (Holloway 2002, 71), "real abstraction" (Sohn-Rethel 1978, 20) or "spectral objectivity" (Heinrich 2012, 52). The social relations humans engage in eventually come to control them by appearing, and functioning, as things independent of those relations. In this context, an appearance is a "concrete social reality created on the basis of a mystified and disguised process" (Dyer-Witheford et al. 2019, 21). Marx stated this clearly:

> Men do not therefore bring the products of their labour into relation with each other as values because they see these objects merely as the material integuments of homogeneous human labour. The reverse is true: by equating their different products to each other in exchange as values, they equate their different kinds of labour as human labour. They do this without being aware of it. Value ... does not have its description branded on its forehead; it rather transforms every product of labour into a social hieroglyphic. Later on, men try to decipher the hieroglyphic, to get behind the secret of their own social product: for the characteristic which objects of utility have of being values is as much men's social product as is their language. (Marx 1990, 166–167)

The commodity and capital thus really do have "a life of their own" (Marx 1990, 165) at the same time that that life is made up of the social relations of humans. Capital is a subject or "higher-order alien power" (Smith 2009, 123) even while it is a process consisting of humans socially relating in particular ways.

In sum, Marx's critique of political economy depicts capital as a potentially infinite process of valorization which systemically occludes its true nature through the generation of efficacious real illusions. Valorization requires the exploitation of labour to capture surplus-value, but capital appears as productive of value itself—and it is, insofar as value takes an objectified form which is recursively applied to labour, from whence it came. The capital which is used to purchase labour-power is itself the result of previous labour which has been objectified. Capital is "dead labour which, vampire-like, lives only by sucking living labour, and lives the more, the more labour it sucks" (Marx 1990, 342). Valorization depends on this recursive process of converting labour into the means for purchasing labour-power.

However, labour-power is not the only necessary input for valorization. Valorization requires that labour-power be combined with the means of production, including raw materials, facilities, tools, and machines. To see how machines fit into Marx's theory of capital, we will switch perspectives from the valorization process to the labour process. These two processes together constitute production: "Just as the commodity itself is a unity formed of use-value and value, so the process of production must be a unity, composed of the labour process and the process of creating value" (Marx 1990, 293). Since value is a non-physical real abstraction, the valorization process necessarily supervenes on the physical substratum of the concrete production of use-values. But while the valorization process requires a labour process on which to supervene, each labour process is determined in its nature by the exigencies of valorization. The machine is capital's preferred means for determining the nature of the labour process.

Marx on Machines

While I refer to capital as such, it is important to remember that capital consists of many individual capitals competing with one another and struggling against their respective labour forces. The valorization imperative generates anarchy among individual capitals: "the immanent laws of capitalist production ... assert themselves as the coercive laws of competition" (Marx 1990, 433). Competition between individual capitals takes many forms, but is founded on surplus-value extraction. The simplest way for capital to increase its harvest of surplus-value is to lengthen the working day; necessary labour stays the same while the surplus increases. Such "absolute surplus-value" is necessarily limited by the finite length of the day (Marx 1990, 432). However increased quantities of surplus-value can also be obtained by decreasing necessary labour time, entailing a relative increase in surplus labour time. The augmentation of "relative surplus-value" is a major technique of capitalist competition (Marx 1990, 432). Since necessary labour time is contingent on the cost of the reproduction of labour-power, the first can be decreased by reducing the cost of the second. Capital thus has an "immanent drive, and a constant tendency, towards increasing the productivity of labour, in order to cheapen commodities and, by cheapening commodities, to cheapen the worker himself" (Marx 1990, 436–437). One prominent method for increasing the productivity of labour is the division of labour, another is machinery.

Marx held that the alleviation of the burden of work is "by no means the aim of the application of machinery under capitalism" (1990, 492). On the contrary, the machine is a "means for producing surplus-value" by "cheapen[ing] commodities and, by shortening the part of the working day in which the worker works for himself, to lengthen the ... part he gives to the capitalist for nothing" (Marx 1990, 492). In theorizing machines, Marx distinguishes between circulating and fixed capital. Since capital is defined as value undergoing valorization, capital is therefore "constantly in circulation ... in this sense all capital is circulating capital" (Marx 1992, 238). But Marx also defines a particular type of circulating capital. Circulating capital, in this specific sense, refers to means of production which are used up in the production process and which wholly pass on their value to the product. An example of this is fuel for a machine. On the other hand, fixed capital refers to means of production which pass on their value incrementally over their lifespans, in inverse proportion to their average depreciation (Marx 1990, 509).[3] A machine with a lifespan of ten years doles out its value over the course of that decade. The value of fixed capital thus "acquires a dual existence" with one part fixed in its physical form while the other "trickles down" into circulation via the sale of the commodity (Marx 1992, 243). Circulating and fixed capital thus both circulate, albeit in different ways. Both are distinguished from variable capital (i.e. purchased labour-power) in that neither can generate surplus-value. Labour-power is an exclusively human attribute (Marx 1990, 274). Machinery, on the other hand, "creates no new value but yields up its own value to the product it serves to beget" (Marx 1990, 509). So what exactly is a machine?

The human body is limited in terms of the type and number of tools it can wield and the forces it can exert, but machines as such have no "organic limitations" (Marx 1990, 495). Machines may be linked together to form a "complex system of machinery" (Marx 1990, 499) which becomes a "vast automaton as soon as it is driven by a self-acting prime mover" (Marx 1990, 502). Although the state of industrial machinery was rudimentary in his time, Marx recognized the process of mechanization in the emerging "mechanical monster" (1993, 503). He elaborates that once a machine "executes, without man's help, all the movements required to elaborate the raw material, and needs only supplementary assistance from the worker, we have an automatic system of

[3] It is incorrect to refer to all machines as fixed capital. Fixed capital is defined by the "particular way in which the means of labour gives up its value to the product ... It is only the function of a product as a means of labour in the production process that makes it fixed capital" (Marx 1992, 239–240).

machinery, capable of constant improvement in its details" (Marx 1990, 503). He recognized that constant improvement in machinery is necessitated by valorization. Driven by its hunger for relative surplus-value, the "tendency and the result of the capitalist mode of production is steadily to increase the productivity of labour" (Marx 1990, 959). Since this is achieved largely through the introduction of machines, capital tends towards an increasingly machinic state. This Marx called the increasing "organic composition of capital", defined by the relative increase of fixed, opposed to variable, capital (1990, 762). He described machinery as "capital's material mode of existence" and the "material foundation of the capitalist mode of production" (Marx 1990, 554) and reasoned that the "development of the means of labour into machinery is not an accidental moment of capital, but is rather the historical reshaping of the traditional, inherited means of labour into a form adequate to capital" (Marx 1993, 694).

Machinery's adequacy to capital is best explained by reference to Marx's notion of subsumption, of which there are two types. Formal subsumption occurs when an existing labour process comes under the control of a capitalist and becomes part of a circuit of valorization (Marx 1990, 1019). This does not alter the labour process itself, and, as such, can only produce absolute surplus-value via a lengthened working day. However, it is possible to increase the production of relative surplus-value by reconfiguring entire labour processes such that a "*specifically capitalist form of production* comes into being" (Marx 1990, 1024, emphasis original). For example, the assembly line broke down complex labour processes into their constituent components and reconfigured the entire layout of factories. This is real subsumption, in which "capitalist social relations ... achieve technical embodiment" (Mackenzie 1984, 488).[4] Marx held that the real subsumption of his time had intensified the pace of work and that it had, by allowing women and children into the industrial workforce, driven wages down (1990, 517–533).

The capitalist use of machines thus confronts labour as a threat. The division of labour devalues labour-power by reducing it to a specialized focus on a particular tool, but when it "becomes the job of the machine to handle this tool, the use-value of the worker's labour-power

[4] Formal and real subsumption should not be considered as stages in a definite historical order (formal followed by real) but rather as complementary techniques which continue to be applied and facilitate each other's application (see Endnotes 2010).

vanishes, and with it its exchange-value" (Marx 1990, 557). In other words, the "instrument of labour, when it takes the form of a machine, immediately becomes a competitor of the worker himself" (Marx 1990, 557). Machines under capital are "dead labour" (Marx 1990, 342) and "devourers of living labour"(Marx 1990, 983) which intensify the adversariality of the exploitation relationship into "complete and total antagonism" (Marx 1990, 558). Marx (1990) even suggested that it "would be possible to write a whole history of the inventions made since 1830 for the sole purpose of providing capital with weapons against working-class revolt" (563). This book, I hope, makes a small contribution to that hypothetical volume.

The logic of fetishism, in which a social relation appears as an independent thing, applies also to machines under capital. In general, the "social character of his labour confronts the worker as something not merely alien, but hostile and antagonistic; when it appears before him objectified and personified in capital" (Marx 1990, 1025). With machines, labour confronts its own creations turned against it. This takes a particularly vivid and literal form with machines which exhibit the capacity to move (and today, emulate cognitive processes): "(P)ast labour – in the automaton and the machinery moved by it – steps forth as acting apparently in independence of [living] labour, it subordinates labour instead of being subordinate to it, it is the iron man confronting the man of flesh and blood" (Marx quoted in Smith 2009, 125). The Marxist understanding of machinery thus seems clear. It is capital's favoured weapon in its ongoing struggle to control and exploit labour. While this is so, capital's machinic tendency is not without complications. One of the most hotly debated topics in the history of Marxism—what Marx called the tendency of the profit rate to fall—is directly related to the increasing organic composition of capital:

> Since the mass of living labour applied continuously declines in relation to the mass of objectified labour that it sets in motion ... the part of this living labour that is unpaid and objectified in surplus-value must also stand in an ever-decreasing ratio to the value of the total capital applied. But this ratio between the mass of surplus-value and the total capital applied in fact constitutes the rate of profit, which must therefore steadily fall. (Marx 1991, 319)

This tendency is important because it contains the perpetual threat of capitalist crisis, yet it is "simply the expression, peculiar to the capitalist mode of production, of the progressive development of the social productivity of labour", which is achieved primarily through the introduction of machines (Marx 1991, 319). There are a variety of ways capital can mitigate this tendency, such as increasing the intensity of exploitation, decreasing wages below the cost of reproduction of labour-power and decreasing the value of constant capital. Much of the historical debate over the tendency centres around how these factors and the tendency interact. The details are beyond the scope of this book, but I submit that if the basic Marxist model of capital obtains, then so must the tendency. The tendency and the counteracting factors are not, in fact, distinct. As Jehu (2015) explains:

> the counteracting influences themselves are the immediate, real and historically relevant expression of the law of the tendency of the rate of profit to fall … they do counter the law, but … the counteracting influences on the profit rate reverse the tendency toward decline of the profit rate only at the cost of accelerating the tendency, precisely because they are ultimately aimed at increasing the productivity of labor and of expanding that portion of the labor day that is unpaid.

The tendency of the profit rate to fall proceeds by a series of convolutions, not a linear trajectory. The tendency of capital towards an increasingly machinic state is both contributor to and consequence of the tendency of the profit rate to fall. Machines are introduced to increase the extraction of relative surplus-value, but by reducing living labour they reduce total potentially extractable surplus-value, necessitating the opening of new markets. The technological history of capital can be schematized as a series of mutations propelled by this paradoxical dynamic. Capital attempts to solve its central problem through the further application of the same techniques which gave rise to this problem. This, according to some readings of Marx, necessitates an ultimate crisis of capital.

The Fragment on Machines

In a passage from *Grundrisse* known as "The Fragment on Machines" Marx imagines a highly automated future capitalism. It is striking to remind oneself that this passage was written in 1857–1858. Marx asserts that the "full development of capital" occurs:

> only when the means of labour has not only taken the economic form of fixed capital, but has also been suspended in its immediate form, and when fixed capital appears as a machine within the production process, opposite labour; and the entire production process appears as not subsumed under the direct skillfulness of the worker, but rather as the technological application of science. (Marx 1993, 699)

Capital achieves maturity as human labour in production is replaced by machines. As Land (2012) puts it, capital "only retains anthropological characteristics as a symptom of underdevelopment" (445–446). The direct labour of workers becomes an "indispensable, but subordinate moment, compared to general scientific labour, technological application of natural sciences … and to the general productive force arising from social combination" (Marx 1993, 700). The collective knowledge of society, embodied in machines, becomes the most significant component of production and the "human being comes to relate more as watchman and regulator to the production process" (Marx 1993, 705). In this speculative context, Marx deploys the peculiar term "general intellect":

> The development of fixed capital indicates to what degree general social knowledge has become a direct force of production, and to what degree, hence, the conditions of the process of social life itself have come under the control of the general intellect and been transformed in accordance with it. (Marx 1993, 706)

Social knowledge—the "social brain" (Marx 1993, 694)—becomes a direct force of production once it has been captured by capital and implemented in machinery. Capital's machinic emulation of the social brain constitutes the general intellect, or the manifold of skill and knowledge possessed by capital as machinery (Dyer-Witheford et al. 2019, 63–64). This is not a widely held interpretation of general intellect. But, I believe it more accurately describes the contemporary technological milieu than the popular *post-operaismo* reading discussed in the next chapter (see Hardt and Negri 2000; Virno 2001). Since machines cannot produce surplus-value, as the general intellect takes over production, there is less and less labour to exploit. Capital "presses to reduce labour time to a minimum, while it posits labour time, on the other side, as sole measure and source of wealth" (Marx 1993, 706). By mechanizing and automating labour processes, capital "works towards its own dissolution as the form dominating production" (Marx 1993, 700).

This spectacular passage is notable for its divergence with the more sober tone of *Capital*. It seems to assert that capital will cut off its supply of surplus-value and automate itself out of existence. Recall the Time Travelling Terminator of Full Automation from the introductory chapter, who heralds the collapse of capital under the weight of its own contradictions. As we will see in the next chapter, this is how *post-operaismo* thinkers have interpreted "The Fragment", as a Marxian prophecy about machines that is happening in our time (Hardt and Negri 2000, 364). But since "The Fragment" is a rather cryptic text which was never published in Marx's lifetime, it is uncertain whether it really was a prediction, some sort of thought experiment, or something else entirely. My reading of this passage accords with that of Christian Fuchs (2016) who argues that "when [Marx] speaks of a breakdown in 'The Fragment' he does not mean an automatic collapse of capitalism, but rather that exchange value collapses within communism" (370). This means that any notion of collapse through the mechanisms gestured to in the "The Fragment" must be preceded by a revolutionary overthrow of the domination of capital. It is not a prophecy which is coming true today, but a description of something that could occur if the mode of production is changed.

The futural musing of "The Fragment" concludes our introduction to Marx. With this foundation in place, the following sections survey several different interpreters of Marx for whom machinery has been a central interest.

Marxism(s)

As our brief look at "The Fragment" indicates, there is no universally accepted reading of Marx. Far from it. Any use of Marx's theory should therefore make clear which reading(s) of Marx it adheres to. My research, as I discuss in the conclusion of this chapter, draws primarily upon labour process theory (LPT) and the New Reading of Marx (NRM). In this and the following chapter, I distinguish these lines of thought from orthodox,

Soviet and Western Marxisms and the influential paradigms of *operaismo* and *post-operaismo*.[5] I also consider a variety of Marxists who have dealt specifically with information technology. All of these interpreters of Marx have differently constructed Marxism's constellation of labour, capital and machine.

It is worth first addressing the allegation of technological determinism which has long been levelled at Marxism (Hansen 1921; Heilbroner 1967). Often cited in this context is the following passage from Marx's *The Poverty of Philosophy*: "In acquiring new productive forces men change their mode of production; and in changing their mode of production, in changing the way of earning their living, they change all their social relations. The hand-mill gives you society with the feudal lord; the steam-mill, society with the industrial capitalist" (Marx 1955, 49). However, as Mackenzie (1984) correctly points out, the determinist interpretation of this passage only holds if productive forces refer only to technology (476). In fact, the forces of production include the social relations in which labour-power is arranged, as well as technology: "co-operation is itself a 'productive force'" (Marx and Engels 1845). The critique of Marx as determinist does not hold much water. This is not to say, however, that there has been no technological determinism in the history of Marxism.

Marx, who died in 1883, only lived to see the publication of Volume 1 of *Capital*. The early diffusion of Marxism was driven by his friend and collaborator Frederick Engels' editing, publication and interpretation of Marx's work after his death, as well as the interpretive work of the philosopher Karl Kautsky. The readings of Marx advocated by Engels and Kautsky are today often referred to as orthodox Marxism. Elbe (2013) argues that for the orthodox Marxist, Marx's achievement was to have achieved a scientific understanding of the historical laws which govern social development. The orthodox reading of Marx posits a teleological, deterministic character to social and natural development, with communism standing at the end of history as the necessary resolution of the contradictions of capitalism. For Elbe (2013), in this interpretation of Marx, "humanity is subordinated to a 'scientifically verifiable' automatism of liberation".

Indeed, Kautsky (1989 [1929]) suggested that "social development is in the last analysis conditioned by technical progress and not by the class

[5] For a study of Chinese Marxism, which is not dealt with here, see Chan (2003).

struggle". Kautsky's "always mechanistic" Marxism (Bronner 1982, 580) understood revolutions as "objective phenomena that socialists should patiently wait for, rather than actively preparing for" (Flakin 2019). The legacy of Engels is subject to more debate. Elbe (2013) derides orthodox Marxism as "Engelsism" because of his purported pernicious influence, but others contest such evaluations (Rees 1994). The contributions of Engels go beyond the scope of this book, but it is worth noting that early on he marked the emerging conjunction of capital and technology, noting that capital enjoys the "assistance of science … against labour" and that "mechanical inventions" can act as competitors to workers (Engels 1844). While few Marxists today endorse an orthodox perspective, as Heinrich (2012) correctly notes, most ideas "in general circulation today concerning Marx and Marxian theory – whether these are appraised positively or negatively – are essentially based upon" the orthodox interpretation (26).

Soviet Marxism

While this book cannot do justice to the wealth of Marxist material on technology produced in the Soviet world, a brief look at some major figures is necessary if we are to adequately situate contemporary Marxist theory. In 1914, Vladimir Lenin (1972 [1914]) was no technological optimist, describing Taylorism as "Man's Enslavement by the Machine". But four years later, after signing the 1918 Treaty of Brest-Litovsk with the Central Powers, he wrote that he had learned from the First World War that "those who have the best technology, organization, discipline and the best machines emerge on top … It is essential to learn that without machines … it is impossible to live in modern society. It is necessary to master the highest technology or be crushed" (quoted in Bailes 1978, 49). Lenin elaborated that without "grasp[ing] all the science, technology and art, we will not be able to build life in a communist society" (quoted in Bailes 1978, 52). Lenin's (1920) famous dictum "Communism is soviet power + electrification of the whole country" expresses his conviction that a new mode of production must be built by embracing the existing technological infrastructure and pushing it beyond its capitalist limitations. Lenin also came to believe that communism must incorporate capitalist techniques for managing labour by treating humans as machines. He asserted that the "Taylor system, properly controlled and intelligently applied by the working people themselves, will serve as a reliable means of further reducing the obligatory working day for the entire working population" (Lenin 1971 [1918]).

Lenin's reevaluation of Taylorism reflects the larger Soviet attitude towards machines, which became one of the enthusiastic embrace (Sochor 1981; Cooper 1977). The appropriation of capitalist machines would become a central tenet of the Soviet project. Leon Trotsky held that a hypertrophic industrialization was necessary to allow the USSR to achieve autonomy from the capitalist world market (Mandel 1991). Aleksei Gastev espoused a "blanket endorsement" of Taylorism, arguing that its practice was distorted under capital, but could be perfected in a socialist economy (Sochor 1981, 250). Yevgeni Preobrazhensky called for a "socialist primitive accumulation" in which peasants would be intentionally and rapidly, yet humanely, transformed into industrial workers (Krassó 1967, 82; Goldner 1995, 75). While the notion of the wholesale appropriation of capitalist technology (and culture) was disputed by figures such as Alexander Bogdanov, who advocated for the development of specifically proletarian technology and culture (Wark 2015), the Soviet technological impetus was amplified with the implementation of "war communism" from 1918 to 1921 which saw all factories nationalized and put under militarized central control. Leon Trotsky (1957 [1924]) even waxed poetic about the aesthetic possibilities of technology: "Faith merely promises to move mountains; but technology, which takes nothing 'on faith', is actually able to cut down mountains and move them. Up to now this was done for industrial purposes … in the future this will be done on an immeasurably larger scale, according to a general industrial and artistic plan".[6]

Technological advancement remained a central theme in Soviet thought throughout the Second World War and beyond. While cybernetics was initially demonized by Stalinist thought, by the time of the third five-year plan (1961–1966), the cybernetic automation of production was a central goal (Gerovitch 2002). It was generally held that automation would play a "crucial role in the creation of the material and technical basis of communist society" while undermining the conditions

[6] Despite Trotsky and Preobrazhensky's good intentions, Soviet industrialization ended up being implemented, after Lenin's death in 1924, in less aesthetic terms, by Joseph Stalin via forced collectivization. In 1928, Stalin implemented the first five-year plan which aggressively developed the industrial and agricultural capacities of the USSR.

for the existence of capitalism (Cooper 1977, 152). The Soviet view of automation was thus mixed up with the orthodox Marxist belief in the teleology of history, culminating in communism. As the USSR degenerated in subsequent decades, such views came to be viewed with skepticism by many Marxists outside the Soviet world, who would then develop very different readings of Marx.[7]

Western Marxism

The year before Lenin's death, two European philosophers, György Lukács (1972 [1923]) and Karl Korsch (2013 [1923]) published foundational works for what would come to be known as Western Marxism. Other notable thinkers in this area include Antonio Gramsci and Frankfurt School critical theorists like Theodor Adorno, Herbert Marcuse and Max Horkheimer. Western Marxism rejects teleological formulations of history and the notion of Marxism as a science of the objective laws of society and nature. It places Marxism somewhere closer to philosophy, and often draws on Freudian psychoanalysis and Marx's Hegelian philosophical roots. Economics is displaced from centre stage by concerns with art, ideology, historical contingency and social critique—in general, culture. This switch in content was accompanied by a shift in tone, from orthodox triumphalism to a "latent pessimism" (Anderson 1979, 88). This pessimistic tone is especially evident in Western Marxist discussions of technology.

Western Marxists did not entirely reject the orthodox thesis that the technological rationalization of production was necessary and desirable for communism (Marcuse 2013 [1964]; Gramsci 1992 [1971]). However, they were more cautious in their prognoses, holding that technology could also enable unprecedented forms of domination over labour. Adorno and Horkheimer held that the technological mastery of nature led, via the Enlightenment, to capitalism and fascism, both expressions of the technological-rational domination of the human (Adorno

[7] That is not to say that all Marxists outside the USSR rejected the Soviet version of Marxism. Some Marxist economists in the West elaborated an orthodox Marxism focused on the quantification of value. This reading of Marx sought to produce rigorous models of how prices derive from the value of commodities and in general, to make Marxism an effective competitor to mainstream economics. Some examples of this view include Dobb (1940) and Sweezy (1968 [1942]). For an overview see Saad-Filho (1997).

and Horkheimer 1997 [1947]). For Marcuse, the technological advances of capitalism made communism theoretically possible by potentially producing an abundance of needs and wants, but he held that this theoretical possibility was denied by historical developments. Instead, the proliferation of machines had wrought a widespread "technological rationality" defined not by critical thought but "adjustment and compliance" (Marcuse 1998 [1941], 146). This produced a "one-dimensional" working class unable to see itself as distinct from capital (Marcuse 2013 [1964]). Lukács (1972 [1923]) elaborated Marx's discussion of fetishism with his notion of reification, arguing that capital systematically disguised social relations between people as things, allowing subjectivity itself to be treated as a "technical relation" (Feenberg 2015, 493). Gramsci (1992 [1971]) contributed the concept of hegemony to explain how capital maintains control via consent rather than coercion, through media technologies and cultural institutions like schools.

According to Western Marxism, capital had successfully infiltrated culture and technology and was employing both to render workers increasingly docile and machinelike. This was a very different configuration of labour, capital and machine than previous Marxisms. But skepticism about orthodox Marxism ramified in other ways as well.

Labour Process Theory

In the 1970s, Harry Braverman (1998) popularized an approach that came to be known as labour process theory. Labour processes are, as we saw above, the series of actions necessary for producing products and services. Labour process analysis focuses on particular concrete labour processes to show how they are structured and restructured by both the larger-scale exigencies of valorization and the creative and militant capacities of labour. Labour process analysis is thus interested in the workplace practices of workers and the ways in which management, as the representative of capital, seeks to control them. Labour process studies have verified Marx's claim that one of capital's most effective means for controlling labour are machines.

Braverman, who worked as a coppersmith for years, witnessed firsthand the deskilling of craft labour processes and their gradual replacement by machines. Like Western Marxists, he was dissatisfied with the use of machines for the industrialization of labour in the USSR. His central goal was to show that the Taylorist reconfiguration of labour processes, as a product of capitalism, was designed to serve the goals of capital. He thus argued that the assumption that socialist or communist modes of production should rely on such an approach was flawed (Braverman 1998, 15–16). To adopt a blindly Taylorist approach to the labour process is to adopt the perspective of capital.

Braverman's argument is based on a historical study of Taylorist scientific management in the late nineteenth century.[8] Taylorism subjected the movements and knowledge of industrial workers to fine-grained scrutiny and documentation (using time-motion study, for instance) and made them available for analysis, and control, by management. This resulted in complex craft labour processes being broken down into components that could be performed by less skilled (and less well paid) workers, and eventually automated. Braverman (1998) summed up this process with three principles. The first is the "dissociation of the labor process from the skills of the workers" (78). Management captures the knowledge and skills of workers through observation or interrogation and makes them available to capital. The second principle is the "separation of conception from execution" (79). Planning, organization and creative functions are shifted to management, while workers simply follow orders. The third principle is the "use of [the] monopoly over knowledge to control each step of the labor process and its mode of execution" (82). Captured knowledge allows capital to specify precisely how work should be done, at a fine grain, so as to maximize productivity and limit worker control.

Via the application of these principles, Taylorism "render[ed] conscious and systematic, the formerly unconscious tendency of capitalist production" (Braverman 1998, 83). The extraction of knowledge and skills from labour, the emulation of them with machines, and the reconfiguration of labour processes on the basis of these machines, became programmatic. The technological reconfiguration of labour processes then allows capital "the opportunity to do by wholly mechanical means that which it had previously attempted to do by organizational and disciplinary means" (Braverman 1998, 134). The supervisory and disciplinary function of management can be increasingly executed automatically through the "progressive elimination of the control functions of the worker, insofar as possible, and their transfer to a device which is controlled,

[8] Rosenthal (2019) shows that scientific approaches to the management of labour predate Taylorism and were first used to track and increase the productivity of slaves in the antebellum southern USA.

again insofar as possible, by management from outside the direct process" (Braverman 1998, 146). As a witness to the early days of information technology (i.e. numerical control machine tools) Braverman took a dark view of the future. For him, the recursive capacity of software heralded a new "universality of the machine" because "control is no longer dependent upon … specialized internal construction" (Braverman 1998, 132). Already in the 1970s, clerical and office work was subject to Taylorist management. Braverman (1998) suggested that the future would see the extension of Taylorism to programmers (227–228) as well as "draftsmen and technicians, engineers and accountants, nurses and teachers" (282).

Labour process theory received substantial criticism for purportedly neglecting considerations of worker subjectivity, favouring instead structural relations of control. This conflict, and others, have been documented in several collections (Knights and Willmott 1990; Wardell et al. 1999; Thompson and Smith 2010). Notable for labour process analyses which clearly include consideration of worker subjectivity is the work of David Noble (1986) for whom labour process analysis is inseparable from class struggle. Labour process theory was also criticized for its central deskilling thesis, even by those working within the tradition (Wood 1982). Some critics held that Braverman neglected to account for how the introduction of new technologies in production actually produces new skills and types of work (Attewell 1987; Burris 1998). Against these critiques, it is important to note that Braverman's work was not meant to provide a "precise specification of the organization and control of each and every form of capitalist labour process" but rather a thesis about work under capital in general, that manifests differently in various labour processes (Knights and Willmott 1990, 11).

The editors of a recent volume on labour process theory and digital work note that new technologies and their applications for automation have renewed interest in the question of deskilling (Briken et al. 2017, 2). However, little work has been done on the AI labour process, other than the broad strokes given in Dyer-Witheford et al. (2019). Chapter 6 of this book aims to contribute to closing this gap.

In the absence of labour process studies of AI, my research has been informed by labour process analyses of software production. Kraft (1977, 1979) was the first to conduct a labour process analysis of software workers whom he argued were not exempt from deskilling. Kraft and Dubnoff (1986) concluded that "software work replicates rather than revolutionizes traditional relationships between managers and managed"

(184). Much early labour process work on software development echoed these sentiments (Cooley 1980, 1981; Duncan 1981; Orlikowski 1988; Greenbaum 1979, 1998; Ensmenger and Aspray 2002). Other voices dissented, arguing that there was no evidence of deskilling in software work (Tarallo 1987; Ainspain 1999; Hounshell 2000).

Rowena Barrett has presented a more complicated picture, arguing that while traditional forms of direct control via deskilling may not be evident in software development, these labourers are subject to control via "'responsible autonomy' which attempts to 'harness the adaptability of labour power by giving workers leeway and encouraging them to adapt to changing situations in a manner beneficial to the firm'" (Friedman 1977, 78 cited in Barrett 2005, 79). Rasmussen and Johansen (2005) agree that "autonomy can be used as a strategy for increased control over the workers ... by devolving responsibility" (118). One manifestation of responsible autonomy is what Barrett (2005) calls "technical autonomy" or "management allowing software developers autonomy to develop the 'best' program using their skills and expertise" (82). Such subtler forms of control help elucidate how management attempts to remain master of a labour process not amenable to Taylorism. But some labour process theorists have argued that software work presents an even greater challenge for management.

According to one labour process analysis of work in software startup companies, it is "difficult to equate the practices and processes ... with an industrial assembly line. At every stage human rather than machine intervention predominates ... each project requires fresh planning and decisions. This reality stands in sharp contrast to the 'one-best-way' of Taylorized work settings" (Andrews et al. 2005, 66). According to this analysis, software production is "dependent upon the skills of individuals and the synchronization of their disparate efforts" in ways management cannot implement from above (Andrews et al. 2005, 59). Software production is thus "craft rather than ... technical-oriented" and not at threat of deskilling and automation because to "fully standardize computer programming ... would require the seemingly omniscient knowledge of both the emergent problems and the associated solutions" (Andrews et al. 2005, 67). According to Andrews, Lair and Landry, software work evinces a fundamental reconfiguration of labour, capital and machine; in the software industry, it would seem, capital cannot capture labour's skills and knowledge. While this is by no means the consensus view of labour process theorists, it provides a compelling starting point for an analysis of labour in the AI industry nearly twenty years later.

The New Reading of Marx

In the 1920s, the Soviet economist Isaak Rubin disputed popular interpretations of Marx which tried to quantify value and concrete labour. Rubin (1978 [1927]) argued that "labour is only [the] substance of value, and that in order to obtain value in the full sense of the word we have to add something to labour as the substance of value, namely the social form of value". By the social form of value, he meant that value (in Marx's sense) can arise only insofar as labour is conducted, and products are produced, within a system of social relations premised on the exchange of commodities. Social relations must have a particular form for the real abstraction of value to obtain. Socially necessary labour time determines the magnitude of value, but the "abstract character of a commodity" by which it has value and can be exchanged for other commodities derives not only from the of magnitude value it represents, but from the social relations by which it is produced and exchanged as a commodity (Rubin 1978 [1927]). This refers back to the point, emphasized earlier in the section on Marx and value, that value is not simply produced at the point of production, but has also to be realized in exchange. This at the time unorthodox approach ruffled ideological feathers because it "could be seen as tantamount to a defense of the market" and Rubin was executed in the Stalinist purges of 1937 (Boldyrev and Kragh 2015, 372). Rubin's focus on the form of value was revived in the 1960s by West German students of Horkheimer and Adorno, such as Hans-Georg Backhaus (1980), Alfred Schmidt (1981) and Helmut Reichelt (1982). Their approach would come to be known as *Neue Marx-Lektüre* or the New Reading of Marx (NRM). While NRM has an expanding presence in English, many of its important publications have not yet been translated from German (i.e. Heinrich 1991). NRM argues that orthodox Marxism did not reflect on Marx's theoretical depth, understanding Marx as an extender, rather than critic, of classical political economy. NRM aims to excavate, from beneath what it considers shallow, orthodox readings, an "esoteric" Marx (Elbe 2013).

The early work of Backhaus (1980) argued that reading Marx as elaborating Ricardo's conception of value is untenable because it cannot explain what it is that undergoes, and remains constant throughout, the fundamental formula of capital, M-C-M' (114). In other words, the formal conception of value was unrecognized. Reichelt points out that such a perspective is also unable to explain how it is that social relations come to be taken as things. He relates how he and his fellows "systematically plagued" their teacher Horkheimer to tell them what reification "really is" (Reichelt 1982, 166). The problem was again, following in the steps of Rubin, an inadequate understanding of the form of value. In this context, form does not mean a form of thought, but a complex of concrete social relations, reproduced over time, by which value manifests in, and has effects on, the world. Value is not just a pure quantity but "something which unfolds itself in differentiations" (Backhaus 1980, 112). To focus on the form of value is thus to focus on value's "mode of existence" (Holloway 2002, 51), an essential component of which is commodity exchange. NRM insists that the realization of value in exchange is essential to understanding how value works. Therefore it expands focus from orthodox concerns with production to situate labour processes amid longer processes distributed across "the social totality" by which value is realized (Heinrich 2007).

For NRM, capital's subsumption of the social totality beyond production, via the value-form, is hard to overestimate. NRM often discusses this by expanding on the moments where Marx attributed autonomy to capital. For Bonefeld (2014), value-form analysis "amounts to an exposition of the law of value as a process of social 'autonomization', which economics analyses in terms of price movements, stock market developments and other such macro-economic analyses of, in themselves, incomprehensible economic quantities" (8). This is why Backhaus (1980), echoing Marx, calls value a "subject" (112). The recursive process of valorization subordinates human social intercourse to "self-moving economic forces that assert themselves behind the backs of the acting subjects, indifferent and indeed hostile to their needs" (Bonefeld 2014, 21–22). Capital's occult power, by which it achieves this autonomy, is the value-form, which NRM holds manifests concretely via money.

NRM thinkers argue that Marx's conception of value pertains specifically to capitalist economies, which assume widespread production for commodity exchange, and therefore money to act as a universal equivalent. Heinrich (2012) states that "only with the money form does an adequate form of value exist" because the "act of measuring [value] can only be conducted by means of money" (63–65). This perspective, like that of Rubin, has met and continues to meet with resistance for many reasons, but one notable one is its insistence that circulation, as well as production, is essential to the extraction of surplus-value.[9] As Pitts (2018) puts it, value is a "category of social mediation expressed in money. It springs from the exchange of commodities by means of money in the sphere of circulation" (3). Before exchange occurs "the magnitude of value can only be more or less estimated" (Heinrich 2012, 55). This would seem to conflict with the essential Marxist notion that the substance of value is abstract labour which is harvested by capital during exploitation in production. Indeed, taken to an extreme, the monetary view of value entails that "value does not refer to the expenditure of labour in production, but to the validation in exchange of the labour performed; and there is no intrinsic relation between the performance of labour and the value of the product" (Saad-Filho 1997, 465). Rubin and Backhaus have been accused of lapsing into such "circulationism" (Starosta and Kicillof 2007) but not many NRM thinkers endorse such an extreme view.

The more prevalent perspective (and one in accord with Marx's own writings, in my opinion) is that value depends on both production and exchange via money. Value "isn't just 'there' after being 'produced' someplace" it is a "social relationship … constituted in production and circulation … the 'either/or' question is senseless" (Heinrich 2012, 54).[10] Abstract labour is the substance of surplus-value which is captured via exploitation in production. Yet if the commodity produced is never successfully sold for (at minimum) its average socially necessary labour time, then its value is never realized and in effect, it ceases to exist. This seems obviously true, yet the status of realization continues to be the subject of controversy. Fuchs (2014) disputes NRM's insistence on realization because it:

> cannot account for the fact that capitalists may not be able to sell commodities because of market problems, are therefore not able to realize profit, but nonetheless have exploited their employee's labour in the production process … it follows that a commodity that is not successfully exchanged with money … does not have value and therefore also has no surplus value, which logically implies that the workers who produced it have not been exploited. (45)

[9] For details on the "monetarist controversy" see Elson (1979) and Bellofiore (2009).

[10] My support for this perspective does not align me entirely with Heinrich; particularly not with his dismissal of the tendency of the profit rate to fall (Heinrich 2013). For a succinct reply to Heinrich on this topic, see Jehu (2015).

This reading seems to conflate Marx's analytic concept of exploitation with an ethical one. Exploitation is one moment in a longer process of valorization which occurs over time and which might not be completed for any number of factors. Exploitation defines capital's appropriation of the difference between the value of labour-power and the surplus-value generated by labour. If capital fails to realize the value of its commodity via exchange, that does not change the character of work that has already been done within a relation of exploitation. It simply means that valorization has been aborted. Surplus-value is not a substance inhering in the freshly produced commodity; prior to realization in exchange, it is "ideally anticipated money", but this anticipation may fall flat (Bellofiore 2009, 17). Capital tries its utmost to avoid this contingency with practices ranging from marketing to logistics to subscriptions.

Marx (1991) pointed out that the "conditions for immediate exploitation and for the realization of that exploitation are not identical. Not only are they separate in time and space, they are also separate in theory. The former is restricted only by the society's productive forces, the latter by the proportionality between the different branches of production and by the society's power of consumption" (352). A commodity produced with exploited labour has, for all intents and purposes, no value if no one can or will buy it. Particular values within the system of capital may change if relevant social relations change. Saad-Filho (1997) refers to "synchronization" to explain how the value of a commodity is determined by the average labour time "presently necessary for production (instead of that necessary when production may have occurred)" (470). As social relations, "values are not established once and for all when the commodities are produced; rather they are socially attributed at every moment" (Saad-Filho 1997, 470). The nature of value as social relation means that individual values may fluctuate as relevant social relations change, but it also entails a larger point: that value, in Marx's sense, is a phenomenon specific to capitalism.[11] Marx states it clearly:

> The value-form of the product of labour is the most abstract, but also the most universal form of the bourgeois mode of production; by that fact it stamps the bourgeois mode of production as a particular kind of social production of a historical and transitory character. If then we make the

[11] For a reading of Marx which contrarily understands value as a transhistorical phenomenon, see Cockshott (2019).

> mistake of treating it as the eternal natural form of social production, we necessarily overlook the specificity of the value-form, and consequently of the commodity form together with its further developments, the money form, the capital form, etc. (Marx 1990, 174)

While other modes of production may generate economic surpluses, these are not all identical. The term value has a plethora of uses in different fields, but the specifically capitalist form of value should not be conflated with these. Neglect of the specificity of value as contingent on a particular ensemble of social relations is one aspect of my critique of *post-operaismo*.

However, even as I hold up NRM as an important and useful way to read Marx, I recognize that it is not immune to critique. Its focus on the form of value entails attention to social relations, however, NRM tends to underplay the fundamental social relation of class antagonism. NRM has often neglected to connect its form analysis to messy, concrete social relations (Bonefeld 2014, 6). Pitts (2018) calls on NRM to recognize that "socially mediate forms are rooted in real relations of antagonism, coercion, domination and dispossession" (5). Further, as NRM overlooks concrete social relations it also tends to spend little time attending to the details of concrete (especially computational) technologies and their applications in labour processes. I submit that the emphasis on the form of value has led NRM to focus on the continuities of capital's valorization process rather than changes in its technological infrastructure. While one should not focus solely on the technological milieu, neither should one ignore it entirely, since it is an important aspect of the material conditions, as the authors in the following section show.

Cybernetic Capitalism

The previous sections looked at only a few lines of Marxist thought. There are also many important Marxist authors who are more difficult to categorize. This section considers some of these more difficult to categorize authors who wrote about technology in the era of "cybernetic capitalism" (Robins and Webster 1988). While there is no consensus definition for the term cybernetic capitalism, I use it to refer roughly to a period from the end of the Second World War until the present (2021), characterized by the proliferation of information and automation technologies.[12] Marxist thought of the cybernetic era has retained the ambivalent evaluation of technology characteristic of earlier Marxist analyses. For some, machines are seen as capital's most effective weapon against labour, but for others, machines represent capital's Achilles heel and the key to communism. For example, in the mid-twentieth century, Marxist estimations of new automation technologies (discussed in Chapter 4) varied widely. On the one hand, the Italian communist Amadeo Bordiga (2019 [1957]) effused that "*we have been waiting for this* [the advent of automation] *for a hundred years*" since he deduced, from a reading of "The Fragment" that automation entails the "necessity of communism" (462, emphasis original). On the other hand, the militant black American auto worker James Boggs (1963) warned that automation would, by eliminating overall jobs and creating surplus workers, "sharpen the conflicts among the various sections of the population, particularly between those working and those not working" and weaken the working class.

Beyond automation technologies, Marxist authors of the cybernetic era have revealed the diverse interconnections between information technology and capital. They have charted how a capital-military joint effort drove the digital networking of the world and the invention of now ubiquitous information technologies (Schiller 1999, 2014). Marxist and Marx-influenced media scholars have also elaborated new theories of digital labour which track the specificities of increasingly computational forms of work and life (Mosco and Wasco 1988; Huws 2003; Terranova 2004; Mosco and McKercher 2009; Burston et al. 2010; Fuchs 2014). Others have applied Marxist theory to the study of information technologies and the internet, social media, big data and the platform economy (Dyer-Witheford 1999; Fuchs and Dyer-Witheford 2013; Fuchs and Mosco 2015; Fuchs 2019). Despite the diversity of their interventions, few Marxists have engaged substantially with AI.

When the first commercial AI systems were deployed in the early 1980s, Marxists discerned in them the possibility for a new extension of Taylorist control over labour (Cooley 1981). Positing the need for a forum to discuss the social and political implications of "the deluge of quasi-expert systems [and] artificial-intelligence software tools", the engineer and militant trade unionist Mike Cooley founded the journal

[12] A more detailed, though still schematic, technological periodization of capitalism is proposed in Dyer-Witheford et al. (2019, 51).

AI & Society, which still exists today (Cooley 1987, 179). A number of other Marxist voices agreed with Cooley's early analysis. Tom Athanasiou (1985) described AI as "cleverly disguised politics". Bruce Berman (1992) held that:

> the ideological importance of AI can best be understood as analogous to the role played by scientific management in the second industrial revolution … AI seeks to achieve the same control over mental processes that scientific management sought to achieve over physical labour through a process of rationalization, fragmentation, mechanization and routinization". (104–105)

Some other Marxists, however, saw in AI a tool that labour might wield against capital. Following in the footsteps of the failed attempts of both the USSR (Peters 2016) and socialist Chile (Medina 2011) to apply cybernetics to centralized economic planning, Paul Cockshott (1988) held out a renewed optimism based on techniques "developed in artificial intelligence" (1). More recently, he has asserted that big data and supercomputers are the "foundations of Cybercommunism" (Cockshott 2017; see also Dyer-Witheford 2013).

Three other Marxist authors are especially relevant for reconfiguring Marx's triangulation of labour, capital and machine for a study of the AI industry. In different ways, they all grappled with the new technological capacities for recursion of capital increasingly suffused with computers, AI and other information technologies in the 1980s and 1990s.

Tessa Morris-Suzuki (1984) held that the "separation of hardware from software … may be seen as constituting a revolutionary fission of the labour process itself" (1984, 112). When the worker's knowledge can be represented as digital information it "may be separated from the physical body of the worker and may itself become a commodity" (Morris-Suzuki 1984, 113). Morris-Suzuki predicted that capital would reorganize itself around software production: "information … which contributes to productive processes—will become a commodity churned out by corporate enterprises almost as routinely and monotonously as cars flowing from an assembly line" (1984, 114–115). All kinds of intellectual labour, including software production, would be subject to Bravermanian deskilling and "the forces of automation" (Morris-Suzuki 1984, 118–120). This book offers support for her predictions. We will see that software production was industrialized decades ago and the recently industrialized production of AI already evinces deskilling.

Second comes George Caffentzis (1997), for whom Turing's mechanization of thought, by showing how cognitive processes can be broken down into discrete stages, provides the grounds for a new computational Taylorism. But his most compelling intervention comes from his ruminations on capital's drive to automation pushed to an extreme. Caffentzis holds that capital's need for valorization entails its pursuit of a "logical escape" from human labour via technological "self-reflexivity" or machines which can autonomously produce machines (2013, 128). Only "when automata create automata ... when the elements of automata systems become products of automata systems" can capital "find its fitting foundation" (Caffentzis 2013, 128). Such an "automatization of automation" implies the elimination of surplus-value producing labour and is thus incompatible with valorization (Caffentzis 2013, 129). Yet, Caffentzis does not ascribe to this scenario a collapse of capital analogous to *post-operaismo* readings of "The Fragment". Rather, he shows that the automatization of automation could occur in a limited sector of industry if it is counterbalanced by other sectors with low organic compositions and high rates of surplus-value production (Caffentzis 2013, 133–134). In other words, a highly automated software sector in the rich world (producing near-zero surplus-value) could be counterbalanced by a proliferation of super-exploited labour elsewhere. Such a situation is today adumbrated by the contrast between Silicon Valley software production and brutal labour in African mines harvesting the precious metals necessary for computing hardware. Caffentzis' point is that highly automated future scenarios should not be immediately dismissed as implausible nor as leading to the automatic breakdown of capital.

The third important thinker is Ramin Ramtin, whose unfortunately overlooked *Capitalism and Automation* develops, with great attention to technological detail, a Marxist theory of automation.[13] Ramtin held that

[13] Ramtin makes the important point that software in general poses a novelty for Marxist theory of technology: "Software as a means of production has a peculiar characteristic: it can never wear out" (1991, 117). Since fixed capital transfers value to its product in inverse proportion to its degradation and software does not in-itself wear out, software's "life is entirely dependent upon the rate of innovation" (Ramtin 1991, 177) which referred to Marx (1991) as "moral depreciation" (118–119). Of course, software requires hardware, so this must also be factored in (Ramtin 1991, 117).

"Automate or die" is an "objective necessity imposed by the very functioning of the capitalist mode of production itself, in accordance with and as a result of the law of value" (1991, 101). This book may be read as a lengthy elaboration of, and argument in support of, this statement. Automation is the use of computers for the "systemic application of the principle of feedback" (Ramtin 1991, 60) which enables machines to "directly accept objectified information" without the "mediation of human labour-power" (53). For Ramtin, the significance of this capacity cannot be overstated:

> It is this characteristic which no previous instrument, network of devices or even whole technological systems had ever possessed. It is ... a technology that potentially can be utilized to perform any task which a worker (manual and intellectual) can perform in a production process, and, from capital's standpoint, much faster and more reliably. (Ramtin 1991, 50–51)

Automation thus presents the possibility of machines doing cognitive types of work. Ramtin (1991) noted, thirty years ago, that "there is increasing pressure to raise the productivity of software specialists ... the main path to the raising of efficiency here lies in the development of new software packages as a replacement for the skilled labour involved in software production itself" (113). Early AI was a herald of this new use of software to produce software. It offered capital new techniques for real subsumption, tending towards the "externalization or the complete abstraction of control systems through objectification" which could allow "the objectification of the collective labourer in total ... the complete dissociation of living labour ... from the production process" (Ramtin 1991, 58). Ramtin (1991) suggested that the "purpose and aim behind the whole AI industry" was to "reduce the role and quantity of 'intellectual' labour" (65–66). AI would be pursued by capital because it gave substance to the "ultimate vision" of capital as an "automated system" wherein "conception, co-ordination and execution" are fused into one "all-embracing purely *managerial* function" (Ramtin 1991, 61–65, emphasis original). The boss would simply delegate tasks to an intelligent, docile machine. To evaluate Ramtin's prescience, consider an article in *Harvard Business Review* which effuses that "machine intelligence will let us all work like CEOs", delegating tasks to an array of autonomous agents (Zilis 2016).

Conclusion

Theory is a tool for thinking and doing, but one must have the right tool for the job. Theory must be adequate to the material conditions of the particular context to which it is applied. This chapter has considered how classical political economy's concern with labour, capital and machines ramified over more than two centuries, through Marx's critique of political economy, into the diverse tradition of Marxist theory. While far from a comprehensive survey, this chapter shows how Marxist thought evolved along with changing technological milieus, although it has engaged relatively little with AI so far.

With this theoretical landscape set out, we can now return to the journalistic articles cited in the introductory paragraph of this chapter, in which Marx and AI are discussed together. All three present a similar thesis: AI-powered automation poses a great danger to the existing capitalist mode of production. While Avent (2018) suggests that AI should motivate a reformation of capitalism into one "Marx might enjoy", Del Corro (2017) holds that AI "is driving humanity towards socialism" and Xiang (2018) assert that AI will "spell the end of capitalism". Underlying all three is a narrative similar to that of the Time Travelling Terminator of Full Automation and the prophetic interpretation of Marx's "Fragment on Machines", with which I disagreed above. The idea is that capital, by progressively automating the labour on which it depends, will cut off its supply of surplus-value and self-destruct. AI is understood as an accelerant for that process. *Post-operaismo* thinkers have been influential popularizers of this narrative, via their understanding of "The Fragment". While I do not purport to know how the authors of the journalistic articles cited above came to their conclusions, we can better understand them, and their conjunction of Marx and AI, by interrogating *post-operaismo* thinkers who have been fascinated by the revolutionary implications of information technology. That is the task of the next chapter. But first, a note on my own theoretical perspective.

If theory is a tool, one of the tasks of theoreticians is to improve on existing tools. *Post-operaismo* is the object of critique in this book, but this critique is intended to be constructive. The goal of all work in the Marxist tradition should be to change the material world, not merely to defeat rival factions. My theoretical position is best described as a reading of Marx filtered through a blend of LPT and NRM with an appreciation for the technological enthusiasm of *post-operaismo*. This blend is intended to remedy some of the faults attributed to both labour process theory and NRM, as well as *post-operaismo*. I am indebted to *post-operaismo*'s insistence that technological change is an essential component of any analysis of capital. By focusing on the labour process, as LPT demands, I foreground the concrete in opposition to *post-operaismo*'s high-level generalizations and NRM's formal focus. However, by retaining the value-form perspective elaborated by NRM while doing so, my labour process analysis remains situated within the broader valorization dynamics of capital rather than positing a historical rupture of these, as does *post-operaismo*, or attributing a special craft status to software work, as does some LPT work. Let us turn now to *post-operaismo*.

Bibliography

Adorno, Theodor W., and Max Horkheimer. 1997 [1947]. *Dialectic of Enlightenment*. London: Verso.

Ainspain, Nathan David. 1999. The Geek Shall Inherit or Leave the Money and Run? Role Identities and Turnover Decisions among Software Programmers and the High-Technology Employees. PhD Diss, Cornell University.

Anderson, Perry. 1979. *Considerations on Western Marxism*. London: Verso.

Andrews, Chris K., Craig D. Lair, and Bart Landry. 2005. The Labor Process in Software Startups: Production on a Virtual Assembly Line? In *Management, Labour Process and Software Development: Reality Bites*, ed. Rowena Barrett. New York: Routledge.

Athanasiou, Tom. 1985. Artificial Intelligence: Cleverly Disguised Politics. In *Compulsive Technology: Computers as Culture*, ed. Tony Solomonides and Les Levidow, 13–35. London: Free Association Books.

Attewell, Paul. 1987. The Deskilling Controversy. *Work and Occupations* 14 (3): 323–346.

Avent, Ryan. 2018. A Digital Capitalism Marx Might Enjoy. *MIT Technology Review*. June 27. https://www.technologyreview.com/2018/06/27/141746/a-digital-capitalism-marx-might-enjoy/.

Babbage, Charles. 2003 [1832]. *On The Economy of Machinery and Manufactures*. https://www.fulltextarchive.com/pdfs/On-the-Economy-of-Machinery-and-Manufactures.pdf.

Backhaus, Hans-Georg. 1980. On the Dialectics of the Value-Form. *Thesis Eleven* 1 (1): 99–120.

Bailes, Kendall E. 1978. *Technology and Society under Lenin and Stalin: Origins of the Soviet Technical Intelligentsia, 1917–1941*. Princeton: Princeton University Press.

Barrett, Rowena. 2005. Managing the Software Development Labour Process: Direct Control, Time and Technical Autonomy. In *Management, Labour Process and Software Development: Reality Bites*, ed. Rowena Barret. New York: Routledge.

Bastani, Aaron. 2019. *Fully Automated Luxury Communism*. London: Verso.

Bellofiore, Riccardo. 2009. A Ghost Turning into a Vampire: The Concept of Capital and Living Labour. In *Rereading Marx: New Perspectives After the Critical Edition*, ed. Riccardo Bellofiore and Roberto Fineschi, 178–194. London: Palgrave Macmillan.

Berman, Bruce. 1992. Artificial Intelligence and the Ideology of Capitalist Reconstruction. *AI & Society* 6: 103–114.

Boggs, James. 1963. The American Revolution: Pages from a Negro Worker's Notebook. https://www.historyisaweapon.com/defcon1/amreboggs.html.

Boldyrev, Ivan and Martin Kragh. 2015. Isaak Rubin: Historian of Economic Thought During the Stalinization of Social Sciences in Soviet Russia. *Journal of the History of Economic Thought* 37 (3).

Bonefeld, Werner. 2014. *Critical Theory and the Critique of Political Economy: On Subversion and Negative Reason*. New York: Bloomsbury.

Bordiga, Amadeo. 2019 [1957]. Who's Afraid of Automation? In *The Science and Passion of Communism: Selected Writings of Amadeo Bordiga (1912–1965)*, ed. Pietro Basso. Leiden/Boston: Brill.

Braverman, Harry. 1998. *Labor and Monopoly Capital: The Degradation of Work in the Twentieth Century*. New York: NYU Press.

Briken, Kendra, Shiona Chillas, and Martin Krzywdzinski. 2017. *The New Digital Workplace: How New Technologies Revolutionise Work*. Basingstoke: Palgrave Macmillan.

Bronner, Stephen Eric. 1982. Karl Kautsky and the Twilight of Orthodoxy. *Political Theory* 10 (4): 580–605.

Burris, Beverly H. 1998. Computerization of the Workplace. *Annual Review of Sociology* 24: 141–57. Accessed February 11, 2020. www.jstor.org/stable/223477.

Burston, Jonathan, Nick Dyer-Witheford, and Alison Hearn. 2010. Digital Labour: Workers, Authors, Citizens. *Special Issue of Ephemera: Theory and Politics in Organization* 10 (3/4): 214–221.

Caffentzis, George. 1997. Why Machines Cannot Create Value; or, Marx's Theory of Machines. In *Cutting Edge: Technology, Information, Capitalism and Social Revolution*, ed. Jim Davis, Thomas Hirschl and Michael Stack. London: Verso.

Caffentzis, George. 2013. *In Letters of Blood and Fire: Work, Machines, and the Crisis of Capitalism*. Oakland, CA: pm Press.

Camfield, David. 2007. The Multitude and the Kangaroo: A Critique of Hardt and Negri's Theory of Immaterial Labour. *Historical Materialism* 15 (2): 21–52.

Chan, Adrian. 2003. *Chinese Marxism*. London: Continuum.

Cockshott, P. 1988. Application of Artificial Intelligence Techniques to Economic Planning. University of Strathclyde. Last accessed 5 May 2020. http://www.dcs.gla.ac.uk/~wpc/reports/plan_with_AIT.pdf.

Cockshott, P. 2017. Big Data and Supercomputers: Foundations of Cyber Communism. 26–28 September. Presented at The Ninth International Vanguard Scientific Conference on 100 Years of Real Socialism and the Theory of Post-Capitalist Civilization, Hanoi, Vietnam.

Cockshott, Paul. 2019. *How the World Works: The Story of Human Labor from Prehistory to the Modern Day*. New York: Monthly Review Press.

Cooley, Mike. 1980. Computerization: Taylor's Latest Disguise. *Economic and Industrial Democracy* 1 (4): 523–539.

Cooley, Mike. 1981. On The Taylorisation of Intellectual Work. In *Science, Technology and the Labour Process Volume 2*, ed. Les Levidow and Robert Young. London: CSE Books.

Cooley, Mike. 1987. *Architect or Bee? The Human Price of Technology*. London: Hogarth Press.

Cooper, Julian M. 1977. The Scientific and Technical Revolution in Soviet Theory. In *Technology and Communist Culture: The Socio-Cultural Impact of Technology Under Socialism*, ed. Frederic Fleron, 146–179. New York: Praeger.

Deleuze, Gilles, and Félix Guattari. 1987. *A Thousand Plateaus: Capitalism and Schizophrenia*, trans. Brian Massumi. Minneapolis: University of Minnesota Press.

Del Corro, Luciano. 2017. Is AI Driving Humanity Towards Socialism? *Hacker Noon*. January 30. https://hackernoon.com/is-ai-driving-humanity-towards-socialism-307c98c87fff.

Dinerstein, Ana C., and Mike Neary, eds. 2002. *The Labour Debate: An Investigation into the Theory and Reality of Capitalist Work*. Aldershot: Ashgate.

Dobb, Maurice. 1940. *Political Economy and Capitalism*. London: Routledge and Kegan Paul.

Duncan, Mike. 1981. Microelectronics: Five Areas of Subordination. In *Science, Technology, and the Labour Process Volume 2*, ed. Les Levidow and Robert Young. London: CSE Books.

Dyer-Witheford, Nick. 1999. *Cyber-Marx: Cycles and Circuits of Struggle in High-Technology Capitalism*. Champaign: University of Illinois Press.

Dyer-Witheford, Nick. 2001. Empire, Immaterial Labor, the New Combinations, and the Global Worker. *Rethinking Marxism* 13 (3–4): 70–80.

Dyer-Witheford, Nick. 2005. Cyber-Negri: General Intellect and Immaterial labor. In *The Philosophy of Antonio Negri Volume 1*, ed. Timothy Murphy and Abdul-Karim Mustapha. London: Pluto Press.

Dyer-Witheford, Nick. 2013. Red Plenty Platforms. *Culture Machine* 14: 1–27.

Dyer-Witheford, Nick. 2015. *Cyber-Proletariat: Global Labour in the Digital Vortex*. London: Pluto Press.

Dyer-Witheford, Nick, Atle Mikkola Kjøsen, and James Steinhoff. 2019. *Inhuman Power: Artificial Intelligence and the Future of Capitalism*. London: Pluto Press.

Elbe, Ingo. 2013. Between Marx, Marxism, and Marxisms—Ways of Reading Marx's Theory. *Viewpoint Magazine*. October 21, 2013. https://www.viewpointmag.com/2013/10/21/between-marx-marxism-and-marxisms-ways-of-reading-marxs-theory/.

Elson, Diane. 1979. The Value Theory of Labour. In *Value: The Representation of Labour in Capitalism*, ed. Diane Elson. London: CSE Books.

Endnotes. 2010. The History of Subsumption. *Endnotes* 2. https://endnotes.org.uk/issues/2/en/endnotes-the-history-of-subsumption.

Engels, Frederick. 1844. Outlines of a Critique of Political Economy. In *Deutsch-Französische Jahrbücher.* https://www.marxists.org/archive/marx/works/1844/df-jahrbucher/outlines.htm.

Ensmenger, Nathan and William Aspray. 2002. "Software as a Labor Process." In *History of Computing: Software Issues*, ed. Ulf Hashagen, Reinhard Keil-Slawik, and Arthur L. Norberg, 139–166. New York: Springer-Verlag.

Feenberg, Andrew. 2015. Lukács's Theory of Reification and Contemporary Social Movements. *Rethinking Marxism* 27 (4): 490–507.

Flakin, Nathaniel. 2019. An Introduction to the Kautsky Debate. *Left Voice*. July 23. https://www.leftvoice.org/an-introduction-to-the-kautsky-debate.

Fuchs, Christian. 2014. *Digital Labour and Karl Marx*. New York: Routledge.

Fuchs, Christian. 2016. *Reading Marx in the Information Age: A Media and Communications Studies Perspective on Capital*, vol. 1. New York: Routledge.

Fuchs, Christian. 2019. Karl Marx in the Age of Big Data Capitalism. In *Digital Objects, Digital Subjects: Interdisciplinary Perspectives on Capitalism, Labour and Politics in the Age of Big Data*, ed. David Chandler and Christian Fuchs. London: University of Westminster.

Fuchs, Christian, and Vincent Mosco. 2015. *Marx in the Age of Digital Capitalism*. Leiden: Brill.

Fuchs, Christian, and Nick Dyer-Witheford. 2013. Karl Marx@ Internet Studies. *New Media & Society* 15 (5): 782–796.

Gerovitch, Slava. 2002. *From Newspeak to Cyberspeak: A History of Soviet Cybernetics*. Cambridge: MIT Press.

Goldner, Loren. 1995. Amadeo Bordiga, the Agrarian Question and the International Revolutionary Movement. *Critique: Journal of Socialist Theory* 23 (1): 73–100.

Gramsci, Antonio. 1992 [1971]. *Selections from the Prison Notebooks of Antonio Gramsci*, ed. and trans. Quintin Hoare and Geoffrey Nowell Smith. New York: International Publishers.

Greenbaum, J. 1979. *In the Name of Efficiency: Management Theory and Shopfloor Practice in Data-Processing Work*. Philadelphia: Temple University Press.

Greenbaum, J. 1998. On Twenty-Five Years with Braverman's 'Labour and Monopoly Capital' (Or, How Did Control and Coordination of Labor Get into Software so Quickly). *Monthly Review* 50 (8).

Hansen, Alvin H. 1921. The Technological Interpretation of History. *The Quarterly Journal of Economics* 36 (1): 72–83.

Hardt, Michael, and Antonio Negri. 2000. *Empire*. Cambridge, MA: Harvard University Press.

Heilbroner, Robert L. 1967. Do Machines Make History? *Technology and Culture* 8 (3): 335–345.

Heinrich, Michael. 1991. *Die Wissenschaft vom Wert: Die Marxsche Kritik der Politischen Ökonomie Zwischen Wissenschaftlicher Revolution und Klassischer Tradition*. Westfälisches Dampfboot.

Heinrich, Michael. 2007. Invaders from Marx: On the Uses of Marxian Theory, & the Difficulties of a Contemporary Reading. *Left Curve* 31.

Heinrich, Michael. 2012. *An Introduction to the Three Volumes of Karl Marx's Capital*. New York: Monthly Review Press.

Heinrich, Michael. 2013. Crisis Theory, the Law of the Tendency of the Profit Rate to Fall, and Marx's Studies in the 1870s. *Monthly Review*. April 1. https://monthlyreview.org/2013/04/01/crisis-theory-the-law-of-the-tendency-of-the-profit-rate-to-fall-and-marxs-studies-in-the-1870s/.

Holloway, John. 2002. *Change the World Without Taking Power: The Meaning of Revolution Today*. London: Pluto Press.

Hounshell, David. 2000. Are Programmers Oppressed by Monopoly Capital. In *or Shall the Geeks Inherit the Earth? Commentary on Nathan Ensmerger & William Aspray, 'Software as Labor Process' in History of Computing: Software Issues*, ed. Ulf Hashagen, Reinhard Keil-Slawik, and Arthur L. Norberg, 167–175. New York: Springer.

Huws, Ursula. 2003. *The making of a cybertariat: Virtual work in a real world*. New York: Monthly Review Press.

Jehu. 2015. Schrodinger's Capital: Heinrich's Hilarious 'Refutation' of Marx on the Falling Rate of Profit. *The Real Movement*. December 4. https://therealmovement.wordpress.com/2015/12/04/schrodingers-capital-heinrichs-hilarious-refutation-of-marx-on-the-falling-rate-of-profit/#more-4041.

Jordan, Tim. 2015. *Information Politics: Liberation and Exploitation in the Digital Society*. London: Pluto Press.

Kautsky, Karl. 1989 [1929]. Nature and Society. *International Journal of Comparative Sociology* 30 (1–2).

Knights, David, and Hugh Willmott, eds. 1990. *Labour Process Theory*. London: Macmillan.

Korsch, Karl. 2013 [1923]. *Marxism and Philosophy*. London: Verso.

Kraft, Philip. 1977. *Programmers and Managers: The Routinization of Computer Programming in the United States*. New York: Springer.

Kraft, Philip. 1979. The Industrialization of Computer Programming: From Programming to 'Software Production.' In *Case Studies on the Labor Process*, ed. Andrew S. Zimbalist. New York: Monthly Review Press.

Kraft, Philip. 1999. To Control and Inspire: US Management in the Age of Computer Information Systems and Global Production. In *Rethinking the Labour Process*, ed. Mark Wardell, Thomas L. Steiger and Peter Meiksens. Albany, NY: SUNY Press.

Kraft, Philip, and Steven Dubnoff. 1986. Job Content, Fragmentation, and Control in Computer Software Work. *Industrial Relations: A Journal of Economy and Society* 25 (2): 184–196.

Krassó, Nicolas. 1967. Trotsky's Marxism. *New Left Review* 1 (44). July/August.

Kurz, Heinz D. 2010. Technical Progress, Capital Accumulation and Income Distribution in Classical Economics: Adam Smith, David Ricardo and Karl Marx. *The European Journal of the History of Economic Thought* 17 (5): 1183–1222.

Land, Nick. 2012. *Fanged Noumena: Collected Writings 1987–2007*. Falmouth: Urbanomic.

Land, Nick. 2017. A Quick and Dirty Guide to Accelerationism. *Jacobite*. May 25, 2017. https://jacobitemag.com/2017/05/25/a-quick-and-dirty-introduction-to-accelerationism.

Lazzarato, Maurizio. 1996. Immaterial Labor. In *Radical Thought in Italy: A Potential Politics*, ed. Paulo Virno and Michael Hardt, 133–147. Minneapolis: University of Minnesota Press.

Lenin, Vladmir Ilich. 1920. Report on the Work of the Council of People's Commissars. December 22, 1920. http://soviethistory.msu.edu/1921-2/electrification-campaign/communism-is-soviet-power-electrification-of-the-whole-country/.

Lenin, Vladmir Ilich. 1971 [1918]. The Immediate Tasks of the Soviet Government. In *Collected Works* Volume 42. Moscow: Progress Publishers.

Lenin, Vladmir Ilich. 1972 [1914]. *Collected Works* Volume 20. Moscow: Progress Publishers. https://www.marxists.org/archive/lenin/works/1914/mar/13.htm.

Lukács, Georg. 1972 [1923]. *History and Class Consciousness: Studies in Marxist Dialectics*. Cambridge: MIT Press.

Mackenzie, Donald. 1984. Marx and the Machine. *Technology and Culture* 25 (3): 473–502.

Mandel, Ernest. 1991. Trotsky's Economic Ideas and the Soviet Union Today. *Bulletin in Defense of Marxism* 84: 24–26.

Marcuse, Herbert. 1998 [1941]. Some Social Implications of Modern Technology. In *Technology, War and Fascism: Collected Papers of Herbert Marcuse Volume 1*, ed. Douglas Kellner and Peter Marcuse. New York: Routledge.

Marazzi, Christian. 2008. *Capital and Language: From the New Economy to the War Economy*, trans. Gregory Conti. Los Angeles: Semiotext [e].

Marcuse, Herbert. 2013 [1964]. *One-Dimensional Man: Studies in the Ideology of Advanced Industrial Society*. New York: Routledge.

Marx, Karl. 1955. *The Poverty of Philosophy*. Moscow: Progress Publishers. https://www.marxists.org/archive/marx/works/download/pdf/Poverty-Philosophy.pdf.

Marx, Karl. 1990. *Capital*, vol. 1. New York: Penguin.

Marx, Karl. 1992. *Capital*, vol. 2. New York: Penguin.

Marx, Karl. 1991. *Capital*, vol. 3. New York: Penguin.

Marx, Karl. 1993. *Grundrisse*. New York: Penguin.

Marx, Karl and Frederick Engels. 1845. *The German Ideology*. https://www.marxists.org/archive/marx/works/1845/german-ideology/index.htm.

Medina, Eden. 2011. *Cybernetic Revolutionaries: Technology and Politics in Allende's Chile*. Cambridge, MA: MIT Press.

Morris-Suzuki, Tessa. 1984. Robots and Capitalism. *New Left Review* 147: 109–121.

Mosco, Vincent, and Catherine McKercher. 2009. *The Laboring of Communication: Will Knowledge Workers of the World Unite?* Lanham: Rowman & Littlefield.

Mosco, Vincent and Janet Wasco, eds. 1988. *The Political Economy of Information*. University of Wisconsin Press.

Moulier, Boutang, and Yann . 2012. *Cognitive Capitalism*. Cambridge: Polity.

Noble, David. 1986. *Forces of Production: A Social History of Industrial Automation*. Piscataway, NJ: Transaction Publishers.

Orlikowski, W.J. 1988. The Data Processing Occupation: Professionalization or Proletarianization? *Research in the Sociology of Work* 4: 95–124.

Pasquinelli, Matteo. 2017. Machines That Morph Logic: Neural Networks and the Distorted Automation of Intelligence as Statistical Inference. *Glass Bead Journal* 1 (1).

Peters, Benjamin. 2016. *How Not to Network a Nation: The Uneasy History of the Soviet Internet*. Cambridge: MIT Press.

Pitts, Frederick Harry. 2017. Beyond the Fragment: Postoperaismo, Postcapitalism and Marx's 'Notes on Machines', 45 Years on. *Economy and Society* 46 (3–4): 324–345.

Pitts, Frederick Harry. 2018. *Critiquing Capitalism Today: New Ways to Read Marx*. London: Palgrave Macmillan.

Ramtin, Ramin. 1991. *Capitalism and Automation: Revolution in Technology and Capitalist Breakdown*. London: Pluto Press.

Rasmussen, Bente and Birgitte Johansen. 2005. Trick or treat? Autonomy as Control in Knowledge Work. In *Management, Labour Process and Software Development: Reality Bytes*, ed. Rowena Barret. New York: Routledge.

Reichelt, Helmut. 1982. From the Frankfurt School to Value-Form Analysis. *Thesis Eleven* 4 (1): 166–169.

Rees, John. 1994. Engels' Marxism. *International Socialism Journal* 65.

Ricardo, David. 2001 [1821]. *On The Principles of Political Economy and Taxation*. Kitchener: Batoche Books.

Ricardo, David. 1951–1973. *The Works and Correspondence of David Ricardo*, 11 Vols, ed. Piero Sraffa with collaboration of Maurice H. Dobb. Cambridge: Cambridge University Press.

Robins, Kevin, and Frank Webster. 1988. Cybernetic Capitalism: Information, Technology, Everyday Life. In *The Political Economy of Information*, ed. Vincent Mosco and Janet Wasko, 44–75.

Rosenthal, Caitlin. 2019. *Accounting for Slavery: Masters and Management*. Cambridge, MA: Harvard University Press.

Rubin, Isaak Illich. 1978 [1927]. Abstract Labour and Value in Marx's System. *Capital & Class* 2 (2): 107–109.

Saad-Filho, Alfredo. 1997. Concrete and abstract labour in Marx's theory of value. *Review of Political Economy* 9 (4): 457–477.

Schiller, Dan. 1999. *Digital Capitalism: Networking the Global Market System*. Cambridge, MA: MIT Press.

Schiller, Dan. 2014. *Digital Depression: Information Technology and Economic Crisis*. Urbana: University of Illinois Press.

Schmidt, Alfred. 1981. *History and Structure, an Essay on Hegelian-Marxist and Structuralist Theories of History*. Cambridge: MIT Press.

Smith, Adam. 1991 [1776]. *Wealth of Nations*. Amherst, NY: Prometheus Books.

Smith, Tony. 2009. The Chapters on Machinery in the 1861–63 Manuscripts. In *Re-reading Marx: New Perspectives After the Critical Edition*, ed. Riccardo Bellofiore and Roberto Fineschi, 112–127. London: Palgrave Macmillan.

Sochor, Zenovia A. 1981. Soviet Taylorism Revisited. *Soviet Studies* 33 (2): 246–264.

Sohn-Rethel, Alfred. 1978. *Intellectual and Manual Labour: A Critique of Epistemology*. London and Basingstoke: Macmillan.

Srnicek, Nick, and Alex Williams. 2015. *Inventing the Future: Postcapitalism and a World Without Work*. London: Verso.

Starosta, Guido, and Axel Kicillof. 2007. On Materiality and Social Form: a Political Critique of Rubin's Value-Form Theory. *Historical Materialism* 15 (3): 9–43.

Sweezy, P.M. 1968 [1942]).*The Theory of Capitalist Development*. New York: Monthly Review Press.

Tarallo, Bernadette Mary. 1987. *The Production of Information: An Examination of the Employment Relations of Software Engineers and Computer Programmers*. PhD Diss: University of California, Davis.

Terranova, Tiziana. 2004. *Network Culture: Politics for the Information Age*. London: Pluto Press.

Thompson, Paul, and Chris Smith. 2010. *Working Life: Renewing Labour Process Analysis*. London: Palgrave McMillan.

Trotsky, Leon. 1957 [1924]. *Literature and Revolution*. New York: Russel and Russel.

Ure, Andrew. 1835. *The Philosophy of Manufactures, or an Exposition of the Scientific, Moral, and Commercial Economy of the Factory System of Great Britain*. London: Charles Knight.

Virno, Paulo. 2001. On General Intellect. https://libcom.org/library/on-general-intellect-paulo-virno.

von Mises, Ludwig. 1935. Calculation in the Socialist Commonwealth. In *Collectivist Economic Planning*, ed. F.A. Hayek. London: Routledge.

Wardell, Mark, Thomas L. Steiger, and Peter Meiksins, eds. 1999. *Rethinking the Labor Process*. New York: State University of New York Press.

Wark, McKenzie. 2015. *Molecular Red: Theory for the Anthropocene*. London: Verso.

Wood, Stephen. 1982. *The Degradation of Work? Skill, Deskilling, and the Labour Process*. London: Hutchinson Radius.

Xiang, Feng. 2018. "AI will spell the end of capitalism." *The Washington Post*. May 3. https://www.washingtonpost.com/news/theworldpost/wp/2018/05/03/end-of-capitalism/.

Zilis, Shivon. 2016. Machine Intelligence Will Let Us All Work Like CEOs. *Harvard Business Review*. June 13. https://hbr.org/2016/06/machine-intelligence-will-let-us-all-work-like-ceos.

Zimmerman, Andrew. 1997. The Ideology of the Machine and the Spirit of the Factory: Remarx on Babbage and Ure. *Cultural Critique* 37: 5–29.

CHAPTER 3

Post-Operaismo and the New Autonomy of Immaterial Labour

Introduction

This chapter continues the exploration of Marxist theory via the conceptual triad of labour, capital and machine. Here the focus switches to *post-operaismo*, the object of critique for this book. To understand *post-operaismo*, we must first look at what it originated from, and from what exactly it garnered the prefix post-: the line of thought known as *operaismo*. First, I outline *operaismo* and *post-operaismo*. Then I discuss an important existing criticism that has been levelled at the theoretical grounds of immaterial labour. Next, I reconstruct the argument for immaterial labour's new autonomy. This is a specifically technological argument, relying centrally on purported changes in technology's mediating function between capital and labour. The technological argument consists of three cyclically repeated stages: human–machine hybridization, abstract cooperation and new autonomy from capital. In closing, I briefly consider the significance of immaterial labour's purported new autonomy, but my critique is reserved until Chapter 7, after the case study of the AI industry in the next three chapters.

J. Steinhoff, *Automation and Autonomy*, Marx, Engels, and Marxisms,
https://doi.org/10.1007/978-3-030-71689-9_3

From *Operaismo* to *Post-Operaismo*

In 1950s Italy, a group of thinkers that would come to be known as *operaismo* (workerism) diverged from Marxist orthodoxy in a way distinct from the philosophical pessimism of Western Marxism. Some of the most prominent members were Mario Tronti, Raniero Panzieri, Romano Alquati and Antonio Negri. Initially, *operaismo* thinkers, like labour process theorists, directed their attention to the industrial workplace. But while labour process theory often depicts workers as reactively resisting a monolithic capital which surveils, controls and reconfigures their work, *operaismo* conducted a categorical class inversion, arguing that in technologically advanced capitalism, it is capital that is essentially reactive. Tronti (1964) held that putting:

> capitalist development first, and workers second … is a mistake … we have to turn the problem on its head, reverse the polarity, and start again from the beginning: and the beginning is the class struggle of the working class. At the level of socially developed capital, capitalist development becomes subordinated to working class struggles; it follows behind them, and they set the pace to which the political mechanisms of capital's own reproduction must be tuned.

Labour pushes forward while capital scrambles to adapt. Automation was understood as capital's reaction to the collective power of the industrial mass worker. Panzieri pursued this idea in his writings on capitalist planning, or the organization of production through technological means. Panzieri critiqued Lenin, whom he argued believed that capital was too anarchic to engage in widespread, planned social organization. Panzieri (1976) held that in fact the use of machines in production constitutes capitalist planning, and not some neutral technological progress, because such machines are "moulded" by capital to serve its interests (12). Alquati (2013 [1961]) elaborated how information technologies allow capital to capture worker's knowledge and decision-making processes, asserting that the "universal diffusion of capitalist despotism … realizes itself above all through its technology, its 'science'".

Capital's planned deployment of technology led *operaismo* thinkers to be dubious of the notion that capital would automate itself out of existence. Panzieri (2017 [1961]) insisted that there is no "occult factor, inherent in the characteristics of technological development or planning in the capitalist society of today, which can guarantee the 'automatic' transformation or 'necessary' overthrow of existing relations". The best that could be expected were changed possibilities for class struggle. The introduction of new machines by capital would be met with new modes of attack and defence by labour (Holloway 2002, 161–162). Capital's organic composition increases, but the "class composition" of labour also continually changes, producing new social capacities unanticipated by capital (Zerowork 1975). Rather than a linear trajectory towards communism, *operaismo* thus conceived of history as a "cycle of struggles" throughout which both capital and labour skirmish, retreat, regroup and mutate to fight again (Dyer-Witheford 1999).

Its focus on the changing composition of labour led *operaismo* to dispute narrow and static conceptions of class. Observing that capitalist planning was extending beyond the industrial workplace, *operaismo* thinkers held that the proletariat must also be expanding. Tronti (1966) held that capital increasingly "sees society as a means and production as an end". He and other *operaismo* thinkers deployed the concept of the "social factory" to describe how society at large was being reconfigured to support the exigencies of production (Dyer-Witheford 1999, 134). *Operaismo*'s initial focus on the industrial mass worker was replaced by the new category of "socialized worker" (Dyer-Witheford 2005, 137–138). The socialized worker describes the new level of social cooperation wrought in the social factory, in which all kinds of work formerly considered unproductive are drawn into circuits of valorization. Ultimately, some *operaismo* thinkers concluded that society was not only being organized around the factory, but was becoming coextensive with it as a "factory without walls" (Negri 1989, 89). The revolutionary significance of this was debated within *operaismo*. Some, like Tronti, remained convinced of the centrality of a communist party representing workers while others came to believe that no subgroup of society had revolutionary primacy. For Negri, the locus of antagonism between capital and labour exploded across society at large, "fractally replicat[ing], manifesting in myriad new movements that contest the logic of capital not only in workplaces" (Dyer-Witheford 2005, 138). This line of thought within *operaismo* led to *post-operaismo*.

Amid the proliferation of personal computing and other information technologies, Negri came to extol technology as empowering labour: "[t]hough initiated for purposes of control and command, as the system grows it becomes an 'ecology of machines'— an everyday ambience of potentials to be tapped and explored by the socialized worker, a techno-habitat whose uses can no longer be exclusively dictated by capital" (Negri 1989, 93, cited in Dyer-Witheford 2005, 140). What exactly are these emergent potentials of the socialized worker? As Dyer-Witheford (2005) notes, on this Negri was "characteristically abstract" (140). Negri (1989) asserted vaguely that productive capacities for the socialized worker centre on "science, communication and the communication of knowledge" (116). Despite this lack of clarity, the new capacities of the socialized worker were the foundation on which *post-operaismo* would be built.

On the basis of the emergent technological milieu, Negri rejected Marx's value theory as a "legacy of the classics and of ... bourgeois mystification" (Negri 1991, 23). He argued that in high-technology capitalism, value is produced socially by the whole of the population, while Marx's theory is based on the work of the individual and is thus "heavily reductive" (Negri 1991, 29) and "objectivist, atomized, and fetishist" (Negri 1991, 64). The *operaismo* notion of the social factory and the primacy of labour over capital, along with Negri's affirmative orientation to technology and dismissal of Marx's value theory, paved the way for *post-operaismo*, which further elaborated these positions and brought them into widespread use in academia and beyond.

Post-Operaismo

Prominent figures in *post-operaismo* include Michael Hardt, Antonio Negri, Paolo Virno, Carlo Vercellone, Yann Moulier Boutang,[1] Maurizio Lazzarato and Matteo Pasquinelli.[2] Lazzarato's (1996) essay "Immaterial Labour" laid out the purportedly novel situation of work in post-Fordism and was followed by Hardt and Negri's enormously popular *Empire* (2000) which has been followed by three sequels (Hardt and Negri 2005, 2009, 2017). *Post-operaismo* draws not only from Marxism but also from post-structuralist theorists such as Gilles Deleuze and Felix Guattari (1983), though I will not delve into such influences here.

[1] Moulier-Boutang (2012) and Vercellone (2005) are advocates of "cognitive capitalism theory" which is aligned, or overlaps, with *post-operaismo* on the theory of immaterial labour.

[2] Pasquinelli is the only *post-operaismo* thinker to engage directly with AI. He has a stated mission to "fill the gap between Marxism and cybernetics" (2015, 50). See also Pasquinelli (2016, 2017).

Post-operaismo begins with technological change. A fundamental tenet of *post-operaismo* is its claim for a "change in the quality and nature of labor … [wherein] information and communication have come to play a foundational role in production processes" (Hardt and Negri 2000, 289). This shift is contingent on the computer becoming "the universal tool, or … central tool, through which all activities might pass" (Hardt and Negri 2000, 292). Computerization entails the new era of capitalist production of post-Fordism with a new class composition called immaterial labour. For *post-operaismo*, the proliferation of computers in post-Fordism drastically redefines the relationship between labour, capital and machines.

In theorizing immaterial labour, *post-operaismo* draws on a prophetic understanding of "The Fragment on Machines". Their reliance on this passage is of such importance that Pitts (2017) has suggested calling *post-operaismo* "fragment-thinking" (328). Hardt and Negri (2000) interpret "The Fragment" as a prophecy: "[w]hat Marx saw as the future is our era. This radical transformation of labor power and the incorporation of science, communication, and language into productive force have redefined the entire phenomenology of labor and the entire world horizon of production" (364). The radical transformation of the post-Fordist era holds the "potential for a kind of spontaneous and elementary communism" (Hardt and Negri 2000, 294). However, sometimes *post-operaismo* offers more qualified interpretations. For instance, Virno (2001) asserts that in post-Fordism, "the tendency described by Marx is actually realised but surprisingly with no revolutionary or even conflictual implication. Rather than a plethora of crises, the disproportion between the role of the knowledge objectified in machines and the decreasing relevance of labour time gave rise to new and stable forms of domination". For Hardt and Negri (2000), "[n]ew communication technologies hold out the promise of a new democracy and a new social equality" even if so far they have "in fact created new lines of inequality and exclusion" (300). These more nuanced statements, however, are overwhelmed by broad assertions of a greater tendency towards radical change, as I will demonstrate.

One of *post-operaismo's* strengths is its insistence that the computer presents promising affordances for a society not based on commodity production. One significant aspect of the computer for *post-operaismo* is that it can be assembled into digital networks which allow for speedy communication and coordination over a distance. The "cooperation of brains working on computers" (Moulier-Boutang 2012, 104) allows for a "dramatic decentralization of production" (Hardt and Negri 2000, 294). Another significant aspect of the computer is that software, being "non-rival and non-excludable", has the status of a "quasi-public" good (Moulier-Boutang 2012, 104). Information products, which are easily and cheaply replicable, undermine the notion of private property, present problems for commodification, and present new possibilities for communal resources or "the commons" (Hardt and Negri 2000, 300–303). Free- and open-source software is interpreted as one manifestation of the new digital commons (Moulier-Boutang 2012, 79–91). *Post-operaismo* thinkers do acknowledge that capital has ways of exploiting these promising capacities for its own ends, but I argue, they underestimate the extent to which this is true. One reason for this underestimation is a lack of appreciation for the recursive capacity of the computer. Hardt and Negri (2000) recognize the recursive properties of software, noting that a "computer ... can continually modify its own operation through its use. Even the most rudimentary forms of artificial intelligence allow the computer to expand and perfect its operation based on its interaction with its user and its environment" (291). However, they do not think we should be concerned about "Digital Taylorism" because even if it "sometimes seems as though computer systems, artificial intelligence, and algorithms are making human labor obsolete ... in fact, there are innumerable digital tasks that machines cannot complete" (Hardt and Negri 2017, 131). The recursive capacity of the computer is limited in scope. Immaterial labour refers to those tasks which are reserved for humans; it is labour which relies on the computer, but which cannot be reduced to a computer program. How exactly is immaterial labour defined?

Immaterial labour is described as work in which the computer becomes "the universal tool" (Hardt and Negri 2000, 292). This is enabled by a "new 'mass intellectuality' [having] come into being" (Lazzarato 1996, 134). Moulier-Boutang (2012) thus refers to the "cognitariat" (96) and deems it appropriate to speak of a "cognitive" capitalism which can "only take place on the basis of collective brain activity mobilised in interconnected digital networks" (Moulier-Boutang 2012, 56). However, immaterial labour is not only computer work. It is usually formulated as possessing a dual nature. Lazzarato (1996) defines immaterial labour in this way:

> [o]n the one hand … it refers directly to the changes taking place … where the skills involved in direct labor are increasingly skills involving cybernetics and computer control (and horizontal and vertical communication). On the other hand … immaterial labor involves a series of activities that are not normally recognized as 'work' – in other words, the kinds of activities involved in defining and fixing cultural and artistic standards, fashions, tastes, consumer norms, and, more strategically, public opinion. (133)

The first aspect of immaterial labour is digital or informational labour, understood as any work involving the use of computers and/or other information technologies. This is itself a broad category. But it is exceeded in breadth by the second aspect, which Lazzarato (1996) sums up as communication and the production of subjectivities (134–140). Immaterial labour thus refers to an aristocracy of high-technology workers but also to "the form of activity of every productive subject within postindustrial society" (Lazzarato 1996, 136).

Hardt and Negri (2000) define immaterial labour in similarly expansive and bipartite terms. In the first case, immaterial labour is labour "that produces an immaterial good, such as a service, a cultural product, knowledge, or communication" (290). Hardt and Negri (2000) posit three types of this kind of immaterial labour. There is industrial production that "has incorporated communications technologies in a way that transforms the production process itself", such as just-in-time manufacturing (293). There is also analytical and symbolic work; either "creative and intelligent manipulation" or "routine symbolic tasks". This refers to computer work, but also to how "[e]ven when direct contact with computers is not involved, the manipulation of symbols and information along the model of computer operation is extremely widespread" (291). Finally, there is the production and manipulation of affect, which "requires (virtual or actual) human contact, labor in the bodily mode" including care work, entertainment and any "services of proximity" (293). More recently, Hardt and Negri have restated their position as follows:

> the nature and conditions of labor have changed radically from the industrial forms that Marx analyzed … First, people work in ever more flexible, mobile, and precarious arrangements … Second, labor is increasingly social and based on cooperation with others, embedded in a world of communicative networks and digital connections … Capital is valorized through cooperative flows in which language, affects, code, and images are subsumed in the material processes of production. (2017, 93)

As in Lazzarato's formulation, for Hardt and Negri, immaterial labour is not limited to various computerized types of work, as the mention of affective labour above shows. At times Hardt and Negri (2004) refer to immaterial labour as "biopolitical labor" or "labor that creates not only material goods but also relationships and ultimately social life itself", echoing Lazzarato's notion of the production of subjectivities (109). In this second sense, immaterial labour is performed by a new productive force called the multitude (Hardt and Negri 2000). The multitude extends beyond populations conventionally classified as workers. It represents the "claim that there is no political priority among the forms of labor: all forms of labor are today socially productive, they produce in common, and share too a common potential to resist the domination of capital" (Hardt and Negri 2004, 106–107). The multitude's "new productive forces have no place … because they occupy all places, and they produce and are exploited in this indefinite non-place" (Hardt and Negri 2000, 210). Labour as a class becomes distributed across the entire social field.

Post-operaismo's new figure of labour has a contradictory dual character, referring simultaneously to high-tech workers and nearly every person on earth. *Post-operaismo* evinces, as Camfield (2007) asserts of Hardt and Negri in particular, a "conceptual slippage" between these two disparate formulations of immaterial labour (30). This book focuses primarily on the narrower formulation of immaterial labour as computational, high-tech labour. This is justified because, while the multitude is a putatively universal category, its universality is contingent on total computerization. The multitude is distinguished by its "universal capacity to produce" (Hardt and Negri 2000, 209) but this capacity is engendered by a "real homogenization of laboring processes" (Hardt and Negri 2000, 292) wrought by the "computer and communication revolution of production" which has "transformed laboring practices in such a way that they all tend toward the model of information and communication technologies" (Hardt and Negri 2000, 291). The "computerization of production" allows "different laboring activities be brought together and seen in a homogeneous way" as the "manipulation of symbols and information" (Hardt and Negri 2000, 292). Immaterial labour has thus "become hegemonic in qualitative terms and has imposed a tendency on other forms of labor and society itself … today labor and society have to informationalize, become intelligent, become communicative, become affective" (2004, 109). The multitude's universality obtains insofar as the multitude approximates currently existing high-tech labour. As Dyer-Witheford (2005) asserts, for *post-operaismo*, the "cyborg, high-tech form of … labor continues to be the privileged point of reference" (152–153). Since immaterial labour tends, supposedly, towards this cyborg figure at the heights of networked, computational mediation, it is there that my critique of immaterial labour will focus. Labour in the AI industry is immaterial labour *par excellence*. A case study of such labour should therefore provide an empirical means of evaluating immaterial labour theory.

Along with its redefinition of labour, *post-operaismo* advocates for a redefinition of value. Since the products of immaterial labour "tend to exceed all quantitative measurement and take common forms", *post-operaismo* argues that Marx's theory of value no longer obtains (Hardt and Negri 2009, 135–136). In other words, because immaterial labour takes on an informational, communicative form, capital encounters a "crisis of measurability" (Marazzi 2008, 43). Immaterial labour cannot be controlled by capital via labour-time in the same ways that labour historically has been; it entails "post-Taylorist production" (Lazzarato 1996, 140). However, this is not to say that *post-operaismo* abandons the notion of value completely. Hardt and Negri hold that "[e]ven if in postmodern capitalism there is no longer a fixed scale that measures value, value nonetheless is still powerful and ubiquitous" (2000, 356). However, value is now produced "in some sense, *externally* to [capital]" (Hardt and Negri 2009, 141). Valorization, a term Marx used to describe the process of capital augmentation, is coopted by Hardt and Negri (2000) to describe a process by which the proletariat increases its own capacities (358). Value no longer refers to the average socially necessary labour-time for the production of a commodity; it instead tracks the autonomy of labour from capital. This is the central premise of immaterial labour theory—that information technology enables for labour a new autonomy from capital. This central premise is the focus of my critique in this book, and the rest of this chapter examines it in some detail. But first, I consider an important existing criticism of immaterial labour theory and distinguish it from mine.

Immaterial Labour Theory

How immaterial is immaterial labour, really? Paul Thompson (2005) has pointed out the necessary materiality of labour, which is "never immaterial. It is not the content of labour but its commodity form that gives 'weight' to an object or idea in a market economy" (84). Thompson points out that labour has a dual existence, both concrete and abstract, under capital. The significance of different types of labour to capital does not derive from their concrete specificity but from how their products, as bearers of value, may support circuits of valorization. To speak of computerized work as immaterial is, in this sense, trivial. From a perspective cognizant of the value-form, all forms of capitalist work have concrete specificity and abstract significance and there is "little difference between material and immaterial labours" (Pitts 2017, 333). Taking the value-form into account thus undermines *post-operaismo*'s argument against Marx's labour theory of value.

According to *post-operaismo*, immaterial labour collectively produces, often outside the workplace. Since it exists beyond the purview of the punchclock, immaterial labour cannot be quantified, like traditional labour was, and therefore value can no longer be measured (Marazzi 2008, 43; Hardt and Negri 2009, 135–136). However, Pitts (2017) shows how this argument relies on a premise which it simultaneously denies: "postoperaist claims of the Fragment's realization rest on a disavowed orthodoxy. Despite their professed anti-productivism, they advocate a conventional labour theory of value … as a means by which it can be dismissed as historically redundant" (329). The value theory which *post-operaismo* declares dead is a Ricardian one which focuses solely on the time of embodied labour in production, even though it also asserts that value no longer arises "from a determinate place" or "specific productive activities" but rather from the "universal capacity to produce" (Hardt and Negri 2000, 209). Rather than adapting Marx's theory of value to situations of networked, computerized labour (see, for example, Fuchs 2014, 127–132), Hardt and Negri explode the theory of value, transforming it into the all-encompassing notion of the "self-valorization" of labour (2017, 119). However, from a perspective which acknowledges the form of value, there is already a mechanism built-into capital for capturing value, even from networked, dispersed sorts of labour. As discussed in the previous chapter's section on NRM, value is calculated in practice by its realization in exchange, even if an individual capital cannot quantify precisely the number of hours put into producing a particular commodity. Immateriality is always a property of labour under capital because value, as a non-physical real abstraction, consists of social relations between people (Pitts 2018).

Post-operaismo's claim for a new autonomy of immaterial labour has received less attention than the descriptor of immateriality. The few assessments autonomy has received in this context have been conducted on primarily theoretical, rather than empirical, grounds. Nicholas Thoburn (2001) notes that *Empire* and Negri's earlier solo work seem "to equate a tendency toward the productivity of communication with an emerging freedom—as if the more fluid and immaterial production becomes, the more it escapes control" (86–87). This is contradictory, Thoburn argues, because at the same time as this emerging autonomy is posited, Hardt and Negri discern "Foucauldian and Deleuzian conceptions of the immanence of [capital's] power to all social relations" (87). David Camfield (2007) frames the same contradiction between autonomy and an all-encompassing capital in terms of subsumption: "Hardt and Negri's claim amounts to a contention that the real subsumption of labour to capital is retreating, making capital parasitically exploitative of autonomous production. They do not attempt to reconcile this with their contention that the real subsumption of society as a whole to capital has taken place" (35). The contradiction pointed out by these critiques is not regarded as such by *post-operaismo*, because, in the era of immaterial labour, labour is purported to undergo an ontological change. Even though capital has subsumed all aspects of society, creating a global social factory, the new autonomy of immaterial labour produces a new type of value, which limits capital to the role of parasite. This book is not, however, primarily concerned with pointing out contradictions in the theoretical foundations of *post-operaismo*.

New autonomy is purported to be a result of post-Fordist technological change. It is logically possible that new autonomy might obtain whether or not *post-operaismo*'s theoretical foundations are consistent. We can thus ask how well immaterial labour theory maps onto the real world. Although it is often taken as describing a tendency, potentiality or as a "provocation" (Fuchs 2017), I want to gauge the capabilities of immaterial labour theory, as it presents itself, as an empirical description. In the following sections, I reconstruct the argument for immaterial labour's new autonomy. This is a specifically technological argument, as we will see, relying centrally on purported changes in technology's mediating function between capital and labour. In my reconstruction, the technological argument comprises three cyclically occurring stages: human–machine hybridization, abstract cooperation and new autonomy from capital.

Human–Machine Hybridization

Post-operaismo argues that in post-Fordism the balance of technological power shifts in favour of labour, contrary to the grim depictions of workers becoming appendages of machines in *Capital* Volume 1. Capital increases its organic composition, but "the changing composition of capital … contributes, subjectively, to strengthening the position of labor" (Hardt and Negri 2017, 114). Because technology and labour are no longer at odds with one another the "repressive use of technology, including the automation and computerization of production", which capital relied on in previous eras, becomes increasingly difficult (Hardt and Negri 2000, 267). Traditional disciplinary techniques and "Taylorist and Fordist mechanisms [can] no longer control the dynamic of productive and social forces" (Hardt and Negri 2000, 268). Rather than being subjected to increased domination, labour gains increasing control over, and even merges with, machines: "the hybridization of humans and machines is no longer defined by the linear path it followed throughout the modern period" and labour obtains "the capacity to take control of the processes of machinic metamorphosis" (Hardt and Negri 2000, 367). Capital loses control over technology and therefore the logic of increasing organic composition of capital outlined by Marx is no longer valid. Instead, it is labour that becomes increasingly machinic:

> The scientific, affective, and linguistic forces of the multitude aggressively transform the conditions of social production … This consists above all in a complete revision of the production of cooperative subjectivity; it consists in an act … of merging and hybridizing with the machines that the multitude has reappropriated and reinvented; it consists … in an exodus that is not only spatial but also mechanical in the sense that the subject is transformed into (and finds the cooperation that constitutes it multiplied in) the machine. (Hardt and Negri 2000, 366–367)

Hardt and Negri restate this notion in their latest book where they argue that it should be recognized "perhaps now beyond Marx, as production is increasingly socialized, how fixed capital tends to be implanted into life itself, creating a machinic humanity" (2017, 114). It is important to note here that while Hardt and Negri certainly draw on the broad conception of the machine developed by Deleuze and Guattari (1983), not all their references to machines can be understood in this register (see Hardt and Negri 2017, 110). Deleuze and Guattari's notion of the machine was intended to express how human labour is always already enmeshed with technologies, institutions and various non-humans:

> What is critical ... in the concept of the machine, as both Deleuze and Guattari employ it, is a consideration of the organisation of the variety of components in relation to each other that comprises any given machine. For that reason machines can and do exist on any scale and can be both material and immaterial ... visible or invisible ... the key focus was on the assemblage as a collective machine and not ... on the actual technical object. (Savat 2009, 2–3)

In contrast to this transhistorical conception of the machine, Hardt and Negri describe a *new* process of human–machine merging, specific to the post-Fordist era. In the past, "the productive process ... severely restricted the actualization of the potential that exceeds capital's bounds ... The affective and intellectual talents, the capacities to generate cooperation and organization networks, the communication skills" (Hardt and Negri 2009, 151–152). But things are different in the post-Fordist era:

> Ever since industrial civilization was born, workers have had a much more intimate and internal knowledge of machines and machine systems than the capitalists and their managers ever could. Today this process of worker appropriation of knowledge can become decisive: it is not simply realized in the production process but is intensified and concretized throughout productive cooperation and spreads throughout the life processes of circulation and socialization. (Hardt and Negri 2017, 119)

Technology changes from dead labour that confronts the worker to a collective human prosthesis: "[f]ixed capital ... the memory and storehouse of past physical and intellectual labor, is increasingly embedded in 'the social individual'" (Hardt and Negri 2017, 114). This new "machinic exodus" or human–machine hybridization produces a new kind of human (Hardt and Negri 2000, 367). Hardt and Negri (2017) explain: "when we say fixed capital is reappropriated by laboring subjects we do not mean simply that it becomes their possession but instead that it is integrated into the machinic assemblages, as a constituent of subjectivity" (122). This is not metaphorical, nor does it refer to the future: "When we look at young people today who are absorbed in machinic assemblages, we should recognize that their very existence is resistance. Whether they are aware or not, they produce in resistance" (Hardt and Negri 2017, 123). I suggest that this rather perplexing formulation of resistance, and the notion of human–machine hybridity here espoused, are comprehensible only if one elaborates an overlooked aspect of *post-operaismo*—its insistence on an irreducible human element in immaterial labour.

Hardt and Negri (2017) declare it a "mistake" to pose an "ontological division … between human life and machines" (109). However, despite such statements, frequent mention of cyborgs and a general affinity for technology, *post-operaismo* is quite clearly invested in the position that certain capacities of human labour are categorically off-limits to machinic implementation. Only based on this assumption can *post-operaismo* affirm the becoming-machine of labour not as capital's increasing organic composition, but rather as the expansion of labour's self-directed capacities. For Hardt and Negri (2017) "there are innumerable digital tasks that machines cannot complete" (131). Virno (2003) likewise asserts that in post-Fordism, the "means of production are not reducible to machines but consist of linguistic-cognitive competencies inseparable from living labor" (61). Virno emphasizes that with immaterial labour a "decisive role is played by the infinite variety of concepts and logical schemes which cannot ever be set within fixed capital, being inseparable from the reiteration of a plurality of living subjects" (2003, 106). For Moulier-Boutang, without the "power of the living … which is radically distinct from machinery … none of this [immaterial labour] can take place" (2012, 163).

This power of living labour is described as autonomous creativity (Hardt and Negri 2000, 83) or "collective intelligence, creativity distributed through the entirety of the population" (Moulier-Boutang 2012, 34). Capital no longer derives its sustenance from the "expenditure of human labour power, but that of *invention-power* … the living know-how that cannot be reduced to machines and the opinions shared in common by the greatest number of human beings" (Moulier-Boutang 2012, 32, emphasis original). Invention-power is "implicit knowledge that is irreducible to machinism, to standardized and codified human capital" (Moulier-Boutang 2012, 54). Based on the irreducible humanity of such communicative and creative capacities, Hardt and Negri (2017) hold that any "Digital Taylorism" attempted by capital will run into insurmountable limits (131). Interestingly, this position concerning essentially human capacities has considerable similarities to recent business-oriented literature on AI and work.

A common trope in business-oriented literature on AI and work is what I call centaur theory. This name derives from the famous defeat of chess champion Garry Kasparov by IBM's Deep Blue AI in 1997. Kasparov went on to develop a style of chess, played by human–machine teams, called cyborg, advanced or centaur chess (Markoff 2020). Rather than pitting human against machine, centaur chess pits hybrid entities against each other. I mobilize the notion of the centaur to show how both *post-operaismo* and contemporary business literature attempt to reconcile advances in automation technology with optimistic appraisals of the future. Both groups of thinkers propose that the ultimate end of AI will be the augmentation, rather than automation, of human capabilities, because machines just cannot complete certain tasks.

Erik Brynjolfsson and Andrew McAfee are some of the most influential writers on the economic implications of AI. Their work provides a prime example of centaur theory. They assert that the emergence of "real, useful artificial intelligence" is one of the "most important one-time events in our history" comparable to the harnessing of steam power and electricity (Brynjolfsson and McAfee 2014, 90). In their assessment, as AI proliferates "costs will go down, outcomes will improve, and our lives will get better", even as low-skill, routine jobs are largely eliminated (Brynjolfsson and McAfee 2014, 91). A new division of labour will relegate unpleasant drudgery to machines, freeing up humans for fulfilling "idea creation" (Brynjolfsson and McAfee 2014, 192). Similarly, for Ajay Agrawal et al. (2018) and Paul Daugherty and James Wilson (2018), AI will be used to automate routine work for which there is plenty of data available and humans will be employed to use their judgement, which is non-automatable, to make predictions in irregular, low-data scenarios. Richard Susskind and Daniel Susskind (2015) suggest a more limited domain for the human component of the centaur, delegating to it only positions involving moral responsibility (279–284). On the other hand, Malcolm Frank et al. (2017) assert that AI can create a "knowledge economy exoskeleton" (151) for workers and go as far as arguing that "for the vast majority of professions, [AI] will actually enhance and protect employment" (8). Exactly what type of labour is left to the human component of the centaur varies from author to author. But the central idea remains that there are some things that machines just cannot do. The sentiment of both *post-operaismo* and business centaur theory is clear: becoming a component of a cyborg assemblage is fine because essentially human capacities will be preserved. I will contest this assumption in the pages to come, but first let us lay out the two other stages of the technological argument for new autonomy.

Abstract Cooperation

Post-operaismo attempts to conceptualize the un-automatable capacities of immaterial labour with a reconfigured version of Marx's notion of general intellect. In Marx's original formulation, the general intellect refers to capital's armamentarium of knowledge and capacities captured from labour and implemented in technology; the extensive objectification of "general social knowledge" in fixed capital which becomes a "direct force of production" (Marx 1993, 706). *Post-operaismo* reworks Marx's notion of general intellect to describe the new technologically enabled capacities of immaterial labour. Hardt and Negri define the general intellect as a "collective, social intelligence created by accumulated knowledges, techniques and know-how" (2000, 364). This definition does not necessarily contradict Marx's formulation of general intellect. It could be referring to fixed capital. But when Hardt and Negri (2000) assert that in the post-Fordist era, "labour is the productive activity of a general intellect and a general body outside measure" it is evident that, for them, general intellect means something completely different (358). Virno's (2003) explanation for this change is as follows:

> Marx conceives the 'general intellect' as a scientific objectified capacity, as a system of machines. Obviously, this aspect of the 'general intellect' matters, but it is not everything. We should consider the dimension where the general intellect, instead of being incarnated (or rather, cast in iron) into the system of machines, exists as attribute of living labor. The general intellect manifests itself today, above all, as the communication, abstraction, self-reflexion of living subjects. It seems legitimate to maintain that, according to the very logic of economic development, it is necessary that a part of the general intellect not congeal as fixed capital but unfold in communicative interaction, under the guise of epistemic paradigms, dialogical performances, linguistic games. (65)

On this account, machines are a minor component of the general intellect. The general intellect refers also, and more importantly, to the new capacities of networked labour; it is "one and the same as cooperation, the acting in concert of human labour, and the communicative competence of individuals" (Virno 2003, 65). General intellect "should not necessarily mean the aggregate of the knowledge acquired by the species, but the faculty of thinking: potential as such" (Virno 2003, 66). Individual workers no longer matter as much as the newly social mass of immaterial labour: "today the general intellect is becoming a protagonist of economic and social production" (Hardt and Negri 2017, 114). This newly social labour entails a new kind of exploitation:

> The dialectic between productive forces and the system of domination no longer has a determinate place. The very qualities of labor power (difference, measure, and determination) can no longer be grasped, and similarly, exploitation can no longer be localized and quantified. In effect, the object of exploitation and domination tend not to be specific productive activities but the universal capacity to produce ... abstract social activity and its comprehensive power. (Hardt and Negri 2000, 209)

Post-operaismo thus posits both a broadening and softening of exploitation: broadening because all social existence is now productive labour and therefore exploitation is a net cast wide across society; softening because there is no definite moment of exploitation—it is "omnipresent" but "there is nothing miserablist about it" (Moulier-Boutang 2012, 92). Exploitation is not eliminated, just redefined as "the expropriation of cooperation" (Hardt and Negri 2000, 385) or the "capturing [of] positive externalities" (Moulier-Boutang 2012, 55) or "the private appropriation of part or all of the value that has been produced as common" (Hardt and Negri 2004, 145). Capital can only survive by parasitically feeding on the results of this newly social form of production: "capital expropriates cooperation ... at the level of social production and social practice" (Hardt and Negri 2009, 140–141). Capital can no longer command labour; it is "increasingly external and has an ever less functional role in the productive process" (Hardt and Negri 2009, 142).

On the basis of this new social mode of production, Hardt and Negri (2017) discern "a challenge or even a potential threat to capital because the primary role in the social organization of production tends to be played by the living knowledges embodied in and mobilized by labor rather than the dead knowledges deployed by management and management science" (115). Immaterial labour thus exhibits a novel way of "becoming common" (Hardt and Negri 2004, 129). This new mode of cooperation Hardt and Negri (2000) call "abstract cooperation" (296). It is "completely immanent to the laboring activity itself" while in previous eras of capitalism, cooperation was imposed by capital (Hardt and Negri 2000, 294). Abstract cooperation is decentralized and diffused. For Lazzarato (1996), "immaterial labor constitutes itself in forms that are immediately collective, and we might say that it exists only in the form of networks and flows" (154). The communicative and creative capacities on which immaterial labour is based are enabled by machines but cannot be implemented in machines. Networked labourers combine their efforts without the organizing command of capital and generate a surplus which capital can at best hope to appropriate after the fact. Capital's control over technology is confounded and its drive towards an increasingly machinic state runs into an obstacle.

New Autonomy from Capital

The upshot of human–machine hybridization and abstract cooperation is a capacity for "autonomous production" (Hardt and Negri 2000, 276). This is also formulated as "real (and increasing) productive powers and capacities for autonomy" (Hardt and Negri 2017, 77) as well as the "radical autonomy of the productive synergies of immaterial labor" (Lazzarato 1996, 140). Hardt and Negri (2017) assert that to "the same degree that capital, as this process [of human-machine hybridization] proceeds, loses the capacity for self-realization, the social individual gains autonomy" (114). Immaterial labourers, having "incorporated the tools of production, having been metamorphosed anthropologically, act and produce machinically, separately and autonomously from capital" (Hardt and Negri 2017, 133). Immaterial labour thus "becomes in cooperation increasingly abstract from capital—that is, it has a greater ability to organize production itself, autonomously, particularly in relation to machines" (Hardt and Negri 2017, 117). The historical bias of machines in the labour–capital relation is flipped. The "productive social cooperation of workers endowed with fixed capital … poses the potential for the autonomy of workers, inverting the relation for force between labor and capital" (Hardt and Negri 2017, 115). Labour has obtained "such a level of dignity and power that it can potentially refuse the form of valorization that is imposed on it and thus, even under command, develop its own autonomy" (Hardt and Negri 2017, 117). The notion of "self-valorization" which Marx used to describe the recursive circuit of capital is inverted to describe how the multitude autonomously expands its capacities (Hardt and Negri 2017, 119). In this development, *post-operaismo* discerns the kernel of a social future beyond capital.

Autonomous production "exceeds capitalist relations ... grants labor increasing autonomy and provides the tools or weapons that could be wielded in a project of liberation" (Hardt and Negri 2009, 137). Lazzarato (1996) sees a "silent revolution" in the "anthropological realities of work and within the reconfiguration of its meanings" (140). But this is not only a liberation from work. For Hardt and Negri (2000), immaterial labour "seems to provide the potential for a kind of spontaneous and elementary communism" (294). Workers have "incorporated the productive tools and knowledges into their own minds and bodies ... are transformed and have the potential to become increasingly foreign to and autonomous from capital. This process injects class struggle into productive life itself" (Hardt and Negri 2017, 115). Emerging is a "new productive nature ... a new form of life that is at the base of a new mode of production" (Hardt and Negri 2017, 119). This autonomy is qualitatively novel:

> Is this autonomy the same as the forms of worker autonomy we spoke of in earlier phases of capitalist production? Certainly not, because now there is a degree of autonomy not only in regard to the processes of production, but also in an ontological sense—labor gains an ontological consistency, even when still completely subordinated to capitalist command. (Hardt and Negri 2017, 117)

This ontological consistency is "simply ... the power to act" (Hardt and Negri 2000, 358) or the immanent "potentiality of the multitude" (Hardt and Negri 2000, 82). Capital cannot emulate this potentiality, which is the sum of all of labour's other capacities which cannot be implemented in machines. This implies the end of capitalism because the condition for its existence, exploitable labour, is disappearing.

The Technological Argument for New Autonomy

We can sum up the technological argument for new autonomy with a one sentence quotation: "the powers of the new technical composition of labor-power cannot be contained by the capitalist modes of control" (Hardt and Negri 2009, 143). The proliferation of information technologies and technical skills enables a machinic hybridization of immaterial labour (which is inherently resistant to total machinic takeover by capital). Hybridization enables a new capacity for social self-organization or abstract cooperation which is not amenable to traditional control and exploitation, so capital can only parasitically collect value produced autonomously by labour. Immaterial labour thus facilitates the collapse of capital.

It is important to note, however, the ambiguity with which this argument is formulated in *post-operaismo* writings. It tends to be unclear whether the revolutionary changes described have already occurred, are underway, or will or might occur in the future. Immaterial labour is often described as fully hegemonic, but in other passages we are told that some "propositions have to be understood as indicative of a tendency" (Hardt and Negri 2017, 118). Sometimes immaterial labour is depicted as already beyond the control of capital and at other moments it is described as possessing only "certain limited margins of autonomy" (Hardt and Negri 2017, 133). Sometimes capital is described as having been reduced to parasitism on autonomous production, while in other formulations, labour remains "subordinated to the mechanisms of the extraction of value by capital" although they no longer function properly (Hardt and Negri 2017, 117).

In the interest of having the most productive engagement possible with immaterial labour theory, I want to "steel man" the argument for new autonomy. This means to represent it as strongly as possible, as opposed to making a "straw man" or weak misrepresentation. The first step towards steel manning the argument for new autonomy is to establish that labour as a global totality has definitely not achieved full autonomy from capital. I do not believe anyone will dispute that. It is more plausible that some limited degree of autonomy has been obtained by some subset of labour. We can then interpret *post-operaismo*'s contradictory statements about immaterial labour as referring to the uneven development of new autonomy. I suggest that the most coherent way to model this development is as a cycle. The cycle goes like this: human–machine hybridization enables abstract cooperation which enables a new degree of autonomy for immaterial labour. Whatever increased level of autonomy has been obtained in the course of this process allows for the appropriation of more technology, which augments human–machine hybridity, thereby expanding capacities for abstract cooperation and restarting the cycle. Eventually, the notion is, labour will or could achieve full autonomy (i.e. communism). This reconstruction seems to be the best way to understand what the *post-operaismo* inversion of the notion of "self-valorization" means (Hardt and Negri 2017, 119). If we grant that information technology has provided the working class with limited new capacities to produce beyond the circuits of capital, then, on this reading, immaterial labour's new autonomy is currently partially achieved and is set to increase in the future. However, even this qualified reading runs into difficulties, as I show in Chapter 7.

Conclusion

This chapter has outlined *operaismo*, *post-operaismo* and elaborated the technological argument for immaterial labour theory. With this, our sketch of the Marxist theoretical landscape is complete (if far from comprehensive). We are now prepared to engage with actually existing AI. The next three chapters shift focus from theory to study the AI industry and particularly work therein, before returning, in Chapter 7, to assess the theory of immaterial labour by the lights of the AI industry.

Bibliography

Alquati, Romano. 2013 [1961]. Organic Composition of Capital and Labour-Power at Olivetti. *Viewpoint Magazine*, September 27, 2013. https://www.viewpointmag.com/2013/09/27/organic-composition-of-capital-and-labor-power-at-olivetti-1961/. Accessed 25 Apr 2018.

Agrawal, Ajay, Joshua S. Gans, and Avi Goldfarb. 2018. *Prediction Machines: The Simple Economics of Artificial Intelligence*. Boston: Harvard Business Review Press.

Brynjolfsson, Erik, and Andrew McAfee. 2014. *The Second Machine Age: Work, Progress, and Prosperity in a Time of Brilliant Technologies*. New York and London: W. W. Norton & Company.

Camfield, David. 2007. The Multitude and the Kangaroo: A Critique of Hardt and Negri's Theory of Immaterial Labour. *Historical Materialism* 15 (2): 21–52.

Daugherty, Paul R., and H. James Wilson. 2018. *Human + Machine: Reimagining Work in the Age of AI*. Boston: Harvard Business Review.

Deleuze, Gilles, and Félix Guattari. 1983. *Anti-Oedipus: Capitalism and Schizophrenia*, trans. Robert Hurley, Mark Seem, and Helen R. Lane. Minneapolis: University of Minnesota Press.

Dyer-Witheford, Nick. 1999. *Cyber-Marx: Cycles and Circuits of Struggle in High-Technology Capitalism*. Champaign: University of Illinois Press.

Dyer-Witheford, Nick. 2005. Cyber-Negri: General Intellect and Immaterial Labor. In *The Philosophy of Antonio Negri*, vol. 1, ed. Timothy Murphy and Abdul-Karim Mustapha. London: Pluto Press.

Frank, Malcolm, Paul Roehrig, and Ben Pring. 2017. *What to Do When Machines Do Everything: How to Get Ahead in a World of AI, Algorithms, Bots, and Big Data*. New York: Wiley.

Fuchs, Christian. 2014. *Digital Labour and Karl Marx*. New York: Routledge.

Fuchs, Christian. 2017. Reflections on Michael Hardt and Antonio Negri's Book 'Assembly'. *tripleC: Communication, Capitalism & Critique*. Open Access Journal for a Global Sustainable Information Society 15 (2): 851–865.

Hardt, Michael, and Antonio Negri. 2000. *Empire*. Cambridge, MA: Harvard University Press.

Hardt, Michael, and Antonio Negri. 2004. *Multitude: War and Democracy in the Age of Empire*. London: Penguin.

Hardt, Michael, and Antonio Negri. 2009. *Commonwealth*. Cambridge, MA: Harvard University Press.

Hardt, Michael, and Antonio Negri. 2017. *Assembly*. Oxford: Oxford University Press.

Holloway, John. 2002. *Change the World Without Taking Power: The Meaning of Revolution Today*. London: Pluto Press.

Lazzarato, Maurizio. 1996. Immaterial Labor. In *Radical Thought in Italy: A Potential Politics*, ed. Paulo Virno and Michael Hardt, 133–147. Minneapolis: University of Minnesota Press.

Marazzi, Christian. 2008. *Capital and Language: From the New Economy to the War Economy*, trans. Gregory Conti. Los Angeles: Semiotext[e].

Markoff, John. 2020. A Case for Cooperation Between Machines and Humans. *The New York Times*, May 21. https://www.nytimes.com/2020/05/21/technology/ben-shneiderman-automation-humans.html.

Marx, Karl. 1990. *Capital*, vol. 1. New York: Penguin.

Marx, Karl. 1993. *Grundrisse*. New York: Penguin.

Moulier-Boutang, Yann. 2012. *Cognitive Capitalism*. Cambridge: Polity.

Negri, Antonio. 1989. *The Politics of Subversion: A Manifesto for the Twenty-First Century*. Cambridge: Polity.

Negri, Antonio. 1991. *Marx Beyond Marx: Lessons on the Grundrisse*. Brooklyn: Autonomedia.

Panzieri, Raniero. 1976. Surplus Value and Planning: Notes of the Reading of Capital. In *The Labour Process and Class Strategies*. London: The Conference of Socialist Economists.

Panzieri, Raniero. 2017 [1961]. The Capitalist Use of Machinery: Marx Versus the Objectivists. https://libcom.org/library/capalist-use-machinery-raniero-panzieri.

Pasquinelli, Matteo. 2015. Italian Operaismo and the Information Machine. *Theory, Culture & Society* 32 (3): 49–68.

Pasquinelli, Matteo. 2016. Abnormal Encephalization in the Age of Machine Learning. *e-flux* 75. http://www.e-flux.com/journal/75/67133/abnormal-encephalization-in-the-age-of-machine-learning/.

Pasquinelli, Matteo. 2017. "Machines that Morph Logic: Neural Networks and the Distorted Automation of Intelligence as Statistical Inference." *Glass Bead* 1 (1).

Pitts, Frederick Harry. 2017. Beyond the Fragment: Postoperaismo, Postcapitalism and Marx's 'Notes on Machines', 45 Years on. *Economy and Society* 46 (3–4): 324–345.

Pitts, Frederick Harry. 2018. A Crisis of Measurability? Critiquing Post-operaismo on Labour, Value and the Basic Income. *Capital & Class* 42 (1): 3–21.

Savat, David. 2009. Introduction: Deleuze and New Technology. In *Deleuze and New Technology*, ed. Mark Poster and David Savat. Edinburgh: Edinburgh University Press.

Susskind, Richard E., and Daniel Susskind. 2015. *The Future of the Professions: How Technology Will Transform the Work of Human Experts*. Oxford: Oxford University Press.

Thoburn, Nicholas. 2001. Autonomous Production? On Negri's New Synthesis. *Theory, Culture & Society* 18 (5): 75–96.

Thompson, Paul. 2005. Foundation and Empire: A Critique of Hardt and Negri. *Capital & Class* 29 (2): 73–98.

Tronti, Mario. 1964. Lenin in England. *Classe Operaia* 1. https://www.marxists.org/reference/subject/philosophy/works/it/tronti.htm.

Tronti, Mario. 1966. *Operai capitale*. Einaudi Editore. https://libcom.org/library/operai-e-capitale-mario-tronti.

Vercellone, Carlo. 2005. The Hypothesis of Cognitive Capitalism. No. halshs-00273641. HAL. https://halshs.archives-ouvertes.fr/halshs-00273641/.

Virno, Paolo. 2001. General Intellect. In *Lessico Postfordista*, ed. Adelino Zanini, and Ubaldo Fadini, trans. Arianna Bove. Milan: Feltrinelli. https://www.generation-online.org/p/fpvirno10.htm.

Virno, Paolo. 2003. *A Grammar of the Multitude*. Los Angeles: Semiotext(e).

Zerowork Collective. 1975. Introduction. *Zerowork: Political Materials* 1.

CHAPTER 4

Industrializing Intelligence: A Political Economic History of the AI Industry

Introduction

Artificial intelligence went from a fringe research interest for a handful of engineers, scientists and mathematicians to a feted centrepiece of twenty-first-century cybernetic capital in just over fifty years.[1] By situating AI in its historical and social context, we can see that it has not been a disinterested intellectual endeavour. AI is a technology of automation that has been intertwined with capital and state since its earliest days. AI first appeared alongside the application of early industrial automation technologies to smash the power of organized industrial workers and a few decades after it appeared, AI was applied to capture and automate the knowledge of expert workers in a variety of technical fields. The first era of the AI industry, built around so-called expert systems in the early 1980s, withered away in the 1990s. But since the mid-2010s, a second era of the AI industry, built on machine learning, has grown within the larger tech industry. Today, machine learning is applied to extract models, and solutions to problems, from data; automating, it is hoped, without having to first capture knowledge from living labour. Over the course of this brief history, I also introduce the major schools of AI and show how

[1] For more conventional histories of AI, see Crevier (1993), Nilsson (2010) and for general introductions to AI, see Frankish and Ramsey (2014), Domingos (2015), Kaplan (2016), Alpaydin (2016).

J. Steinhoff, *Automation and Autonomy*, Marx, Engels, and Marxisms,
https://doi.org/10.1007/978-3-030-71689-9_4

they present capacities for technological recursion that capital persistently seeks to direct towards its own ends. This historical sketch sets the stage for the analysis of the contemporary AI industry in the next chapter.

The Historical Context

The notion of a thinking machine goes back to ancient history (Husbands et al. 2008). AI research proper, it is generally held, began less than ten years after the deployment of the first general-purpose digital computer ENIAC and two years after the suicide of Alan Turing, in post-Second World War Massachusetts. There at the 1956 Dartmouth Summer Research Project the term artificial intelligence was coined. Taking off in the post-war USA, AI research began in a political economic context already enamoured with the recursive possibilities of information technology and in which the antagonism between capital and labour was taking on a new, technologically mediated intensity. Let us begin by considering four related characteristics of this social and technological milieu.

The first was the intellectual and technical influence of cybernetics, the interdisciplinary study of how complex systems, from computers to brains to organizations, process information to achieve actions broadly described as "control and communication" (Wiener 2019 [1948]). By arguing that brains and computers employed essentially the same mechanisms, cybernetics blurred boundaries between human and machine. A central concern of cybernetics was feedback, or the process by which a system could form a loop, based on the use of its output as input, to respond to its environment. Cyberneticians, were thus, like Turing, concerned with phenomena of recursion. Cybernetics bloomed in the context of artillery research during the Second World War (Wiener 2019 [1948], 8–11). The increased speed of new aircraft rendered conventional methods of aiming anti-aircraft weapons, contingent on skilled human operators, ineffective, so Norbert Wiener and colleagues devised a machine which could conduct the relevant calculations and aim the artillery automatically. Such cybernetic successes led to the novel belief, in the 1940s and 1950s, that humans could design and build machines more complex than themselves (Johnston 2008, 25). It also led to a flurry of research and applications in all kinds of fields, backed by substantial government and military support (Kline 2015). The influence of cybernetics is hard to overestimate, even if its terminology is not often explicitly used any longer. As John Johnston (2008) argues, cybernetics "formed the historical nexus out of which the information networks and computational assemblages that constitute the infrastructure of the postindustrial world first developed" (25).

Early AI was not cleanly separated from cybernetics. Both fields were interested in intelligence and several attendees of the 1956 Dartmouth workshop were involved with cybernetics. Paul Edwards (1996) argues that by blurring the boundary between human and machine, cybernetics contributed to the emergence of "cyborg discourse" in the wake of the Second World War (2). AI would take up and advance this discourse. While cybernetics drew an analogy between the computer and the brain, early AI researchers proposed an "even more comprehensive and abstract computer-*mind* metaphor" (Edwards 1996, 252, emphasis original). This ended up splitting the community into AI researchers who were concerned with symbol systems, logic and psychology, and cyberneticians interested more in self-organizing systems and neurophysiology (Kline 2011, 6).

A second contextual factor was the massively increased industrial productive capacity of capital in the Allied countries, driven by wartime advances in mechanization and new techniques of automation. In 1946 *Fortune* magazine published an influential article entitled "Machines without Men" which called for the full-scale application of wartime technological advances in automatic machinery to everyday manufacturing (Leaver and Brown 1946). Two years later saw the first published definition of the word automation (Le Grand 1948). New production technologies were accompanied by the intensification of Fordist labour organization. While Henry Ford's feted assembly line had began operation back in 1913, the use of machinery to simplify and speed up work, and to increase managerial control over workers, accelerated after the war (Noble 1986, 39). New production technologies were often disastrous for workers. In the USA, some 88,000 workers were killed and over 11 million were injured in industrial accidents between 1940 and 1945 alone (Noble 1986, 23). Advanced Fordism coincided with the introduction of mainframe computers, used for data processing, and computerized production machinery (Smith 2000, 5). The first commercially available computer numerically controlled (CNC) machine, a lathe, went on the market in 1952 and quickly became a flashpoint for conflict between capital and labour (Noble 1986). In 1959, the first industrial robot, Unimate, was installed at a General Motors factory in New Jersey.

It consisted of a single arm which could be programmed to perform one task at a time. It was in mass production by 1961 and was widely copied, leading to industrial robot proliferation (Wallén 2008, 9–10). The economic potential of the recursive capacities of information technology was becoming increasingly apparent.

A third factor was the changing face of industrial labour. During the Second World War, the composition of the workforce changed dramatically, though temporarily, as women and black people were employed to fill jobs previously reserved for white men. While they were largely dismissed after the war, the remaining mass workers of the Fordist workplace came out of the war in a strong position *vis a vis* capital. The USA's wartime no-strike pledge expired and "newly powerful unions [were] ready to test their strength" (Noble 1986, 24). Labour's power manifested in numerous strikes. During the war there were 14,471 strikes in the USA, involving almost seven million workers (Noble 1986, 22). This militant workforce drove capital to launch a multipronged assault on labour, one powerful arm of which constituted the application of automation technologies. Capital saw "unprecedented opportunities" for "reduced skill requirements, more concentrated management control, and the replacement of workers by machines" (Noble 1986, 36). The cybernetician Wiener (1949) wrote to UAW (United Auto Workers) President Walter Reuther (who never replied) concerned about the possibility of a "factory without employees", noting that "any labor, which is in competition with slave labor, whether the slaves are human or mechanical, must accept the conditions of work of slave labor". In the end, automation technologies of the mid-twentieth century did not achieve the delirious goals of perfection their promoters promised, nor were they apocalyptic for labour. They did, however, allow firms to reduce the number of unskilled and low-skilled workers they employed (Noble 1986). Automation would, combined with the turn, by many capitalist states, to Keynesian welfare and a "class compromise" between labour and capital, contribute to industrial workers trading in revolutionary aggression for benefits and wage increases (Harvey 2007, 10).

A fourth contextual factor, also concerning the changing face of labour, was the rise of a new workforce based around computing technology. One year after the Dartmouth workshop, management theorist Peter Drucker (1957) argued that:

> Today the assembly line is obsolescent ... even mechanical work is best organized as joint effort of men of high skill and knowledge exercising responsible, decision-making, individual judgment in a common effort and for a joint end ... Automation may well eliminate the unskilled worker from the production floor. But it replaces him by an equal number of men of high skill and judgment ... Each of them works in his own field of knowledge with a broad discretionary area of judgment. Each of them, however, must of necessity work closely with all the others - in constant communication with them, constantly adjusting to their decisions and in turn making decisions that affect their work. (67)

On the basis of the automation of manual labour and technologically augmented communication, a new knowledge worker was said to arise. Looking back, we know that what Drucker observed applied only to a small subset of workers in only a few parts of the world. High-skill collaborative and communicative work did appear, but it did not revolutionize work as such. Even as Drucker was writing, computer work was appearing which lacked the shining characteristics he attributed to the knowledge worker.

The early computer labour force was divided by gender. Men worked on engineering hardware for which they received attention from press and academia, while software production or programming was performed by women, was not considered prestigious, and was even concealed from the public (Light 1999). ENIAC, to take one example, was programmed by a team of women led by Jean Jennings and Frances Bilas (Abbate 2012, 24–33). David Alan Grier (2005) argues that in its earliest days during the Second World War, computer work was a "job of the dispossessed, the opportunity granted to those who lacked the financial or societal standing to pursue a scientific career. Women probably constituted the largest number of computers, but they were joined by African Americans, Jews, the Irish, the handicapped, and the merely poor" (276). After the war, early programmers were not easily replaceable. Soldiers returning from war did not possess the relevant skills, so many women stayed in the workforce as demand exploded (Little 2017). In 1950, there were only a few hundred programmers, but five years later there were around 10,000 programmers working with approximately one thousand existing computers. By 1960, "in the midst of a booming commercial computer market" programming would "become a profession in its own right, with about 60,000 practitioners servicing some five thousand machines. Programming began to emerge as a craft" (Edwards 1996, 248).

While far from a complete picture, these factors outline the social context in which AI emerged: one in which a changing working class faced an increasingly cybernetic capital. The rest of this chapter traces how the contemporary AI industry developed from this initial context.

The Advent of AI Research

The organizers of the 1956 Dartmouth workshop (funded by the Rockefeller Foundation and the US Office of Naval Research (ONR)) founded their project on the conjecture that:

> every aspect of learning or any other feature of intelligence can in principle be so precisely described that a machine can be made to simulate it. An attempt will be made to find how to make machines use language, form abstractions and concepts, solve kinds of problems now reserved for humans, and improve themselves. (McCarthy et al. 1955)

They hoped to achieve these goals with a "2 month, 10 man study" (McCarthy et al. 1955). A few years later, some of these researchers proclaimed that "there are now in the world machines that think, that learn, and that create … their ability to do these things is going to increase rapidly until—in a visible future—the range of problems they can handle will be coextensive with the range to which the human mind has been applied" (Simon and Newell 1958, 8). It is not hard to imagine why capital might have found AI, as it was described in these early proclamations, appealing. However, such lofty aspirations went unfulfilled. The workshop did not achieve its goals, and half a century later, machines have yet to achieve coextensive function with the human mind.

Such bold statements did, however, accrue interest (and capital) for a particular approach to AI called symbolic AI or GOFAI (Good Ol' Fashioned AI) (Haugeland 1989). While some attendees of the Dartmouth workshop endorsed a different approach inspired by neurophysiology (which would go on to develop into today's machine learning) GOFAI became, until the mid-1980s, the hegemonic idea of AI. GOFAI aims to implement in machines high-level cognitive functions, such as logical reasoning, through the manipulation of information encoded in a symbolic language (Newell and Simon 1976). It assumed, as the Dartmouth organizers put it, that a "large part of human thought consists of manipulating words according to rules of reasoning and rules of conjecture" (McCarthy et al. 1955). GOFAI therefore aimed "to formalize knowledge of the world, injecting it into computer systems predefined and predigested" (Edwards 1996, 255). A typical GOFAI system solves problems by "generating and progressively modifying symbol structures until it produces a solution structure" (Newell and Simon 1976, 120–121) in a process called "heuristic search" (Boden 2014, 90). The system contains an internal representation of a problem in a symbolic language and performs rule-based manipulations on it. Imagine a chess program. There is a large but finite number of possible states the chess board can be in and a finite set of rules that determine the possible state changes for any given state. However, a good chess player looks not only at the current state of the board, but also considers possible future states. Mentally scrolling through all possible moves both current and future is time-consuming and cognitively wasteful, so a good chess player or program will apply heuristics, or rules of thumb, to curtail search (Hofstadter 1979, 150–151). One might, for instance, eliminate all courses of action that would result in losing one's queen.

The necessity of internal representation led to a serious issue for GOFAI known as the frame problem or "the problem of updating, searching, and otherwise manipulating, a large structure of symbols in realistic amounts of time" (Copeland 2000, see also Dennett 2006). One way to think of this is in terms of common-sense reasoning. If I perceive a plate resting on a table (in the absence of contributing factors such as a meddlesome cat or an earthquake) I do not wonder whether it might suddenly disappear and reappear under the table or spontaneously shatter. Common sense dictates that force must be applied to the plate for these things to happen. Lacking common sense, a GOFAI system must have all such basic knowledge programmed into it as explicit rules, and there are very many rules required to approximate even naïve conceptions of physics, let alone the vagaries of social interaction. Beyond very simple domains, GOFAI therefore ran into problems of complexity. Despite this and other problems, most of AI's early successes can be credited to GOFAI. The first era of the AI industry, discussed below, was based on a GOFAI application called expert systems. While GOFAI's fame has faded, it is still used in the AI subfield of planning which finds applications in video games, route planning, air traffic control and configuring electronics components (Kaplan 2016, 25). Few now see GOFAI as the future of AI since, as Boden reflects, "most of the 'intelligence' involved lies in the choices of actions, operators, and heuristics specified by the programmer" (2014, 90). But in the early years of AI, things were different.

There was not yet an AI industry in the 1950s and 1960s. Those researching the topic worked in both industry and academia and often passed back and forth between the two sectors, which were connected by a foundation of military funding. Edwards (1996) calls the nascent computing industry an "iron triangle" of "self-perpetuating academic, industrial, and military collaboration" (47). By the end of the Second World War, the US Office of Scientific Research and Development (OSRD) had increased yearly military research and development funding from a prewar ~$23 million to over $100 million (Edwards 1996, 46). This outlay continued after the war with the establishment of a number of centres of excellence (some devoted to AI) situated in universities. According to Edwards (1996), AI was "for over two decades almost exclusively a pure research area of no immediate commercial interest, [and it] received as much as 80 percent of its total annual funding from ARPA" (64). The USA's Advanced Research Projects Agency (ARPA) and the Office of Naval Research (ONR) were the largest funders of early AI research. The commercial viability of AI would be built on the foundation provided by their funding.

The ONR (which still exists) funds technology research and development with applications to US naval security. ARPA (now DARPA) was formed in 1958 as a response to the USSR's successful deployment of the Sputnik 1 satellite the year prior. DARPA has a mission of ensuring US technological superiority through organizing and funding scientific and technological research. ARPA opened an Information Processing Techniques Office (IPTO) in 1962, directed by J.C.R. Licklider, who advocated a "symbiosis" between humans and machines (Licklider 1960). Beginning around 1962, IPTO funded AI and other computing projects at several US universities (including MIT, Carnegie Tech and Stanford University) and private research labs in industry, all of which were also based in the USA (Nilsson 2010, 120). Perhaps the most well-known of these is the RAND Corporation.

Headquartered in Santa Monica, California, and originally an Air Force research project, RAND was spun-off in 1948 and developed into one of the most influential research institutions of the twentieth century. RAND researchers were integral to the development of many information technologies including computers, the internet and AI. The very first book on AI, the anthology *Computers and Thought* (Feigenbaum and Feldman 1963), had six of twenty chapters previously published by RAND researchers (Klahr and Waterman 1986, 1). International Business Machines (IBM) has also been involved with the development of nearly all aspects of information technology, AI included. Arthur Samuel, an IBM researcher attributed with the first use of the term machine learning, developed a checkers playing program which was able to improve itself and defeat novice players, in 1956. Samuel (1959) hoped that "[p]rogramming computers to learn from experience should eventually eliminate the need for much of this detailed programming effort" (211). Bell Laboratories was also involved in the development of myriad information technologies, as well as early experiments in AI. Claude Shannon, inventor of information theory, worked for Bell starting in 1941 and developed a robot mouse called Theseus which employed a rudimentary form of machine learning to find its way out of mazes. It is also worth mentioning Systems Development Corporation (SDC), which is considered to be the world's first software company (Campbell-Kelly 2004, 36–41). It began as a project group of the RAND Corporation and was spun off in 1957. SDC specialized in designing and consulting for large networked computer systems. They are perhaps best known for their involvement in the production of the Semi-Automated Ground Environment (SAGE). SAGE was a system of networked radar sites and computers intended to provide comprehensive surveillance of US airspace. AI was used to manage the enormous amount of data the system integrated. SAGE went online in 1958 but was never put to the test.[2]

Early AI researchers moved between these institutions throughout the 1950s and 60s. There is no discernable trend in migrations from academic to industry positions or vice versa. Licklider, for instance, worked first at Lincoln Laboratories and MIT, later went to another firm and eventually, to ARPA (Nilsson 2010, 119). The influential AI researcher Allan Newell

[2] A number of other organizations were also influential in early AI research including BBN Technologies, Lincoln Laboratories and SRI International (formerly Stanford Research Institute). BBN conducted early research in natural language processing. SRI is a research lab established by trustees of Stanford University. In 1966, SRI opened its Artificial Intelligence Center that would develop "Shakey," widely accepted as the first mobile robot with the ability to perceive and reason about its surroundings. Lincoln Laboratories, created in 1951 as a federally funded research and development center at MIT, was meant to remedy perceived inadequacies in the USA's air force. Lincoln Laboratories also contributed to SAGE.

on the other hand, worked at RAND in his early years but spent his later years at CMU (Nilsson 2010, 115). While there were, by the late 1950s and early 1960s, labs devoted to AI at some universities, they were often lacking in hardware and academic AI researchers would often have to gain access to the expensive computers owned by industry research labs for computationally demanding AI projects (Nilsson 2010, 116). MIT owned an IBM 704 which was cutting-edge at its release in 1954, but quickly began to pale as computing research intensified. The first PDP-1 (programmed-data-processer) computer, which possessed magnitudes more computational power, was bought by the research company BBN Technologies in 1960 for $120,000. Such expensive hardware ensured that AI researchers would continue to draw on the deep pockets of military funding.

Throughout the 1950s and 1960s, there were impressive achievements in subfields of AI such as machine vision, robotics and theorem proving. There were, however, no commercial applications, since most of these successes were achieved on "toy problems" in artificially defined, very narrow domains and could not be generalized to the more complex real world (Crevier 1993, 114). Beyond the field of AI, programming evolved from its nascent post-war form into an adolescent profession. In the 1960s, demand for software drove a demand for programming labour. However, even as programming work exploded, it was already being automated. In fact, automation became an essential component of programming, and remains so today. This can be illustrated by considering the development of higher-level programming languages.

Higher-level programming languages allow programming to be done in more-or-less natural languages (Sammet 1969, 1–2). One of the most popular of these was FORTRAN (originally developed by IBM) which became available in the 1950s. Before higher-level languages, programs were written in binary machine code which precisely specifies all functions of a given piece of software in relation to its hardware solely with ones and zeros, making it "extremely difficult to use and even more difficult to debug" (Edwards 1996, 247). Programmers of the day referred to FORTRAN's capacity to automatically translate programs written in roughly natural language into machine code as "automatic programming" (Backus 1981, 25). Mark Campbell (2020) dubs this the "first wave of automated coding" (81). All programming is thus always already the automation of programming. A recursive operation of "recruit[ing] the computer into its own operation" lies at the very foundation of computer work (Chun 2005, 29).

According to John Backus (1981), before 1954, programmers "rightly regarded their work as a complex, creative art that required human inventiveness to produce an efficient program" (25). Higher-level programming languages automated much of the machine code-based labour process and made programming much easier to learn. With this, according to Edwards (1996), not long after programming appeared, "already the amount of mathematical skill it required had begun to diminish" (248–249). This was driven, in part, by capital's valorization imperative. The "cost of programmers associated with a computer center was usually at least as great as the cost of the computer itself ... programming and debugging accounted for as much as three-quarters of the cost of operating a computer" (Backus 1981, 26–27). In addition, "[b]usinesses ... wanted to write their own software without hiring expensive experts ... they had to if they were going to use computers at all, since before the 1960s 'off-the-shelf' software was virtually unknown" (Edwards 1996, 249). Programming labour needed to be deskilled and devalued.

The AI Winter

During the 1960s, the global economy began winding down after the post-Second World War boom, "stagflation" threatened Western economies and civil rights activists upset the social status quo. Early proclamations about AI, such as those made by the Dartmouth workshop researchers, were decried as hubristic. The AI "winter" ensued in which funding for AI research substantially decreased (Crevier 1993, 203). A significant blow came in 1966 with the dire assessment of the ALPAC (Automatic Language Processing Advisory Committee) Report. The report was commissioned by the US National Research Council to evaluate the prospects of computational linguistics and machine translation research (which government agencies had already funded to the tune of $20 million). Preoccupied with the threat of communism, the US government was interested in the automatic translation of Russian language documents. Citing the higher costs, slower speed and lower accuracy of machine, compared to human, translations, the report ended most government funding into machine translation and dampened enthusiasm for AI more broadly in the public sphere (National Research Council and Automatic Language Processing Advisory Committee 1966).

A further blow came in 1969, when the US Congress passed the first Mansfield Amendment which strictly limited the kinds of research government bodies could fund (Laitinen 1970). The amendment "brought about a swift decline in some of the military's support for basic research, often driving it toward the applied realm" (National Research Council 1999, 213). Since AI applications were few, this had the effect of diminishing AI research. Across the Atlantic, 1973 saw the publication of the report "Artificial Intelligence: A General Survey" commissioned by the UK Parliament. The so-called Lighthill Report argued that AI research could only work with toy problems and would remain stymied by the complexity of the real world. This report dampened government funding for AI research in the UK, which did not recover until the early 1980s, and arguably contributed to US dominance in the field.

Throughout the AI winter, AI research continued in subdued tones. Some universities, including Toronto, Rochester, Texas, Maryland, British Columbia, California and Washington, even opened new AI research groups (Nilsson 2010, 207). Into the 1970s, ARPA still provided "as much as 80 to 90 percent of funding for the major AI groups–MIT, Stanford, SRI and Carnegie-Mellon" but overall amounts were diminished (Edwards 1996, 296). Many academic computing researchers turned to applied research while others left academia altogether, contributing to the rise of startups, the proliferation of private research labs and the computing industry in general (Ensmenger and Aspray 2002, 162–163). Microsoft, for instance, was founded in 1974 and would release its influential operating system MS-DOS in 1981.

Expert Systems: The First Era of the AI Industry

The 1970s saw social theorists such as Daniel Bell reconsider the knowledge worker Drucker had written about two decades earlier. Bell (1973) reckoned with not only changes in the workplace but predicted a whole new "post-industrial" society characterized by a shift from producing goods to services and from manual to cognitive labour, all powered by computing technology processing vast quantities of information. Despite the tendency of epochal modes of analysis like Bell's to overemphasize change at the expense of continuity, there did occur substantial changes around that time (Webster 2014). Between 1948 and 1990, employment in the USA increased by nearly 83% with 97% of this increase coming from circulation capital sectors or "nongoods-producing industries" including "services, transportation, communications, utilities, wholesale and retail trade, finance, insurance, and real estate" (US Bureau of Labor Statistics 1993, 7). Between the 1970s and 1990s, the proportion of industrial manufacturing work declined around the world by varied amounts, but in some countries surpassed 20% (Castells and Aoyama 1994, 11).

However, even as diverse types of non-manufacturing labour increased, so did efforts to automate it. By the 1980s, the high skill, communicative knowledge worker imagined by Drucker and Bell was also a target for automation with an AI application called the expert system, which intended to capture expert knowledge about a particular domain and make it available to management and/or workers lacking in said knowledge. Expert systems thus explicitly manifested the Taylorist principle of the "dissociation of the labor process from the skills of workers" (Braverman 1998, 78). Advocates of the expert system approach were not afraid to admit it:

> [t]o make major productivity gains, we discovered that the automation net would have to be cast farther out than the factory floor—to cover the information handlers, those doing the planning, the problem solving, and the decision making. In short, it was necessary to bring the power of automation to the knowledge worker. (Feigenbaum et al. 1988, 4)

Expert systems are made up of two main components: the knowledge base and the inference engine. The knowledge base consists of factual and heuristic knowledge, represented in a symbolic language. It is created via a process called "knowledge engineering" in which engineers interview experts in a given field and encode their knowledge as a set of conditional rules (Feigenbaum et al. 1988). The inference engine defines the steps taken to apply the stored knowledge to solve particular problems. Users can query the expert system to obtain its "expert" opinion.

The first expert system, Dendral, was developed throughout the 1960s by Edward Feigenbaum and Joshua Lederberg at Stanford with the goal of helping organic chemists identify unknown biological molecules (Lederberg 1987, 1). Dendral proved that the expert system concept could work, and while it remained in academia, it spawned many offspring, some of which were commercialized. In 1980, Digital Equipment Corporation (DEC) deployed the "first expert system in daily production use in industry", called XCON (Expert Configurator) (Barker and O'Connor 1989). XCON aided in the configuration and assembly of customizable computer systems. According to Alex Roland and Philip Shiman (2002), by "the middle of the decade [DEC] estimated it was saving $40 million annually by use of XCON" (191). The expert system "Dipmeter Adviser" was developed by oilfield services corporation Schlumberger, in cooperation with academic researchers, starting in 1980. This system analyzed sensor data to infer "subsurface geologic structure" in preparation for drilling (Davis et al. 1981, 846). It was deployed in 1984. Also in 1984, Intellicorp, arguably the first AI startup company, founded in 1980 by Feigenbaum and others, received $1,286,781 from DARPA to produce an "evolutionary new generation" expert system (Roland and Shiman 2002, 198). Feigenbaum also founded Teknowledge, which began as a consulting business, but moved into expert systems with DARPA funding of $1,813,260 from 1984 to 1986 (Roland and Shiman 2002, 201).

Demand for expert systems exploded in the mid-1980s (Crevier 1993, 198). Commenting on the "industrialization of artificial intelligence", the AI entrepreneur Jerrold Kaplan (1984) noted that "[o]ver the past few years, the character of the AI community has changed. AI researchers used to be able to go about their work in peace … As the promise of practical applications of AI has slowly become reality, new players have entered the field, changing its nature forever" (51). According to one contemporary estimate, 1500 expert systems were in commercial use at the end of 1987 (Feigenbaum et al. 1988, x). It is only at this point in the late 1980s that it is fair to say that AI comprised a distinct industry. Daniel Crevier describes the nascent AI industry as composed of three main sectors. The largest sector, comprising over half the market, was specialized expert system computers called LISP machines, the largest producers of which were the corporations Xerox and Texas Instruments along with two startups from Massachusetts (Crevier 1993, 200). The second largest sector was that of expert system "shells" which could be adapted to function on different knowledge bases. The third sector, complete expert system applications, was the smallest sector of the industry.

Expert systems were necessarily bespoke; each had to be built, or at least heavily customized, to suit its particular knowledge base, and it would only work in that narrow domain. DARPA, however, wanted an expert system with "generic or universal application" (Roland and Shiman 2002, 194). DARPA wanted an inference engine that could be deployed to different knowledge bases without its core components needing to be modified. In essence, it was pursuing AGI. The generous funding it provided to Teknowledge and Intellicorp was intended to advance this goal. While a general expert system would prove infeasible, interest in, and funding for, expert systems research and development drew labour to the AI industry. The number of people trained to work in AI dramatically increased throughout the 1980s. New graduate programmes were established, such as Feigenbaum's applied Masters of Science in Artificial Intelligence at Stanford, which aimed not at producing academic researchers, but instead nurturing the basic skills for applied AI development in industry (Roland and Shiman 2002, 196). Membership in the Association for the Advancement of Artificial Intelligence (AAAI) increased from around 5000 in 1979 to 16,421 in 1987 (Nilsson 2010, 271).

By the mid-1980s, the AI industry was booming. In 1986, sales in the USA of "AI-related hardware and software reached $425 million" and forty new companies were formed, with total investments of around $300 million (Crevier 1993, 200). Many large companies established in-house AI teams. In 1987, the conglomerate DuPont "had 100 expert systems in routine operation and 500 in various stages of development" (Crevier 1993, 199). The computing company Digital Equipment Corporation (DEC) had 77 employees in its AI team in 1986 but this ballooned to 700 by 1988 (Crevier 1993, 199). Enthusiasm for expert systems continued throughout the 1990s. The total number of expert systems in use went from 1500 in 1987 to an estimated 12,500 by 1997 (Liebowitz 1997, 118).

Strategic Computing: AI and the State Part I

The 1970s and 1980s saw the rise of neoliberalism, first in Chile, then the UK, USA and elsewhere. David Harvey defines neoliberalism as a "theory of political economic practices that proposes that human well-being can best be advanced by liberating individual entrepreneurial freedoms and skills within an institutional framework characterized by strong private property rights, free markets, and free trade" (Harvey 2007, 2). While neoliberal theory extols the virtues of market freedom from state influence, it has in practice entailed the formation of a "neoliberal state" which implements measures necessary to keep the market operating (Harvey 2007, 7).

According to Harvey (2007), neoliberal states demonstrate an "intense interest in and pursuit of information technologies" because they require "technologies of information creation and capacities to accumulate, store, transfer, analyse, and use massive databases to guide decisions" (3). Support for Harvey's claim is provided by the case of state involvement in computing and AI research in the 1980s. AI became a front of national technological competition, not unlike the Space Race between the USA and USSR in the 1950s and 1960s.

Japan's Ministry of Trade and Industry (MITI) jump started the race for AI with its Fifth Generation Computer Systems project in 1982. MITI created the Institute for Next Generation Computer Technology (ICOT) to carry out a ten-year plan of developing supercomputers for AI. ICOT was backed by a consortium made up of two government research labs and eight Japanese giants of industry including Fujitsu, Hitachi and Toshiba. The project had a budget of approximately $850 million (Feigenbaum and McCorduck 1984, 137). By 1992, some interesting technological developments had been achieved, but commercially viable output and AI supremacy had not, and the project was ended.

Reacting to Japan's computational ambitions, the USA began its Strategic Computing (SC) Initiative in 1983. By 1993, DARPA had spent an "extra $1 billion on computer research to achieve machine intelligence" (Roland and Shiman 2002, 1). SC also failed to meet its ambitious goals and was instead adapted to a project of "high-performance computing" by the end of the 1980s (Roland and Shiman 2002, 325). Like Japan's Fifth Generation project, it did however contribute greatly to improved computing infrastructure and a proliferation of AI skills (Roland and Shiman 2002, 331). Not all USA AI initiatives failed, however. The Dynamic Analysis and Replanning Tool (DART) was developed for DARPA by a team led by an engineer from BBN Technologies. Deployed in 1991, its successful logistical management reportedly "paid back all of DARPA's 30 years of investment in AI in a matter of a few months" according to the director of DARPA at the time (Hedberg 2002, 81–83).

The USA's AI mobilization occurred in direct response to Japan's program, but it was also motivated by fear of the increasingly high-tech spectre of communism. There is little available English literature about

Soviet AI research. Computing got off to a slow and late start in the USSR due to (at least) two factors. One is that the Communist Party concealed the existence of computers in the Union from both its citizens and other nations for the first years of their existence, slowing the diffusion of relevant skills. A second factor is that cybernetics was construed, well into the mid-1950s, as a bourgeois pseudo-science that contradicted Marxism-Leninism (Gerovitch 2004). It was not until after the death of Stalin in 1953 that cybernetics research gradually became acceptable. By 1961, cybernetics was being hailed as "one of the major tools of the creation of a communist society" (quoted in Conway and Siegelman 2006, 316). As in the early days of AI research in the USA, there seems to have been some conceptual blurring between AI and cybernetics in the USSR. According to Boris Malinovsky (2010), the preeminent Soviet cybernetician Victor Glushkov "regarded artificial intelligence as the most promising direction in Cybernetics" (32). Soviet AI practitioners pursued research into theorem proving, pattern recognition, machine learning, speech recognition, heuristic search machine translation and machine vision (Feigenbaum 1961; Gerovitch 2011, 180; Peters 2016, 117). When the expert system pioneer Feigenbaum, visiting from the USA in 1960, surveyed the Soviet AI and computing landscape, he concluded that in the USSR "research on artificial intelligence and other advanced applications of computers is beginning to achieve a priority which it did not seem to have just one year ago" (Feigenbaum 1961, 579). By 1966, at the first machine versus machine chess championship, a Soviet chess-playing AI program defeated 3-1 a program built by AI practitioners from MIT and Stanford, including John McCarthy, lead organizer of the Dartmouth conference (Adelson-Velskii et al. 1970; Feigenbaum 1968). The USSR did not, however, ever achieve influential status in AI.

The British government also reacted to Japan's Fifth Generation program, with the establishment of the five-year Alvey Programme in 1983. AI was the "initial focus" of Alvey, though it also encompassed other computing research (Oakley and Owen 1989, 172). The Programme received £290 million in funding from a combination of public and private sources. It did not posit goals as optimistic as those of Japan or the USA, but whether it constituted a success was still debated (Oakley and Owen 1989, 172). Also in 1983, the Commission of European Communities launched the ten-year European Strategic Program on Research in Information Technology (ESPRIT). This project was designed to develop the industrial potential of European information technology with a focus on AI (Steels and Lepape 1993, 5). It consisted of two phases, the first of which included 32 AI projects funded at a cost of 84 million ECU. By 1993, the ongoing second phase involved 27 more projects involving AI with total funding of around 80 million ECU (Steels and Lepape 1993, 4).

Although each of these strategic computing projects varied considerably in their details, a few useful generalizations can be made. All were driven by national or supranational bodies which recognized a need for direct intervention in research and the commercialization of computing and AI. All involved collaboration across academic, commercial and industrial sectors (and national borders in the case of ESPRIT). All largely failed to achieve their original goals. Despite that, all these projects contributed to the diffusion of AI and computing skills and technological infrastructure, laying ground for the emergence of personal computing and the internet.

Computational enthusiasm and the promotion of expert systems by capital and state during the 1980s generated the first critical backlash against the industry of AI. A spate of Marxist research wary of the capacities of expert systems emerged, as mentioned in Chapter 2 (Cooley 1981, 1987; Athanasiou 1985; Berman 1992; Ramtin 1991). Critics of this period did not see their worst fears for AI realized, however, because by the early 1990s the AI industry went into a decline from which it would not recover for over two decades.

The Decline of Expert Systems

Despite the efforts of capital and state, the AI industry underwent a second AI winter in the early 1990s. Commonly cited reasons for this second AI winter are the "brittleness" of expert systems or how their performance drops to zero when posed a problem beyond their narrow domain (Feigenbaum et al. 1988, 253) as well as their "opacity" or the unpredictable ways they perform as more and more interacting rules are added (Crevier 1993, 204). There was also a shift in the underlying hardware. Expert systems were often run on LISP machines specially built for the purpose, which cost tens of thousands of dollars. In 1977, the Commodore PET ($795) and the Apple II ($1298) were released and personal computing became possible. Cost, ease of use and wide applicability diverted interest from LISP machines, and as cheap computers became more powerful, they could be used for some AI applications as well.

It was not just a technological issue, however. Labour was a problem for expert systems. Some workers resented their knowledge being captured by the knowledge engineering process. Nor was management always enthusiastic about the large expenditures necessary for knowledge engineering and expert system hardware. One of the creators of XCON noted in 1984 that a "lot of missionary work is still needed" (Kraft 1984, 48). There also turned out to be more labour involved in producing expert systems than expected. As expert systems passed from the research lab to commercial applications they were applied to increasingly complex domains and so required more and more rules. DARPA held that "production of the systems had to be dramatically streamlined" (Roland and Shiman 2002, 194). Imagined future expert systems were calculated to require impossibly herculean efforts on the part of knowledge engineers, such that by the mid-1980s, "knowledge engineers were starting to realize that building truly extensive AI systems would require automating the knowledge-acquisition process itself" (Crevier 1993, 205). In addition, the problem of maintenance became apparent. Expert systems need to be updated every time their domains change. With the constant revolutionizing of business processes required by capitalist competition, knowledge engineering was a never-ending task.

The proposed solution was recursive; an expert system which could build expert systems. This meant "codify[ing] for computer use the very knowledge that is helpful in building expert systems" (Feigenbaum et al. 1988, 250). This proved intractable with the available technology, but in 1982, the MIT AI lab (with DARPA funding) released a semi-automated program called The Programmer's Apprentice (Rich and Waters 1988). It began a "second wave" of automated coding in which programs "generate high-level code from human concepts represented in textual or graphical models" (Campbell 2020, 81). So far this field has had limited success, but some believe that machine learning will soon make it feasible (Campbell 2020, 82). Proponents of expert systems came to a similar conclusion in the mid-1980s and admitted that "[l]earning is the 'magic bullet' that is needed to help with the building of the large knowledge bases" (Feigenbaum et al. 1988, 255). However, expert systems could not be made to learn, and by the late 1990s, the industry was in decline. The term "expert system" faded away as its techniques were invisibly embedded within other information technologies (Angeli 2010, 52). The era of GOFAI came to an end.

During this second AI winter, new technologies, such as the internet, took centre stage in public interest while AI research was conducted in academic shadows. The 1990s saw the rise of what Schiller (1999) calls "digital capitalism", defined by capital's reconstitution around the infrastructure of the internet. This period saw a mania of speculative investment in early internet companies. Web browsers improved and internet companies proliferated, with investors happy to throw money at anything purporting to do business on "the net". From 1998 to 2002, around 50,000 companies were formed which aimed to turn profits on the internet (Goldfarb et al. 2005, 2). Several of these internet companies became today's largest AI producers: Amazon, an internet retailer, was founded in 1994 and both Google, initially focused on internet search, and Tencent, initially focused on social media, were founded in 1998.

As the internet diffused throughout industry, making communication and coordination at a global scale easier, industrial production started to change. Theorists inspired by the production model of Toyota promoted "lean" production as a successor to Fordist mass production. Lean production aims for the quality and flexibility of craft production as well as the quantity of mass production. For Womack et al. (1990) lean production "employ[s] teams of multiskilled workers at all levels of the organization and use[s] highly flexible, increasingly automated machines to produce volumes of products in enormous variety" (13). A related development methodology, known as Agile, has since been widely adopted in software and AI production, as we will see in Chapter 6.

The widespread technological optimism of the 1990s was taken down several notches when the "dot com" speculative investment bubble collapsed in 2000, drawing the global economy into a recession the following year. Nearly half of all dot com companies, such as Pets.com, were killed off. Amazon's stock fell from $107 to just $7, although it later recovered, in part by establishing the cloud platform Amazon Web Services (AWS) in 2002 (Edwards 2016). Other surviving internet companies thrived in the post-crash economy and began diversifying. Google acquired YouTube in 2006 and online ad company DoubleClick in 2007.

The Rise of Machine Learning

In the 2000s, AI was no longer an industry buzzword. GOFAI and expert systems had failed to deliver, but competing AI paradigms were on the rise.[3] The machine learning (ML) approach to AI has existed since the 1956 Dartmouth workshop but it was not commercialized until the 1980s and did not become commercially widespread until after 2010 when it became the main force of the AI industry's second era. ML took a back seat to GOFAI for decades. This is often held to have been caused by Marvin Minsky and Seymour Papert (1969) showing how a simple artificial neural network called the perceptron was unable to process the logical function of exclusive disjunction (a proposition that is true if one of its constituent statements is true and one is not). Despite wide scepticism, Geoffrey Hinton, David Rumelhart and James McCelland continued to research ML throughout the 1970s at the University of California, San Diego as part of the PDP (parallel distributed processing) Group. Nilsson (2010) notes that "before about 1980 machine learning ... was regarded by some as on the fringes of AI" (398). Things changed when the PDP Group published influential papers which widely expanded the scope for ML applications (McClelland and Rumelhart 1986).

ML takes a very different approach to AI than GOFAI. While GOFAI was primarily applied to emulate high-level cognitive functions such as logical reasoning, ML has historically aimed to emulate lower-level, pattern-recognition functions of cognition and perception. Early ML researchers argued that AI research should begin by considering how the brain's architecture enables intelligence in the first place, rather than how

[3]Another of these competing paradigms is the situated, embodied, dynamical (SED) framework. SED refers to a variety of approaches to AI, developed since the 1980s, that emphasize the irreducible importance of the body and its perceptual apparatuses to cognition (Beer 2014, 128). Advocates argue that any attempt to engineer intelligence which only emulates disembodied high-level cognition is doomed to fail when presented with the complexities of concrete reality. The SED approach has thus been concerned with robotics as well as AI. Against the symbolic representations of GOFAI, SED pioneer Rodney Brooks (1991) asserts that it is "better to use the world as its own model" (140). Aiming to circumvent the frame problem, SED systems "do not contain a complicated symbolic model of their environment. Information is left 'out in the world' until such time as the system needs it" (Copeland 2000). Sensors may therefore replace symbolic structures, to some degree. The SED approach has enjoyed limited commercial success, although humanoid robots based on SED approaches are produced for industrial settings by companies such as ReThink Robotics. Thus far, the commercial impact of such products has been minimal, so this book does not discuss them.

philosophers and mathematicians attempt to reconstruct intelligence in logic. The PDP Group thus described their work as investigating the "microstructure" of cognition (McClelland and Rumelhart 1986, 79). They sought to emulate the brain's complex network of interconnected neurons in code (Sun 2014). One way of doing so is the artificial neural network (ANN) architecture, which models collections of interconnected neurons organized into hierarchies of layers. The lowest level receives input data. Middle levels—also referred to as hidden layers—process data which is sent up to them. The topmost layer gives an output. Processing occurs in parallel, distributed across the network. In general, the more layers an ANN has, the more complex patterns it can find and the more complex problems it can solve. While popular discourse on contemporary AI often conflates the ANN and ML, the two are not equivalent. The ANN architecture is one possible way of doing ML, which is one way of doing AI.[4] Yet, while there are many other ways to do ML, this book has the ANN architecture in mind when talking about ML, for explanatory ease and also because deep learning, the most hyped approach to AI today, involves very large ANNs.

Beyond its initial ambitions and architecture, ML is distinguished from GOFAI by its much-vaunted capacity to learn. However, learning in the ML sense is unlike what we attribute to humans. Machine learning means using an algorithm to automatically "extract patterns from data" (Kaplan 2016, 27). The extracted pattern takes the form of another algorithm, called a model. Ethem Alpaydin (2014) explains that to "solve a problem on a computer, we need an algorithm ... For some tasks, however, we do not have an algorithm" (1). If we do not know how to create a suitable algorithm, but we have some relevant data, we may be able to use machine learning "to extract automatically the algorithm" from that data (Alpaydin 2014, 2). Once a model is produced, it may then be applied to new data. Models may be descriptive (used for analysis of data) or predictive (used to extrapolate from data) or both (Alpaydin 2014, 3).

Already it should be clear that ML is reliant on data. As we will see, it requires vast quantities. But how does ML use an algorithm to extract a model from data? We will look in more detail at the different types of ML in Chapter 6, in the context of the labour process. For now, it will suffice to know that ML systems learn through training on data. In an

[4] On the diversity of approaches to ML, see Chapter 8 of Mackenzie (2017).

ANN, the synapses which connect the layers of neurons are "weighted" with numeric values representing the strength of the connection. Initially these are set randomly, input data is fed through them and the output that the network gives will likely be wrong or useless. The learning algorithm adjusts the weights of these connections over the course of a process called training with the goal of approaching the correct, or at least useful, output. The model produced should not only work correctly on the data it was trained on, but also on new data. This is called "generalization ability" (Alpaydin 2016, 40). ML models have narrow domains; a facial recognition model will not recognize speech. The best generalization ability today means that a model can be applied to new data of a similar domain. This minimal sense of generality is about as close to AGI as most actually existing AI gets.[5]

The shift described by Alpaydin, from writing an algorithm to solve a known problem to using ML to automatically generate a model from data, indexes a new degree of recursion with new potentials for automation. For Pedro Domingos (2015) the "Industrial Revolution automated manual work and the Information Revolution did the same for mental work, but machine learning automates automation itself" (9–10). From this perspective, ML is "the inverse of programming" because with it, "algorithms ... make other algorithms ... computers write their own programs so we don't have to" (Domingos 2015, 6–7). Such proclamations indeed point out the salient novelty of ML, but should be taken cautiously. We should not think, based on the rhetoric surrounding ML, that it requires no human intervention or that AGI is only a few steps away. We will see in Chapter 6 that although it is already being automated, the production of ML still requires a lot of human work.

We should also avoid drawing unwarranted parallels between ML and human intelligence. While ML is indeed a recursive technique which "recruit[s] the computer into its own operation" (Chun 2005, 29) it achieves this through brute force techniques hard to compare directly to human intelligence. As mentioned in the introduction, the line between AI and computation is a fuzzy one. While humans learn from relatively small amounts of data in short periods of time, advanced ML relies on

[5] A reconsideration of generality and actually-existing AI may be necessary in the near future, based on promising early experiments with OpenAI's diversely applicable language model GPT-3 (Shardin 2020) and DeepMind's impressively general use of reinforcement learning to learn how to play an array of video games (Mnih et al. 2013).

massive datasets and extensive amounts of training, powered by huge arrays of powerful computers (Han and Dally 2018; Press 2018). For example, in 2012, when the ML-based second era of the AI industry was beginning to gather steam, a Google ML system which learned to recognize images of cats drew on 16,000 processors to learn from a dataset made up of 10 million images (Markoff 2012). Today, cutting-edge ML requires far more resources. According to one analysis, the largest ML training processes in 2018 consumed 300,000 times more computing power than those of 2012. The authors assert that "it's difficult to be confident that the recent trend of rapid increase in compute usage will stop" (Sastry et al. 2019).

ML attained its first commercial success in the late 1980s when it was applied to fields such as speech recognition and optical character recognition (Crevier 1993, 215–216; Lisboa and Vellido 2000, vii). By 1989, three hundred companies, "most of them startups founded by researchers, competed for [the ANN] market" (Crevier 1993, 216). One account places the global market for AI in 1994 at "about $900 million, with North America accounting for two-thirds of that total" (Roland and Shiman 2002, 214). However, by the eve of the new millennium researchers admitted that "[a]pplications of neural networks in 'real world' scale are scant. Even though quite a few companies have nurtured neural network prospective studies, not so many make use of neural networks in every-day-business life" (Vellido et al. 1999, 57). That would not happen for another decade. In the meantime, AI slowly reappeared in the public eye. IBM's Chess-playing GOFAI system Deep Blue defeated chess master Gary Kasparov in 1997 and a handful of experimental semi-autonomous vehicles, often employing ML, garnered attention when they demonstrated limited success in controlled environments.

Deep Learning: The Second Era of the AI Industry

In 1987, Hinton of the PDP Group moved from San Diego to The Canadian Institute for Advanced Research (CIFAR) in Toronto where he continued ML research with limited government funding and a small group of students. ML was not a hot topic. By the early 2000s, "the number of researchers who specialized in neural networks dwindled to fewer than half a dozen" (Allen 2015). This was the era of "Web 2.0"—applications and websites defined by the proliferation of user-generated content and increased ease of use for casual users (DiNucci 1999, 32).

More companies which would later become AI giants appeared at this time. In 2000, Baidu was founded with a focus on internet search, while the social network Facebook appeared in 2004. In 2006, Hinton and company demonstrated what came to be known as "deep" machine learning because it uses ANNs possessing as many as a thousand layers (LeCun et al. 2015, 436–444; He et al. 2016). The proliferation of layers enables deep learning systems to find more complex, hierarchical patterns in data (LeCun et al. 2015, 436). As the CIFAR researchers refined their new deep learning approach, the global economy nearly imploded.

The financial crisis of 2007–2008, spurred by subprime mortgage lending and the consequent housing bubble in the USA, and amplified by high-frequency algorithmic trading and diverse high-risk lending practices by banks, culminated in a global economic meltdown. Enormous government bailouts prevented a total collapse of the banks, although the Great Recession still descended on the world in 2009. While it might seem strange to mention this crisis, based as it was on finance, in the context of the AI industry, it was not unconnected to the dot com crash of 2000, in which several of today's AI giants were implicated. Carlota Perez (2009) argues that the two crises should be seen as episodes of the same story: "[t]he first was based on technological innovation, the second on financial innovation, facilitated, accelerated and made global by information technology and the internet" (802). While tech companies thrived after the recession abated, workers, in general, did not.

After 2009, in the USA alone hundreds of thousands of jobs were lost, income inequality between the richest and poorest increased substantially and wealth was concentrated in the richest families (Federal Reserve 2014). Around the world, the fall in labour's share of national incomes, which began in the 1980s, continued (OECD 2012; IMF 2017). While the world was still reeling, Hinton and others demonstrated the potential of deep learning with a record-breaking application to speech recognition (Hinton et al. 2012). It was discovered that graphics processing units (GPUs), intended for computer gaming, work very well for the intensive parallel computation necessary for ML. Companies also began to realize how to capture the increasingly profuse data generated by online activity and mobile device use for training ML models (Kelly 2014).

In the next few years, a market for ML opened and the AI industry began developing its contemporary form. Early on, capital was starving for ML-producing labour. Most of the researchers at CIFAR spun off their research into startups, many of which were bought up by the tech giants. Hinton and two students, Alex Krizhevsky and Ilya Sutskever, formed DNNresearch Inc. in 2012 to market applications of deep learning for image recognition and language processing. DNNresearch won a $600,000 award from Google before being acquired by the tech giant in 2013. The same year, Hinton was hired as a distinguished researcher by Google Brain. Krizhevsy and Sutskever were also hired by Google while Hinton's other students Yann Lecun and Ruslan Salahutdinov were hired to lead Facebook's AI Research Group in 2013 and Apple's AI research program in 2016, respectively. Yoshua Bengio, who also worked with Hinton at CIFAR, was hired by IBM in 2015.

Tracking such developments, *The Economist* (2016) stated that "artificial intelligence is finally starting to deliver on its promises". By 2016, nearly all the Silicon Valley tech giants had opened in-house AI research labs and tech CEOs, such as Google's Sundar Pichai, were proclaiming a shift from "mobile-first" to "AI-first" computing (D'Onfro 2016). Even corporations dating back to the mid-twentieth century, such as General Electric and IBM, became interested in both producing AI and incorporating AI into their production processes (Woyke 2017; Boyle 2017).

Around the same time, China began pouring money into AI research. Kai-Fu Lee (2018) describes the 2016 victory of DeepMind's AlphaGo over Chinese Go champion Ke Jie as a "Sputnik moment" for Chinese government and business which had previously had little interest in AI (1). The following years saw a pivot by China's largest tech companies, Baidu, Tencent and Alibaba, towards AI and the release of the Chinese government's AI plan from which followed policy changes and billions of dollars in investment. At the time of writing, the AI industry is flourishing in its second era. While the AI industry is still relatively young and small, ML is providing tools for a new wave of automation which capital hopes will "capture benefits such as lower labor costs, increased throughput, enhanced quality and lower downtimes" (Statista 2019, 11).

Conclusion

This chapter has sketched a political economic history of the AI industry. It has shown that AI has been implicated with capital, state and military since its inception. AI has not led a purely conceptual or academic life; it has continually been mobilized as an automation technology, though it has yet to provide the full wealth of recursive power hoped for by its advocates. While the hopes of early AI purveyors were largely dashed by limitations inherent to expert systems which made them inefficient automation technologies, the situation may be different with machine learning. The possibility presented by ML, of automating tasks by automatically extracting algorithms to complete them from data, entails a different approach to automation. I return to this topic in Chapter 6.

Bibliography

Abbate, Janet. 2012. *Recoding Gender: Women's Changing Participation in Computing*. Cambridge, MA: MIT Press.

Adelson-Velskii, G.M., et al. 1970. Programming a Computer How to Play Chess. *Russian Mathematical Survey* 25 (221).

Allen, Kate. 2015. How a Toronto Professor's Research Revolutionized Artificial Intelligence. *The Star*, April 17.

Alpaydin, Ethem. 2014. *Introduction to Machine Learning*. Cambridge: MIT Press.

Alpaydin, Ethem. 2016. *Machine Learning: The New AI*. Cambridge: MIT Press.

Angeli, Chrissanthi. 2010. Diagnostic Expert Systems: From Expert's Knowledge to Real-Time Systems. *Advanced Knowledge Based Systems: Model, Applications & Research* 1: 50–73.

Athanasiou, Tom. 1985. Artificial Intelligence: Cleverly Disguised Politics. In *Compulsive Technology: Computers as Culture*, ed. Tony Solomonides and Les Levidow, 13–35. London: Free Association Books.

Backus, John. 1981. The History of FORTRAN I, II and III. In *History of Programming Languages*, vol. 1, ed. Richard L. Wexelblat, 25–45. Academic Press. http://www.softwarepreservation.org/projects/FORTRAN/paper/p25-backus.pdf.

Barker, Virginia E., and Dennis E. O'Connor. 1989. Expert systems for configuration at Digital: XCON and beyond. *Communications of the ACM* 32 (3): 298–318.

Beer, Randall D. 2014. Dynamical Systems and Embedded Cognition. In *The Cambridge Handbook of Artificial Intelligence*, ed. Keith Frankish and William M. Ramsey, 128–148. Cambridge: Cambridge University Press.

Bell, Daniel. 1973. *The Coming of Post-Industrial Society: A Venture in Social Forecasting*. New York: Basic Books.

Berman, Bruce. 1992. Artificial Intelligence and the Ideology of Capitalist Reconstruction. *AI & Society* 6: 103–114.

Boden, Margaret A. 2014. GOFAI. In *The Cambridge Handbook of Artificial Intelligence*, ed. Keith Frankish and William M. Ramsey, 89–107. Cambridge: Cambridge University Press.

Boyle, Alan. 2017. IBM Makes a 10-Year, $240 M Investment in Artificial Intelligence Research at MIT. *GeekWire*, September 6. https://www.geekwire.com/2017/ibm-makes-240m-investment-artificial-intelligence-research-mit/.

Braverman, Harry. 1998. *Labor and Monopoly Capital: The Degradation of Work in the Twentieth Century*. New York: NYU Press.

Brooks, Rodney A. 1991. Intelligence Without Representation. *Artificial Intelligence* 47 (1–3): 139–159.

Campbell, Mark. 2020. Automated Coding: The Quest to Develop Programs That Develop Programs. *Computer* 53 (2, February).

Campbell-Kelly, Martin. 2004. *From Airline Reservations to Sonic the Hedgehog: A History of the Software Industry*. Cambridge: MIT Press.

Castells, Manuel, and Yuko Aoyama. 1994. Paths Towards the Informational Society: Employment Structure in G-7 Countries, 1920–90. *International Labour Review* 133: 5.

Chun, Wendy Hui Kyong. 2005. On Software, or the Persistence of Visual Knowledge. *Grey Room* 18: 26–51.

Cooley, Mike. 1981. On the Taylorisation of Intellectual Work. In *Science, Technology and the Labour Process*, vol. 2, ed. Les Levidow and Robert Young. London: CSE Books.

Cooley, Mike. 1987. *Architect or Bee? The Human Price of Technology*. London: Hogarth Press.

Conway, Flo, and Jim Siegelman. 2006. *Dark Hero of the Information Age: In Search of Norbert Wiener, the Father of Cybernetics*. New York: Basic Books.

Copeland, Jack. 2000. What Is Artificial Intelligence?" *AlanTuring.net*. Accessed 7 Nov 2018. http://www.alanturing.net/turing_archive/pages/reference%20articles/what_is_AI/What%20is%20AI11.html .

Crevier, Daniel. 1993. *AI: The Tumultuous History of the Search for Artificial Intelligence*. New York: Basic Books.

Davis, Randall, Howard Austin, Ingrid Carlbom, Bud Frawley, Paul Pruchnik, Rich Sneiderman, and J.A. Gilreath. 1981. The DIPMETER ADVISOR: Interpretation of Geologic Signals. In *Proceedings of the 7th International Joint Conference on Artificial Intelligence*, vol. 2, 846–849. Morgan Kaufmann Publishers Inc.

Dennett, Daniel. 2006. Cognitive Wheels: The Frame Problem of AI. In *Philosophy of Psychology: Contemporary Readings*, ed. José Luis Bermúdez. New York: Routledge.

DiNucci, Darcy. 1999. Fragmented Future. *Print* 53 (4): 32–33.

Domingos, Pedro. 2015. *The Master Algorithm: How the Quest for the Ultimate Learning Machine Will Remake Our World*. New York: Basic Books.

D'Onfro, Jillian. 2016. Google CEO: We're Headed Towards an 'AI First' World. *Business Insider India*, April 22. https://www.businessinsider.in/Google-CEO-Were-headed-towards-an-AI-first-world/articleshow/51935048.cms.

Drucker, Peter. 1957. *Landmarks of Tomorrow*. New York: Harper and Brothers.

Edwards, Jim. 2016. One of the Kings of the '90s Dot-Com Bubble Now Faces 20 Years in Prison. *Business Insider*, December 6. https://www.businessinsider.com/where-are-the-kings-of-the-1990s-dot-com-bubble-bust-2016-12.

Edwards, Paul N. 1996. *The Closed World: Computers and the Politics of Discourse in Cold War America*. Cambridge: MIT Press.

Ensmenger, Nathan, and William Aspray. 2002. Software as Labor Process. In *History of Computing: Software Issues*, 139–165. Berlin: Springer.

Federal Reserve. 2014. Changes in U.S. Family Finances from 2010 to 2013: Evidence from the Survey of Consumer Finances. *Federal Reserve Bulletin* 100 (4, September). https://www.federalreserve.gov/pubs/bulletin/2014/pdf/scf14.pdf.

Feigenbaum, Edward A. 1961. Soviet Cybernetics and Computer Sciences, 1960. *Communications of the ACM* 4 (12): 566–579.

Feigenbaum, Edward A. 1968. Artificial Intelligence: Themes in the Second Decade. AI-MEMO-67. Stanford University Department of Computer Science. https://stacks.stanford.edu/file/druid:cc421zn5789/cc421zn5789.pdf.

Feigenbaum, Edward A., and Julian Feldman (eds.). 1963. *Computers and Thought*. New York: McGraw-Hill.

Feigenbaum, Edward A., and Pamela McCorduck. 1984. *The Fifth Generation*. London: Pan Books.

Feigenbaum, Edward A., Pamela McCorduck, and Penny Nii. 1988. *The Rise of the Expert Company*. New York: Times Books.

Frankish, Keith, and William M. Ramsey (eds). 2014. *The Cambridge Handbook of Artificial Intelligence*. Cambridge: Cambridge University Press.

Gerovitch, Slava. 2004. *From Newspeak to Cyberspeak: A History of Soviet Cybernetics*. Cambridge: MIT Press.

Gerovitch, Slava. 2011. Artificial Intelligence with a National Face: American and Soviet Cultural Metaphors for Thought. In *The Search for a Theory of Cognition: Early Mechanisms and New Ideas*, ed. Stefano Franchi and Francesco Bianchini. New York: Rodopi.

Goldfarb, Brent D., Michael D. Pfarrer, and David Kirsch. 2005. Searching for Ghosts: Business Survival, Unmeasured Entrepreneurial Activity and Private Equity Investment in the Dot-Com Era. *Robert H. Smith School Research Paper* No. 06-027.

Grier, David Alan. 2005. *When Computers Were Human*. Princeton: Princeton University Press.

Han, Song, and William J. Dally. 2018. Bandwidth-Efficient Deep Learning. In *DAC '18: The 55th Annual Design Automation Conference*, June 24–29, San Francisco, CA, USA. ACM: NY, USA, 6 pages. https://doi.org/10.1145/3195970.3199847.

Harvey, David. 2007. *A Brief History of Neoliberalism*. Oxford: Oxford University Press.

Haugeland, John. 1989. *Artificial Intelligence: The Very Idea*. Cambridge: MIT Press.

He, Kaiming, Xiangyu Zhang, Shaoqing Ren, and Jian Sun. 2016. Deep Residual Learning for Image Recognition. In *Proceedings of the IEEE Conference on Computer Vision and Pattern Recognition*, 770–778. http://openaccess.thecvf.com/content_cvpr_2016/papers/He_Deep_Residual_Learning_CVPR_2016_paper.pdf.

Hedberg, Sara Reese. 2002. DART: Revolutionizing Logistics Planning. *IEEE Intelligent Systems* 17 (3): 81–83.

Hinton, Geoffrey, Li Deng, Yu. Dong, George Dahl, Abdel-Rahman Mohamed, Navdeep Jaitly, Andrew Senior, Vincent Vanhoucke, Patrick Nguyen, Tara N. Sainath, and Brian Kingsbury. 2012. Deep Neural Networks for Acoustic Modeling in Speech Recognition. *IEEE Signal Processing Magazine* 29: 82–97.

Hofstadter, Douglas R. 1979. *Gödel, Escher, Bach: An Eternal Golden Braid*. New York: Basic Books.

Husbands, Philip, Owen Holland, and Michael Wheeler (eds). 2008. *The Mechanical Mind in History*. Cambridge, MA/London: MIT Press.

IMF. 2017. Chapter 3: Understanding the Downward Trend in Labor Income Shares. *World Economic Outlook 2017*. https://www.imf.org/en/Publications/WEO/Issues/2017/04/04/world-economic-outlook-april-2017.

Johnston, John. 2008. *The Allure of Machinic Life: Cybernetics, Artificial Life, and the New AI*. Cambridge, MA: MIT Press.

Kaplan, Jerrold. 1984. The Industrialization of Artificial Intelligence: From By-Line to Bottom Line. *AI Magazine* 5 (2): 51.

Kaplan, Jerry. 2016. *Artificial Intelligence: What Everyone Needs to Know*. Oxford: Oxford University Press.

Kelly, Kevin. 2014. The Three Breakthroughs That Have Finally Unleashed AI on the World. *Wired*, October 27. https://www.wired.com/2014/10/future-of-artificial-intelligence/.

Klahr, Philip, and Donald A. Waterman. 1986. Artificial Intelligence: A RAND Perspective. *AI Magazine* 7 (2): 54.

Kline, Ronald. 2011. "Cybernetics, Automata Studies, and the Dartmouth Conference on Artificial Intelligence." *IEEE Annals of the History of Computing* 33 (4): 5–16.

Kline, Ronald. 2015. *The Cybernetics Moment: Or Why We Call Our Age the Information Age*. Baltimore: Johns Hopkins.

Kraft, Arnold. 1984. XCON: An Expert Configuration System at Digital Equipment Corporation. In *The AI Business: The Commercial Uses of Artificial Intelligence*, ed. P.H. Winston and K.A. Prenderghast. Cambridge: MIT Press.

Laitinen, Herbert A. 1970. Reverberations from the Mansfield Amendment. *Analytical Chemistry* 42 (7): 689.

Leaver, Eric W., and John J. Brown. 1946. Machines Without Men. *Fortune* 34 (11): 165–204.

LeCun, Yan, Yoshua Bengio, and Geoffrey Hinton. 2015. Deep Learning. *Nature* 521: 436–444.

Lederberg, Joshua. 1987. How DENDRAL Was Conceived and Born. In *Proceedings of the ACM Symposium on the History of Medical Informatics*. National Library of Medicine. https://profiles.nlm.nih.gov/ps/access/BBALYP.pdf.

Lee, Kai-Fu. 2018. *AI Superpowers: China, Silicon Valley, and the New World Order*. New York: Houghton Mifflin Harcourt.

Le Grand, Rupert. 1948. Ford Handles with Automation. *American Machinist* 92: 107–109.

Licklider, Joseph C.R. 1960. Man–Computer Symbiosis. *IRE Transactions on Human Factors in Electronics* 1: 4–11.

Liebowitz, Jay. 1997. Worldwide Perspectives and Trends in Expert Systems: An Analysis Based on the Three World Congresses on Expert Systems. *AI Magazine* 18 (2): 115.

Light, Jennifer S. 1999. When Computers Were Women. *Technology and Culture* 40 (3): 455–483.

Lisboa, P.J.G., and Alfredo Vellido. 2000. Preface: Business Applications of Neural Networks. In *Business Applications of Neural Networks: The State-of-the-Art of Real-world Applications*, ed. P.J.G. Lisboa, Bill Edisbury, and Alfredo Vellido. Singapore: World Scientific.

Little, Becky. 2017. The First 1940s Coders Were Women—So How Did Tech Bros Take Over? *History.com*, September 1. https://www.history.com/news/coding-used-to-be-a-womans-job-so-it-was-paid-less-and-undervalued.

Mackenzie, Adrian. 2017. *Machine Learners: Archaeology of a Data Practice*. Cambridge: MIT Press.

Malinovsky, Boris. 2010. *Pioneers of Soviet Computing*, ed. Anne Fitzpatrick, trans. Emmanuel Aronie. Published electronically. http://www.sigcis.org/files/SIGCISMC2010_001.pdf.

Markoff, John. 2012. How Many Computers to Identify a Cat? 16,000. *The New York Times*, June 25. https://www.nytimes.com/2012/06/26/technology/in-a-big-network-of-computers-evidence-of-machine-learning.html.

McCarthy, John, Martin Minsky, N. Rochester, and Claude Shannon. 1955. A Proposal for the Dartmouth Summer Research Project on Artificial Intelligence. Accessed 6 Nov 2018. http://www-formal.stanford.edu/jmc/history/dartmouth/dartmouth.html.

McClelland, J.L., and D.E. Rumelhart. 1986. *Parallel Distributed Processing: Explorations in the Microstructure of Cognition*. Cambridge: MIT Press.

Minsky, Marvin, and Seymour Papert. 1969. *Perceptrons: An Introduction to Computational Geometry*. Cambridge: MIT Press.

Mnih, Volodymyr, Koray Kavukcuoglu, David Silver, Alex Graves, Ioannis Antonoglou, Daan Wierstra, and Martin Riedmiller. 2013. Playing Atari with Deep Reinforcement Learning. *arXiv Preprint*. arXiv:1312.5602.

National Research Council. 1999. *Funding a Revolution: Government Support for Computing Research*. Washington, DC: National Academies Press.

National Research Council and Automatic Language Processing Advisory Committee. 1966. *Language and Machines: Computers in Translation and Linguistics: A Report*, vol. 1416. Washington, DC: National Academies Press.

Newell, Allen, and Herbert A. Simon. 1976. Computer Science as Empirical Inquiry: Symbols and Search. *Communications of the ACM* 19 (3): 113–126.

Nilsson, Nils. 2010. *The Quest for Artificial Intelligence*. Cambridge: Cambridge University Press.

Noble, David. 1986. *Forces of Production: A Social History of Industrial Automation*. Piscataway, NJ: Transaction Publishers.

Oakley, Brian, and Kenneth Owen. 1989. *Alvey: Britain's Strategic Computing Initiative*. Cambridge: MIT Press.

OECD. 2012. Chapter 3: Labour Losing to Capital: What Explains the Declining Labour Share? *OECD Employment Outlook 2012*. https://www.oecd.org/els/emp/EMO%202012%20Eng_Chapter%203.pdf.

Perez, Carlota. 2009. The Double Bubble at the Turn of the Century: Technological Roots and Structural Implications. *Cambridge Journal of Economics* 33 (4): 779–805.

Peters, Benjamin. 2016. *How Not to Network a Nation: The Uneasy History of the Soviet Internet*. Cambridge: MIT Press.

Press, Gil. 2018. The Brute Force of IBM Deep Blue and Google DeepMind. *Forbes*, February 7. https://www.forbes.com/sites/gilpress/2018/02/07/the-brute-force-of-deep-blue-and-deep-learning.

Ramtin, Ramin. 1991. *Capitalism and Automation: Revolution in Technology and Capitalist Breakdown*. London: Pluto Press.

Rich, Charles, and Richard C. Waters. 1988. The Programmer's Apprentice: A Research Overview. *Computer* 21 (11): 10–25.

Roland, Alex, and Philip Shiman. 2002. *Strategic Computing: DARPA and the Quest for Machine Intelligence, 1983–1993*. Cambridge: MIT Press.

Sammet, Jean E. 1969. *Programming Languages; History and Fundamentals*. Englewood Cliffs, NJ: Prentice Hall.

Samuel, Arthur L. 1959. Some Studies in Machine Learning Using the Game of Checkers. *IBM Journal of Research and Development* 3 (3): 210–229.

Sastry, G., J. Clark, G. Brockman, and I. Sutskever. 2019. Compute Used in Older Headline Results. *OpenAI Blog*. Last accessed 5 May 2020. https://openai.com/blog/ai-and-compute/#addendum.

Schiller, Dan. 1999. *Digital Capitalism: Networking the Global Market System*. Cambridge: MIT Press.

Shardin, Anton. 2020. Apps and Startups Powered by GPT-3. *Leta Capital*, October 29. https://medium.com/letavc/apps-and-startups-powered-by-gpt-3-976c55dbc737.

Simon, Herbert A., and Allen Newell. 1958. Heuristic Problem Solving: The Next Advance in Operations Research. *Operations Research* 6 (1): 1–10.

Smith, Tony. 2000. *Technology and Capital in the Age of Lean Production: A Marxian Critique of the 'New Economy'*. Albany, NY: SUNY Press.

Statista. 2019. *In-Depth: Artificial Intelligence 2019: Statista Digital Market Outlook*. Statista.

Steels, Luc, and Brice Lepape. 1993. Knowledge Engineering in Esprit. *IEEE Expert* 8 (4): 4–10.

Sun, Ron. 2014. Connectionism and Neural Networks. In *The Cambridge Handbook of Artificial Intelligence*, ed. Keith Frankish and William M. Ramsey, 108–127. Cambridge: Cambridge University Press.

The Economist. 2016. The Return of the Machinery Question, June 23. https://www.economist.com/special-report/2016/06/23/the-return-of-the-machinery-question.

US Bureau of Labor Statistics. 1993. Labor Composition and U.S. Productivity Growth, 1948–90. https://www.bls.gov/mfp/labor_composition.pdf.

Vellido, Alfredo, Paulo J.G. Lisboa, and J. Vaughan. 1999. Neural Networks in Business: A Survey of Applications (1992–1998). *Expert Systems with Applications* 17 (1): 51–70.

Wallén, Johanna. 2008. *The History of the Industrial Robot*. Linköping: Linköping University Electronic Press.

Webster, Frank. 2014. *Theories of the Information Society*. New York: Routledge.

Wiener, Norbert. 1949. Father of Cybernetics Norbert Wiener's Letter to UAW President Walter Reuther. *LibCom*. https://libcom.org/history/father-cybernetics-norbert-wieners-letter-uaw-president-walter-reuther.

Wiener, Norbert. 2019 [1948]. *Cybernetics*. Cambridge, MA: MIT Press.

Womack, James P., Daniel T. Jones, and Daniel Roos. 1990. *The Machine That Changed the World*. New York: Macmillan.

Woyke, Elizabeth. 2017. General Electric Builds an AI Workforce. *MIT Technology Review*, June 27. https://www.technologyreview.com/s/607962/general-electric-builds-an-ai-workforce/.

CHAPTER 5

Machine Learning and Fixed Capital: The Contemporary AI Industry

Introduction

Contemporary artificial intelligence commodities of the AI industry's second era are products of a relatively small, yet highly concentrated and competitive industry, a growing sector within the larger tech industry. In this chapter I survey its structure and dynamics. The first half discusses the capital side of the industry, including its size, spatial distribution and characteristics that distinguish it from other industries, including the involvement of the state, the centrality of cloud computing, the emerging proprietary AI hardware market and the open-source AI phenomenon. The second half discusses the labour side. I distinguish the different roles in the industry, from generously remunerated data scientists to ghost workers who sometimes earn mere dollars a day. I also discuss how the AI industry is stratified by both gender and race, characterized by rampant sexism, and how these features have unique consequences for an industry built around machine learning, which extracts patterns from data. Finally, I discuss how workers in the AI industry, and the larger tech industry, have bucked a historical trend of apoliticism and begun organizing around such issues as racism, sexism and the militarization of AI.

But first, let us begin, as in the previous chapter, by sketching some important elements of the larger political economic context in which the contemporary AI industry exists. The first of these is the platform, both the technology and the business model, which many companies, including

J. Steinhoff, *Automation and Autonomy*, Marx, Engels, and Marxisms,
https://doi.org/10.1007/978-3-030-71689-9_5

all the major AI producers, reconfigured around in the wake of the 2008 financial crisis. The platform model revolves around gathering and using data. Nick Srnicek (2017) defines platforms as "digital infrastructures" that "enable two or more groups to interact" and which usually "come with a series of tools that enable their users to build their own products, services, and marketplaces" (43). Platform capitals capture the data which passes through their platforms, sell it and use it as input to produce other commodities. Data is an especially imporant input to the valorization processes of AI producers who peddle machine learning commodities. Machine learning and platforms form a virtuous loop. Platforms gather data and ML needs data for training. In turn, ML offers diverse ways to optimize the functioning of platforms (via microtargeted ads, for example). Data collection entails surveillance, so when valorization depends on data collection, capital depends on surveillance. The voracious collection of data is not an unfortunate side effect of the platform model, but rather one of its necessary components. Surveillance and AI go hand in hand.

A second factor is the shrinking availability of cheap labour on the global market, particularly in China. Since China's opening to the world market in 1978, capital from the Global North grew accustomed to accessing its abundant supply of cheap manufacturing labour. However, since 2005 the cost of Chinese labour has increased at least threefold and since 2017, exceeds the cost of labour in Brazil, Argentina and Mexico (Gao 2017). Despite dissidence often being met with militaristic force, Chinese worker strikes and protests are on the rise with "more than 1,700 incidents [in 2018], up by 36 percent from 1,250 in 2017" (Symonds 2019). It is not difficult to see capital's enthusiasm for AI as, at least in part, a reaction to such increased labour costs. As the cost of labour rises, the incentive to automate increases. As researchers from the think tank Brookings note laconically, "[r]ising wages make computers cost-effective for an increasing number of low-skill tasks" (Karsten and West 2015). Already in China, large capitals are feeling the pressure. The Swedish-Swiss corporation ABB Robotics reported a "90% surge in robot sales in China" at the end of 2020 (Revill 2021). Labour costs are also a problem for US capitals trying to "reshore" their operations. An almost humorous illustration of this occurred in 2016 when US President Trump ballyhooed his success in pressuring the manufacturer Carrier to cancel its planned move of 1000 jobs from Indiana to Mexico. However, the president of Carrier later admitted that "to continue to be competitive" the company would be investing $16 million USD in automation, which "ultimately means … there will be fewer jobs" (Turner 2016).

A third factor is renewed interest in military applications of AI. The USA's war on terror was already invested heavily in cyberwarfare, but revelations of Russian interference in the 2016 US elections brought renewed attention to the ways information technologies might be offensively mobilized. The past decade has also seen the military-funded development of martial technologies incorporating various types of AI, including drones, battlefield robots and cyborg soldier augmentation technology (Scharre 2018; Surber 2018). In 2017, Russian President Putin declared, "Whoever leads in AI will rule the world" (RT 2017). Other national governments seem to agree. The US Department of Defense formed the JAIC (Joint Artificial Intelligence Center) in 2018 with a mission to "transform the DoD by accelerating the delivery and adoption of AI" (CIO DoD 2018). The top five US defence contractors, including Lockheed Martin, all have AI projects underway (Roth 2019) and major AI producers, such as Google, have been (often clandestinely) accepting contracts from military agencies, to the chagrin of many of their employees. While Google has pledged not to work on offensive weapons, Oberhaus (2018) argues that the interaction between the military and AI is unlikely to cease because AI producers must continue to sell commodities: "once you've dominated civilian markets, the capitalist imperative to grow doesn't just magically stop". How exactly the AI industry will ramify remains to be seen. Certainly, platforms, rising labour costs and militarized AI are only a few relevant contextual factors. However, they provide a frame for our study of the contemporary AI industry.

Charting the AI Industry

Today's AI industry is global, although unevenly concentrated, with the largest AI firms located in the USA and China. As of 2018, the four countries with the most AI companies were the USA (2028), China (1011), the UK (392) and Canada (285) (China AI Development Report 2018). In the USA, AI production is dominated by big tech companies Google, Amazon, Microsoft, Facebook, Intel and Apple, along with some older companies like IBM and Siemens as well as startup companies like DataRobot and Uber. In China, the AI industry revolves around the so-called BAT, made up of the big tech companies Baidu, Alibaba and Tencent and powerful startups such as SenseTime (Table 5.1).

Table 5.1 The AI Tech Giants and Dinosaurs

2019							
Company	*Sales*	*Profits*	*Assets*	*Market value*	*Employees*	*Country*	*Global rank by assets*
Apple	$261.7 B	$59.4 B	$373.7 B	$961.3 B	132,000	USA	6
Amazon	$232.9 B	$10.1 B	$162.6 B	$916.1 B	647,500	USA	28
Alphabet	$137 B	$30.7 B	$232.8 B	$863.2 B	98,771	USA	17
General Electric	$121.6 B	(−)$22.4 B	$317.7 B	$81.4 B	283,000	USA	389
Microsoft	$118.2 B	$33.5 B	$258.9 B	$946.5 B	131,000	USA	16
Siemens	$98.3 B	$5.5 B	$164.2 B	$97 B	379,000	Germany	64
IBM	$ 78.7 B	$8.6 B	$130.9 B	$124.9 B	381,100	USA	60
Intel	$70.8 B	$21.1. B	$128 B	$263.1 B	107,400	USA	44
Facebook	$55.8 B	$22.1 B	$97.3 B	$512 B	35,587	USA	63
Alibaba	$51.9 B	$10.3 B	$133.7B	$480.8 B	101,958	China	59
Tencent	$47.2 B	$11.9 B	$105.4 B	$472.1 B	54,309	China	74
Baidu	$15.4 B	$4.2 B	$43.3 B	$59.7 B	42,267	China	297

Data from Murphy et al. (2019)

While figures vary widely from study to study, the AI industry is definitely growing. The global revenue of the AI industry was around $5 billion in 2015 and by 2019 had increased to somewhere between $15 and $37 billion (Statista 2020). Tractica (2019) projects global AI industry revenue to grow to $89.85 billion by 2025, but another analysis puts it at over $125 billion by the same year (Statista 2020). One can confirm the industry's growth by looking at startup companies. In 2014, less than a thousand AI startups received venture capital funding, but by 2018 this had increased to over 3000 (Perrault et al. 2019, 88). Investment in AI startups increased from $1.3 billion in 2010 to $40.4

billion by 2018 (Perrault et al. 2019, 88). One projection expects investment to reach $52.2 billion by 2021 (International Data Corporation 2018). Such predictions should be taken with a grain of salt, but they do accurately indicate capital's enthusiasm for AI.

The AI industry is new and far away from maturity, by any measure. A 2016 study, including 1548 AI companies, reported that 62% were still in the "lab project" stage while a mere 5.6% were ready for "strategic direction for business" (Naimat 2016, 6). No follow up study has yet been done, though it is certain that more companies now have AI commodities on the market. According to a more recent study based on 1388 responses, in 2019 more than 50% of companies queried were using AI in production or for analysis (Magoulas and Swoyer 2020). This is certainly not representative of all firms in the world, but it is a surprisingly high number regardless.

While media coverage tends to focus on cutting-edge AI research, like the deep learning employed in DeepMind's AlphaGo, most commercial applications of AI today use simpler approaches. Tolu, a startup CEO I interviewed, told me that "there's an increasing mismatch between the requirements of industry and the progress in academia ... a lot of these fancy neural network approaches ... nobody wants them. Businesses ... need text processing, speech recognition, they need the bottom floor. Not the 400th floor". However, as deep learning advances and its cost decreases, this may change.

ML is being applied in too many domains to exhaustively discuss. Some common applications include "friend suggestions, ad targeting, user interest prediction, supply/demand simulation and search result ranking" (Dong 2017). However, AI commodities are available for industries as varied as education, agriculture and logistics (Zilis and Cham 2016). According to one study, the most popular fields are advertising and customer resource management (Pham 2017). According to another, healthcare, finance and marketing are predominant (Faggella 2019). For our purposes, it is sufficient to follow Brynjolfsson and McAfee (2017) in heuristically mapping the AI industry as two broad and overlapping domains of perception and cognition.

Perception, in this context, is the machinic implementation of sensory apparatuses. It comprises subfields such as object, facial, character and speech recognition and machine translation. AI perception has surpassed human performance in a few narrow domains. In 2016, an object classification system achieved an error rate of less than 3% for the task of labelling the ImageNet dataset, a collection of images used to train machine learning models that is also often used as a benchmark. The human average is 5% (Perrault et al. 2019, 67). In 2018, a Microsoft system reportedly achieved human-level quality and accuracy in translating news stories from Chinese to English (Perrault et al. 2019, 68). AI perception software for images, video, documents and speech are now commercially available. For example, Google sells image recognition capacities through the Google Cloud AI Platform. Customers can embed pre-trained ML models into their websites or applications to automatically detect emotions, objects or explicit content in photos. Both Google and Microsoft provide free online translation services but also sell more powerful versions for businesses. In addition to these general-use options, there are at least a dozen companies offering specialized translation systems for particular domains from medicine to military.

What Brynjolfsson and McAfee refer to as cognition, in the context of today's AI industry based around ML, is more precisely described as classification and prediction. Classification is a popular commercial application of ML because there are many possible situations in which it might be useful and profitable to automatically determine whether a given entity or data point belongs to category X or Y. For example, insurance companies are using ML-powered classification to aggregate real-time phone data from drivers to achieve fine-grained "behavioural premium pricing" based on whether they qualify as a good driver or not (Faggella 2020). Prediction involves extrapolating from a classification to make a guess about what is likely to happen in the future or about some situation for which data is lacking. For instance, one might want to predict whether a credit card transaction is or is not fraudulent. The credit agency Equifax claims to have applied ML to improve the predictive ability of its credit scoring models by 15% (Press 2017). In sum, perception and cognition are the main functions, broadly construed, that AI commodities provide today. What kinds of companies produce such commodities?

AI Capital Composition

There are five major types of organization involved in the AI industry. First, a handful of giant tech capitals hailing from the USA and China, such as Google and Baidu. Second, are industrial manufacturing "dinosaurs" such as General Electric and Siemens, which are attempting to modernize by moving into AI production. Third, is a globally distributed horde of startup companies. Fourth are think tanks and research laboratories. These are funded by a combination of philanthropic, academic, industry and governmental sources and some are non-profit. State involvement in AI production is significant enough that it constitutes the fifth type of organization involved. In the following sections, I analyze examples of each type of organization.

AI Tech Giants

In 2016, *The Economist* (2016) noted that in "Silicon Valley a handful of giants are enjoying market shares and profit margins not seen since the robber barons in the late 19th century". These powerful tech capitals have all moved into the production of AI, which as we have seen, has a recursive relationship with the data-centric nature of platforms. The need for data drives these firms to expand rhizomatically into markets and sectors wherever data may be extracted. Concerning this rhizomatic expansionism, Nick Srnicek (2017) proposes a "convergence thesis" or theory that there is a "tendency for different platform companies to become increasingly similar as they encroach upon the same [key] market and data areas" (107). To take only a few examples, the search company Google bought the video streaming site YouTube and has attempted to create a social media platform (Google+), while Facebook, the social media platform, has attempted to move into online retail, which Amazon dominates. Amazon has forayed into both social media with its failed Spark and video streaming with Prime Video. Facebook has even proposed its own cryptocurrency called Libra, which would provide the company with payment data, while Google seeks similar data via Google Pay. Whether Srnicek's convergence thesis proves completely true or not, AI is one case where it seems to be largely verified. The tech giants are all tending towards a cloud-based AI model combined with the provision of free product-services like Gmail, Google Maps and Translate which are provided to users in (more or less tacit) exchange for access to, and ownership of, their data. The data gathered from users of these services is fed back into the applications to improve their functioning.

It is worth noting that, despite vocal excitement for AI, and its increasingly central role in the self-presentation of tech giants, it so far remains a minor contributor to revenue, considered directly. For instance, as recently as 2019, Google still generated around 85% of its overall revenue from advertising and Facebook's percentage is even higher (Schomer 2019). AI is, however, essential to the microtargeted advertising, which is customized to particular users based on data about their actions and preferences, that Google and Facebook rely on, so its indirect contributions are certainly greater.

I will explore typical features of the tech giants by looking at the example of Google.

Founded in 1998, Google weathered the dot com crash of 2000–2002 and rapidly ascended the corporate technology hierarchy thereafter. Based on the early success of the Google search algorithm, the company expanded its digital purview and nows owns the most popular search engine in the world, the most popular web browser (Chrome), the most widely used mobile operating system (Android), the most popular streaming video platform (YouTube) and a very popular email service (Gmail).

Google first publicly delved into AI with the founding of the Google Brain lab in 2011. Google Brain sets its own research agenda and produces both basic and commercializable research. Its employees present and publish their work in academic contexts and share it via the Google AI blog. Google Brain was noticed by the media in 2012 when researchers demonstrated a deep learning system that learned to recognize cats in images (Markoff 2012). This feat was followed by a spate of impactful AI research including a ML-based overhaul of Google Translate which substantially improved its quality. The extent to which Google applies its AI research internally is impossible to estimate, but according to a Google executive, by 2015 Google Brain had generated enough value to counterbalance the company's numerous speculative investments (Dougherty 2015).

Like most of the AI tech giants, Google produces AI for both the consumer commodity (non-productive use) and fixed capital (used in production processes) markets. Google's most visible AI consumer commodity is perhaps the Google Home "smart speaker" first produced in 2016. This is a physical platform for Google Assistant which uses speech recognition to perform entertainment, organization and home automation tasks via spoken word commands, while simultaneously functioning as a data collection device (Langley and Tuohy 2019). Google's most significant AI commodities are, however, sold for use as fixed capital by other capitals. This occurs primarily through Google Cloud Platform which, with a revenue of $1 billion per quarter in 2017, seems to be the fastest growing section within the company (Trefis Team 2019). Google's cloud, however, lags behind that of Amazon which is the dominant cloud provider with a 35% market share (Miller 2017). Other cloud platforms are offered by Alibaba, IBM, Microsoft, Salesforce and Oracle.

Computing power necessary for AI research continues to increase rapidly. Owning the requisite hardware is infeasible for most companies, who instead rent access to it from the cloud providers. Amodei and Hernandez (2018) calculate that the amount of computing power used for training the most powerful ML systems has been doubling every 3.5 months since 2012, with no end in sight. To get an idea of the requisite costs for contemporary AI production, consider that Google researchers are proud to report the success of ***a single*** experiment operating on a minimalist hardware budget of "only 1.2 million USD" compared to a similar effort at Facebook which cost $4.1 million (quoted in Perez 2017).

Google's Cloud AI offerings include a platform for AI developers to train models and a variety of "plug and play AI components" which "make it easy for developers to add sight, language, conversation, and structured data to their applications" (Google, n.d.-a). These offerings help data scientists and other skilled AI workers integrate existing ML models into business processes. Google also offers "prepackaged" solutions to common business problems targeted at users lacking expertise in ML. The "Document Understanding AI" automates the reading and processing of documents while the "Contact Center AI" automates customer service via speech or text (Google, n.d.-b). Finally, as I will discuss in greater detail in the next chapter, Google has since 2018 been offering an "automated way for businesses to build new algorithms" (Metz 2018b). This automated machine learning service aims to make the production of ML models possible for businesses lacking ML expertise.

Like all the tech giants, Google buys up promising startup companies. Google acquired 30 AI startups from 2009 to 2020, the most of any tech giant (Hurst 2020). In 2014, Google acquired the UK company DeepMind, a "startup with no revenue or marketable product" for £400 million (*The Economist* 2017). DeepMind has since produced groundbreaking ML research such as the Go playing AlphaZero. They describe their overarching goal as the creation of AGI, stating a mission to: "Solve Intelligence. Use it to make the world a better place" (DeepMind, n.d.). In the meantime, Google is developing DeepMind's research into healthcare commodities and has applied DeepMind's research to reduce the energy used for cooling a Google data centre by over 40% by predictively adjusting distribution (Evans and Gao 2016).

In sum, Google is typical of the AI giants insofar as it increasingly integrates AI functions into its diverse business processes, most of which give Google access to vast amounts of data that it uses to expand its AI efforts. Like most AI giants, Google produces for both consumer commodity and fixed capital markets, and delivers much of its commodities via a cloud platform. Google is also engaged in the acquisition of AI startups and continually strives to break into new markets. Google is, however, distinguished from the other giants by its sheer size, diversified nature and massive investment in research. It is nearly impossible to use the internet without encountering a Google product or service, unless perhaps, you are in China where, as of July 2020, Google represented only 3.76% of search engine queries, compared to Baidu's 69.55% (Statcounter 2020).

AI Dinosaurs

General Electric (GE), founded in 1892, is a different breed of AI company. Originally a manufacturer of electrical machinery, GE was also a contributor to the early computing industry. Today, GE is a conglomerate invested in sectors from healthcare to aviation. It began investing in AI around 2015. GE and other AI dinosaurs, such as Siemens (founded 1847), are primarily interested in making AI fixed capital products for industrial manufacturing. The tech giants have not delved much into manufacturing, so the dinosaurs have almost free reign for the moment (Walker 2019). GE offers a range of AI consulting services, but its main focus is AI-powered platforms offering capacities for monitoring and simulating production processes. iFIX, a ML-powered system for industrial automation, allows a plant operator to see and control all of the relevant operations of a factory in one app. GE is also selling the Predix Industrial IoT Platform which it markets as an operating system for factories (Passieri 2015). Predix integrates data from production and circulation processes to enable predictive management. Siemens offers a similar product called MindSphere, which it describes as a "cloud-based, open IoT operating system … that connects your products, plants, systems, and machines" (Siemens, n.d.). AI dinosaurs are, like tech giants, eager to buy up startups. Siemens spent $10 billion on acquiring software startups from 2007 to 2017 (Walker 2019). AI dinosaurs buy technology from the AI giants (GE uses Amazon Web Services and Siemens uses IBM's Watson Analytics) and also develop their own in-house. Whether or not these companies will converge with the AI tech giants remains to be seen, though it seems unlikely GE will invest in its own social media network any time soon.

AI Startups

Startups are the lauded epitome of the tech industry. They are smaller companies which often rely on venture capital. The startup companies I interviewed workers from ranged in size from six employees to just over thirty. AI startups operate a variety of business models. They might sell premade ML models, provide insights produced by their own ML models, sell a service or sell specialized hardware. Premade ML models are used in many fields. My interviewees produced voice biometrics systems, predictive models for marketing and advertising and machine vision models for medicine, to take a few examples. Companies which provide insights or services operate a consulting business model or build, or assist in building, bespoke AI systems for other businesses. One of my interviewees did consulting work for banks, while another contributed to a natural language processing system for smart appliances.

Fabian (2018) puts the total number of AI startups in the world in 2018 at 3465. The number of AI startups is always in flux because many go bankrupt while others are acquired by larger firms. Of the 120 AI startups that exited the market in 2017, 115 were acquired (Patrizio 2018). DeepMind was famously acquired by Google without a working product, but this is not always the case. Some startups may develop successful commodities and resist acquisition. In 2018, the Chinese startup SenseTime, founded in 2014, received $600 million in funding, putting its total valuation at more than $4.5 billion and making it the most valuable AI startup in the world at the time (Vincent 2018). Its products focus on machine vision and range from "beautification" filters for social media to autonomous vehicle vision and automated surveillance video analysis. However, even if AI startups are not acquired by a tech giant, most are already connected to them on an infrastructural level, relying on their clouds for computing power and applications.

AI Think Tanks

AI think tanks are private research institutes that are funded by academic, industry, governmental or philanthropic sources. While AI research has been associated with think tanks since its earliest days (i.e. RAND), think tanks devoted specifically to AI only began to appear in the mid-2010s (Think Tank Watch 2018). These organizations vary in nature. Some were founded by transhumanists concerned with the dangers and prospects of future AGI, such as the Machine Intelligence Research Institute (MIRI), a non-profit funded by philanthropic groups including the Thiel Foundation. MIRI is part of the "AI safety" movement which aims to ensure that if AGI appears, it can be controlled.

Other AI think tanks are concerned with actually existing AI and the AI industry. These usually have connections to both industry and academia, such as the AI Now Institute (part of NYU and funded by Google and Microsoft) and the Partnership on AI (partners include MIT Media Lab, Amazon, Facebook and Google). AI Now (n.d.) describes itself as studying the "social implications of artificial intelligence" while the Partnership on AI (n.d.) states that its goal is to "study and formulate best practices on AI technologies, to advance the public's understanding of AI, and to serve as an open platform for discussion and engagement about AI and its influences on people and society". These think tanks have produced valuable research on diverse aspects of the social implications of AI from gender relations and privacy to technical concerns about best practices for development and policy implications. But at least some of them serve other functions as well.

One important function is serving as a vehicle for the so-called "democratization" of AI programs which the tech giants are advancing. These will be discussed below in more detail, but for now it is enough to note that socially concerned think tanks play an important public relations function for the AI industry. This came to light after Google's clandestine agreement to provide drone vision software for the Pentagon's "Project Maven" was revealed. In emails leaked to *The Intercept*, Fei-Fei Li, then head scientist at Google Cloud, worried that the exposure of Project Maven, with which she was centrally involved, could counteract her company's efforts to portray their AI products as socially benevolent:

> I don't know what would happen if the media starts picking up a theme that Google is secretly building AI weapons or AI technologies to enable weapons for the Defense industry ... Google Cloud has been building our theme on Democratizing AI in 2017, and Diane and I have been talking about Humanistic AI for enterprise. I'd be super careful to protect these very positive images. (quoted in Fang 2018)

After employee pressure and public outcry, Li resigned. It would be incorrect to attribute solely public relations functions to such think tanks. But it would also be wrong to deny that this function exists (Ochigame 2019) and is becoming increasingly important for the industry, as the tech giants come under increasing scrutiny for their dubious practices, as the section on labour below elaborates.

Other think tanks are interesting for different reasons; the case of OpenAI particularly so. OpenAI was founded in 2015 with $1 billion funding from the ilk of Elon Musk and Peter Thiel. Ilya Sutskever, former student of Geoffrey Hinton, is a chief scientist. OpenAI produces cutting-edge ML systems, such as OpenAI Five, a team of five ANNs which has defeated professional players at the competitive video game DOTA2. While initially operating as a non-profit, in 2019 OpenAI announced a shift to a "capped-profit" model necessitated by competition with the AI tech giants. They identified a "need to invest billions of dollars in upcoming years into large-scale cloud compute, attracting and retaining talented people, and building AI supercomputers" (OpenAI 2019). Since then, Microsoft has invested $1 billion USD in the think tank and has become its exclusive cloud provider, with rights to its future research (Brockman 2019). OpenAI's story sums up the difficulties of AI research and development beyond the reach of capital—something I will return to in Chapter 7.

National AI Strategies: AI and the State Part II

Nearly forty years after Japan's Fifth Generation Computing Initiative and the USA's Strategic Computing Program ended, AI is once again a topic of national interest. Governments around the world now agree that, in the words of the Chinese State Council (2017), AI is "a new engine of economic development" (2). The USA had the first national government to explicitly engage with the contemporary AI industry. The US government spent approximately $1.1 billion on unclassified R&D

for "AI-related" technologies in 2015 (Executive Office of the President 2016, 25) and in 2016 the outgoing Obama administration produced two reports on AI. It asserted that a "strong case can be made in favor of increased Federal funding" to the tune of doubling or even tripling, with a lucrative expected payoff in economic growth (Executive Office of the President 2016, 25). In 2017, Canada became the first country to launch an articulated strategic national plan for AI ($125 million CAD), recognizing that AI "has the potential to drive strong economic growth, by improving the way we produce goods, deliver services and tackle challenges like climate change" (Canadian Federal Government 2017, 103). This plan involved the construction of three research institutes across the country and the creation of lucrative "AI Chair" positions to attract expert researchers.

Other countries followed suit. In 2017, the UK made "Artificial Intelligence and Data" one of four Grand Challenges in its Industrial Strategy. French President Macron announced in March 2018 that his government would spend €1.5 billion over five years to advance national AI research. A coalition of researchers from across Europe have written a manifesto which calls for the establishment of a European Lab for Learning & Intelligent Systems (ELLIS) by which to develop AI talent in Europe. In 2019, President Trump signed an executive order to launch the American Artificial Intelligence Initiative. As of 2018, at least 18 countries had announced national AI strategies (Dutton et al. 2018). While details vary from country to country, in general, national AI plans call for the attraction and retention of AI-skilled labour, the establishment of national AI research institutes, the relaxation of regulations around the collection and use of the data requisite for ML and legislative efforts to speed up the commercialization of AI (Dutton et al. 2018). One of the most ambitious national AI strategies comes from China.

In 2017, China's State Council announced its Next Generation Artificial Intelligence Development Plan which aimed to achieve, by 2020, AI capacities "in step with globally advanced levels" (5). By 2030, China aims to be the number one producer of AI with a "gross output of RMB 1 trillion (US $150.8 billion) for the core AI industry and RMB 10 trillion (1.5 trillion) for related industries" (Ding 2018, 7). This plan is significant not only for its unprecedented levels of spending, but also because China is currently the only country with the expertise and resources to contest the USA's AI dominance. China has the second highest quantity

(8.9%) of AI experts in the world after the USA (13.9%) and exceeds the USA in number of AI patents filed and AI papers published (China AI Development Report 2018, 3). More than one analysis argues that countries that fail to invest in AI now will fall economically behind as recursive AI productivity gains compel exponential increases in the economies of China and the USA (Cummings et al. 2018, vi; Lee 2018, 185–186). Kai-Fu Lee (2018) is reluctant to describe this situation in terms of a new national "AI race" because of its zero-sum connotations (246). However, AI is in fact a central component of a new global arms race which could take on a zero-sum logic (Simonite 2017; Allen 2019).

The USA leads spending on AI-powered autonomous weapons systems (AWS), reportedly having spent $4 billion before 2010 with $18 million budgeted for the next ten years (Haner and Garcia 2019, 332). DARPA is working on COMPASS (Collection and Monitoring via Planning for Active Situational Scenarios) which will "leverage advanced AI and other technologies to help commanders make more effective decisions to thwart an enemy's complex, multi-layered disruptive activity" (South 2018). These efforts occur alongside the Chinese People's Liberation Army's endeavours towards AI-powered "intelligentized" warfare (Kania 2017) and Russia's plan to have thirty percent of its combat power "partially or fully autonomous" by 2030 (Haner and Garcia 2019, 334). While, at the time of writing, fully autonomous weapons have yet to be deployed, semi-autonomous weapons are increasingly capable (Scharre 2018). Autonomous weapons are, however, only one way that AI might be weaponized. Autonomous weapons threaten physical security, but AI might also be used to threaten digital security via cyberattacks, and political security via surveillance, persuasion and deception (Brundage et al. 2018, 6).

Despite state interest, Cummings (2018) notes that due to the AI industry's massive salaries and benefits, governments are finding it hard to hire AI experts and are forced to contract out for their AI needs. Cummings (2018) wonders if "defence companies and governments continue down a path of relative AI illiteracy, could this enable a potential power shift such that critical AI services will be leased via Google, Amazon or Facebook?" (17). The dystopian possibility of national militaries beholden to corporate AI lies beyond the scope of this book, but it does not seem wholly implausible if we look at how aggressively the AI industry maintains concentrated control over the technology it produces.

AI Capital Concentration

Despite a hangover of early internet era verbiage of freedom, decentralization and democratization, today's AI industry is dominated by a handful of tech giants. The substantial accumulated wealth of the tech giants enables them to invest heavily in continual research, development and fixed capital improvement, making it "very hard for newcomers to become serious competitors of the established leaders in any of the already occupied core business fields" (Dolata 2018, 91). Only rival giants are capable of engaging in "fierce oligopolistic competition … carried out primarily through aggressive innovation and expansion strategies" (Dolata 2018, 98). My interviewees also noted the relentless competition in their industry. Yimin, a data scientist, told me "we're not living in real free market conditions. There are bigger forces that dominate the market … the fate of the industry is tied to … Google, Amazon … IBM. Giants … they hire most of the advanced graduates". Tolu, a startup CEO, expressed a similar view: "We're financially competing with Facebook and Google for talent … you can't find the right people because Google and Facebook just bought them all". *The Economist* (2017) agrees that "the incumbent tech groups will capture many of AI's gains, given their wealth of data, computing power, smart algorithms and human talent, not to mention a head start on investing. History points to the likelihood of concentration".

The centrality of data to capital based on ML leads even capital-friendly analyses to posit an inherent recursive tendency towards concentration and monopoly in the AI industry:

> AI tools are often characterized by some degree of increasing returns: better prediction accuracy leads to more users, more users generate more data, and more data leads to better prediction accuracy. Businesses have greater incentives to build [AI] if they have more control, but along with scale economies, this may lead to monopolization. (Agrawal et al. 2018, 23)

Lee (2018) argues similarly that the "positive-feedback loop generated by increasing amounts of data means that AI-driven industries naturally tend toward monopoly, simultaneously driving down prices and eliminating competition among firms" (161). This means that companies such as Facebook and Google, which have access to vast quantities of search and social media data, have a decided advantage in the AI industry. One analysis of IBM argues that because the company does not have such data resources it faces difficulties forming a “virtuous circle” of AI commercialization (Kisner et al. 2017, 19–20). Or as Mahir, a startup CEO, put it to me: “large companies that have large amounts of data ... have a huge defensive moat ... it becomes really hard for a startup to come along and disrupt the big one if they don’t have a dataset ... how do they get that dataset if they don’t have any algorithms ... or a deployed product?”. In sum, despite its rhetoric of freedom the AI industry is characterized by “concentration, control and power” (Dolata 2018, 86). The power of the AI tech giants has, however, generated some potential countervailing forces from beyond the industry.

There is a growing social consensus, across the political spectrum, that the tech giants are running amok, even if no one can agree on how to deal with it. At the time of writing, the US Justice Department and Federal Trade Commission are engaged in an antitrust investigation of the tech giants. Commentators argue that competition should be stimulated (Doctorow 2019; *The Economist* 2019) or for new types of regulation (Chen 2019; Cath et al. 2018; Reed 2018). Others, including 2020 US Democratic presidential candidate Elizabeth Warren (2019), argue that the platforms established by the tech giants should be split from their other business ventures and operated as public utilities so that the tech giants “do not crowd out potential competitors, smother the next generation of great tech companies, and wield so much power that they can undermine our democracy”. Precedent for regulating the tech giants is provided by the European Union’s 2018 implementation of the General Data Protection Regulation (GDPR), which put strict rules on how companies can collect, store and use user data. In January 2019, France fined Google €50 million for violating the GDPR. Shortly after, Apple CEO Tim Cook (2019) published an opinion piece in *Time* calling for similar regulations in the USA. How these discussions will play out remains uncertain. It is hard to guess exactly how states will balance the emerging desire to reign in the tech giants with the competitive dynamics of an international AI race driven by those same companies.

Open-Source AI, Clouds, AI Chips

Now we turn to some distinctive technological characteristics of the AI industry. Open-source libraries suitable for ML such as Theano (developed by the Montreal Institute for Learning Algorithms) have been available since 2007. But it was not until 2015 that a wave of open-source AI tools swept the industry, beginning with the release of Keras (privately developed primarily by François Chollet, a Google engineer) and later, Google's proprietary TensorFlow. Google CEO Sundar Pichai (2015) said he hoped open sourcing TensorFlow would help "exchange ideas much more quickly, through working code rather than just research papers. And that, in turn, will accelerate research on machine learning, in the end making technology work better for everyone". Since the release of TensorFlow, nearly all of the AI giants have open-sourced some AI tools, including IBM's SystemML, Baidu's Warp-CTC, Facebook's PyTorch and Amazon's Neo-AI.

According to my interviews, use of open-source tools is near universal in the AI industry. Mahir, a startup CEO, told me "[m]ost startups … use open source technologies. Everything from the programming language that we use, which is primarily Python and Javascript … to the software packages we use". Juan, another CEO, agreed: "all the tools that we actually use for building the product … besides [operating systems], are open source. The couple exceptions, like NVIDIA, have some software … that's proprietary". Several companies also used MathWorks' MATLab, a proprietary software suite, but a vast majority of the tools for producing ML are freely available.

Why would an industry characterized by oligopolistic competition be so eager to open source proprietary software? According to the tech giants, it is out of a benevolent desire to bring AI to the masses, as Pichai's quote above suggests. Concerning its "Democratizing AI" program, Microsoft (2016) asserts that "We're going to infuse every application that we interact with, on any device, at any point in time, with intelligence", while Intel extols the wonders of "ubiquitous artificial intelligence" (Intel Brandvoice 2018). Microsoft (2016) says it will make the "same intelligent capabilities that are infused in our own apps … available to every application developer in the world" with the goal of "helping everyone achieve more — humans and machines working together to make the world a better place". Industry commentators have been more prosaic.

Aside from the free contributions of a community of unpaid developers, Gershgorn (2015) suggests that companies can indirectly benefit from open sourcing by both creating potential future employees skilled with their software and by having their software become the infrastructure on which future applications are built, ensuring its ongoing relevance.

Google deployed this strategy successfully when it open sourced Android, which is now the most popular mobile operating system in the world (Gershgorn 2015; Amadeo 2018). This is, however, only part of the story of the corporate manifestation of open-source AI, and it should be considered alongside two connected markets which many AI giants have entered since 2015: the cloud and specialized hardware.

The second era of the AI industry was enabled in part by the discovery that graphics processing units (GPUs) work well for running the parallel processing necessary for ML (Kelly 2014). Most companies rent access to GPUs via the clouds of the AI giants. Yimin, a data scientist, told me: "Most of the computation in data science is done on the cloud. We have the local servers also running, but most of the heavyweight data solutions [are] on the cloud". GPUs were, however, created with computer graphics, rather than artificial neural networks, in mind. AI producers are now investing in the development of chips specifically designed for ML, in direct competition with historical GPU manufacturers like NVIDIA (Hayes 2020). Since around 2015 Google has been internally using its proprietary Tensor Processing Unit (TPU), a chip which is specially designed for the ANNs used for deep learning and in 2018 it made them available for third party use via the Google Cloud. However, the "performance boost provided by TPUs works only if you use the right kind of machine-learning framework with it. And that means Google's own TensorFlow" (Yegulalp 2017). In other words, one must use Google's software to harness the full benefits of the company's specialized AI chips. In this way, the free distribution of TensorFlow can be leveraged to channel developers towards the Google cloud. Open sourcing functions as a technique for dominating the AI market.

Labour in the AI Industry

We have heard enough about capital. What about the labour that produces AI? The AI industry's growth and the widespread hype around it have generated an enormous demand for labour with AI skills. Microsoft reportedly went from four deep learning experts to seventy between 2011 and 2014 (Vance 2014). While official statistics do not have distinct categories for AI labour, job postings can be used as a proxy measurement. According to AI Index (2017), the number of AI jobs in the USA grew by 4.5 times between 2013 and 2017. Yet, according to one assessment, by 2018 only 22,000 people in the world had the skills to "do serious A.I. research" (Metz 2018a). Demand continues to outpace supply. For the qualified, salaries ranging from substantial to astronomical are available. In 2013, the salary for a "world class" deep learning expert was reportedly comparable to that of a National Football League quarterback (Vance 2014). However, there are a variety of jobs in the AI industry, and not all of them are so lucrative.[1]

To better grasp the composition of the AI labour force, I make a schematic division of AI work into five categories, noting that, like the rest of the nascent industry, these are not rigorously defined and definitely not set in stone. As Martin, a ML scientist, explained to me, AI industry job titles are "not very well defined. And people use them in many different manners". From most remunerated to least, the categories are: data/ML scientist, data/ML engineer, data analyst, service worker and ghost worker. This, of course, focuses only on the technical side of AI work. There are numerous more conventional business roles which may be more or less involved in technical AI matters.

Data/ML scientists occupy the apex of the AI labour hierarchy.[2] We might follow Christian Fuchs (2014) and use the term "labour aristocracy" (229–230), first deployed by Mikhail Bakunin (1971 [1872]), to describe these workers who earn much more than other workers and tend to exist on relatively friendly terms with capital. Data scientists receive most of the AI industry hype. Aghabozorghi and Lin (2016) breathlessly describe the data scientist as the (presumably more successful) "alchemist of the 21st century: someone who can turn raw data into purified insights". Data scientists often come from backgrounds in math, statistics or physics, tend to have graduate degrees, and know how to program (Anderson 2018). They create and deploy machine learning models and conduct research. Martin, a ML scientist, told me "I'm expected to do more modelling and more delivering … machine learning models as opposed to analytics … data comes in, data engineers process them, and then deliver them … to the data scientists".

[1] While not necessarily representative of the entire AI industry, one suggestive study shows that 90% of workers in California's Silicon Valley made less in 2018 than they did in 1997 after adjusting for inflation (Sheng 2018).

[2] Data scientist and ML scientist are often used interchangeably (and are here). However, according to one study, while 90% of data scientists are involved with ML to some degree, only 40% say it constitutes the majority of their work (Theuwissen 2015, 11).

Data scientists receive the highest wages of AI industry workers, even if most do not achieve football player salaries. A survey by the programming community website Stackoverflow (2018) puts the median salary for a data scientist or machine learning specialist in the USA at $102,000, while the global median salary for the same position is $60,000. According to Indeed.com (2019a), data scientists earn an average of $120,301 yearly, but if they are hired by one of the tech giants, they can earn much more. At such firms, recently graduated PhDs can be paid "from $300,000 to $500,000 a year or more in salary and company stock" (Metz 2017) and those who are "exceptional or more experienced ... can net seven-figure salaries" (Bergen and Wagner 2015). Sutskever, the former student of deep learning luminary Hinton, was paid $1.9 million in 2016 for his position at the then-non-profit OpenAI (Metz 2018a). High salaries are one factor motivating a "brain drain" of data scientists from academia to industry. From 2004 to 2018, over 150 AI professors left their posts for industry positions and another 68 took industry positions while retaining part-time positions at a university (Gofman and Jin 2020). The number of professors leaving industry increased steadily over that period from less than 5 per year from 2005 to 2010 to over 40 departures in 2018 alone. Offers to depart academia are abundant. One study reports that nearly "50% of data scientists get contacted at least once a week about a new job opportunity ... 85% get contacted at least once a month" (Theuwissen 2015, 8).

Data engineers are similarly highly educated to data scientists but tend to have stronger programming backgrounds rather than math or physics (Anderson 2018). They specialize "in creating software solutions around big data" and building "data pipeline[s]" by connecting diverse big data technologies (Anderson 2018). They are often characterized as preparing the infrastructure necessary for data science (Aghabozorghi and Lin 2016). According to Indeed.com (2019b), data engineers are paid similarly to data scientists at an average of $129,653 yearly, suggesting that the difference between the two titles is not as clear as the heuristic distinctions sketched here imply.

Data analysts work with pre-existing software and tools to do things with data. They "query and process data, provide reports, summarize and visualize data" (Aghabozorghi and Lin 2016). They typically have less education than data scientists or engineers, usually possessing a bachelor's degree and/or professional certificates in fields such as data mining. According to Indeed.com (2019c), data analysts earn approximately half the wages of data scientists and engineers at $65,502 yearly.

An often-invisible part of the AI labour force is the service workers who provide the perks for Silicon Valley-style tech workplaces. These include shuttle bus drivers, cooks, security and janitorial staff.[3] They are often direly underpaid. According to a report by Working Partnerships USA (2016), in Silicon Valley, service workers earn a yearly average of $19,900 while local rent averages $21,444 USD (1). Beyond often dismal pay, most service workers are employed by subcontracting agencies that offer minimal, if any, job security and benefits. This is perhaps why service workers are the only sector of labour in the AI industry with a formally recognized labour union. This is discussed more below.

Finally, we have ghost workers. The term comes from Mary L. Gray and Siddharth Suri (2019) who define ghost work as the "often intentionally hidden" human work "powering many mobile phone apps, websites, and artificial intelligence systems" (4). Ghost work has become increasingly visible since Sarah Roberts' (2014) exploration of content moderation work done behind the scenes of platforms like YouTube. Ghost workers fill in the gaps that automated systems cannot manage; they label ML training datasets but also identify explicit images and identify hate speech. Many are thus exposed to disturbing content which takes a psychological toll.

Ghost workers are often hired through automated platforms like Amazon's Mechanical Turk to perform piecework for micropayments. Such work typically amounts to less than $5 hourly (Hitlin 2016). The low pay and contingent nature of ghost work means that, for many, long, repetitious hours of work must be taken whenever they are available. Many, though not all, ghost workers come from poorer countries where the low wages can provide some degree of subsistence. According to one study, ghost workers come from "[n]early all regions of the world" but especially "Brazil, India, Indonesia, Nigeria and the United States, as well as Western and Eastern Europe" (Berg et al. 2018, 31).

Ghost work is essential to contemporary AI. ML requires lots of training data, but data must be prepared before it can be used. Nakashima (2018) describes data preparation as "the digital equivalent of needlework—drawing boxes around cars in street photos, tagging images, and transcribing snatches of speech that computers can't quite make out". Due to its repetitive nature, ghost work has been compared to Taylorized "old-fashioned manual labour" (Yu 2017). Sometimes, ghost workers are

[3] For an in-depth exploration of tech industry service work in India, see Chakraborty (2021).

secretly employed to fulfil technological promises which AI companies cannot keep. One example of such "Potemkin AI" (Sadowski 2018) is the company Expensify, which purports to automate business document processing with ML. In 2017, it was revealed that, lacking the requisite technology, the company was outsourcing its supposedly automated processes to ghost workers via Mechanical Turk (Gallagher 2017).

One prominent product of AI ghost work is the dataset ImageNet, which is widely used to train and benchmark image recognition ML models. ImageNet is a set of 14,197,122 images ranging from amphibians to geological formations to people. The images are labelled with a plethora of categories and subcategories. The category "animal" alone has 3822 subcategories. ImageNet was labelled by 49,000 Mechanical Turk ghost workers between 2007 and 2010 (Li 2017). A subindustry has since formed around data labelling. Worker-owned ghost work cooperatives have been proposed (Sriraman et al. 2017) and some companies attempt to describe their data products as "fair trade" because they offer more traditional employment structures and benefits than platforms like Mechanical Turk. However, the title of "fair trade" data is self-appointed and has no standard meaning (Kaye 2019). For the time being, ghost work remains precarious and poorly remunerated.

Labour Composition: Race and Gender

As discussed in Chapter 4, the earliest programmers included many women and other minority groups. But today, data scientist Timnit Gebru describes the AI industry as amid a "diversity crisis" (Snow 2018). Indeed, the figures are stark. At Apple, Microsoft, Google and Facebook white people comprise between 40 and 50% of the technical workforce (data scientists, engineers and coders). People identifying as asian are slightly less well represented with 35% at Apple, 39% at Microsoft, 43% at Google and 52% at Facebook. However, latinx people represent only 8%, 5%, 3% and 4% at the same companies, while black people are represented even more poorly with 6%, 3%, 2% and 2%. Aboriginal peoples barely show up with only Apple and Microsoft reporting 1% (Harrison 2019). Amazon does not release the demographics of its workforce but has reported that 42% of its US workers are black or latinx, although this figure includes both technical workers and its 647,000 minimum-wage earning distribution centre workers (Harrison 2019).

The situation is also dire when it comes to gender. One estimate puts women as making up between 30% and 50% of computer programmers throughout the 1960s (Ensmenger 2012, 237). Over the following decades programming became a prestigious, masculine job and women were pushed out of the programming workforce by a combination of means, including gender biased aptitude testing (Ensmenger 2012, 239–240). In 2013, the share of women working in computing was 26% (West et al. 2019, 10). Even less specialize in AI: only 22% of "AI professionals" in the world are women (Duke 2018). Women represent 15% of the AI research staff at Facebook and 10% at Google (West et al. 2019, 10–11).

Women who do work in AI tend to work on application rather than development. They also tend to work in "'traditionally female' industries … which already have a relatively high share of female workers, such as the nonprofit, healthcare and education sectors" (Duke 2018). In general, women also get paid less for doing the same tech work as their male counterparts. A 2016 US Labor Department investigation found that Google had "systemic compensation disparities against women pretty much across the entire workforce" (Kolhatkar 2017). While Google has disputed this, and refused to disclose all of its employees' earnings, an employee-led investigation (totaling 2% of employees) showed that men do indeed make more than women (Ehrenkranz 2017).

Clearly, the AI industry participates in the larger tech industry's "Brotopia" (Chang 2019). Widespread sexism in the tech industry became visible to the public with the 2015 publication of the study "Elephant in the Valley" which documented how over 200 women experienced a wide variety of discrimination in tech work (Vassallo et al. 2015). 2017 saw the circulation of Google engineer James Danmore's memo that argued for the biological inferiority of women in tech work (Wakabayashi 2017). Danmore was fired, but the same year saw a barrage of disclosures of sexual assault and harassment by women in the industry (Benner 2017). After an outpouring of apologies by various male industry figures, pervasive discrimination continues. According to a recent study, 54% of women in tech have been told that "female brains just aren't as technical" (Forbes 2019). Attempts to increase diversity in the AI industry have been met with substantial criticism. A recent report judges that these attempts have been ineffective due to a narrow focus on white women, as well as a focus on helping women get from school to industry, rather than addressing the sexist and racist power dynamics which characterize working in the industry (West et al. 2019, 3).

Due to the data-centric nature of ML, the consequences of bias and discrimination in the AI industry extend beyond the workplace experiences of women. As Kate Crawford (2016) asserts, AI has a "white guy problem" that is also a "data problem". Since ML models are based on patterns extracted from data, they can "pick up any tendencies that already exist in the data they train on" (Dickson 2018). Crawford (2016) warned that AI "may already be exacerbating inequality in the workplace, at home and in our legal and judicial systems". A few years after Crawford's piece was published, examples of perniciously biased AI systems abound: a Google algorithm categorizes black people as gorillas, predictive policing algorithms target black neighbourhoods disproportionately, an AI beauty contest judge overwhelmingly chooses white winners and an Amazon system for hiring employees was scrapped before deployment when it was found to prefer the resumes of men over those of equally qualified women (Dickson 2018; Cook 2018). One might expect that such palpable discrimination and inequality would entail a highly organized labour force, but this is not the case in the AI industry, nor has it been the case historically in the tech industry at large. There are, however, signs of change. Discrimination is one issue around which AI labour has recently rallied.

AI Labour Organization

From 2014 to 2017, around 5000 contract services workers became unionized in Silicon Valley, but the rest of AI work follows the tech industry at large, where unions are not present (Hyde 2003). There are several contributing factors. One often cited reason is the high wages, benefits and general job satisfaction experienced by tech workers (Milton 2003, 32). Companies like Google famously distribute free perks including "free meals at more than 30 cafes ... nap pods, [and] a concierge service" (ABC 7 News 2018). Another contributing factor is the high demand for, and low supply of, tech workers. Scarcity means it is "as easy for a tech worker to quit their job and find another better one as it is to attempt to organize their coworkers" (Patel 2017). While these are both significant factors, they must be considered alongside a third factor which goes back to Silicon Valley's roots. In the 1960s, Bob Noyce, co-founder of Intel stated:

> Remaining non-union is an essential for survival for most of our companies. If we had the work rules that unionized companies have, we'd all go out of business. This is a very high priority for management here. We have to retain flexibility in operating our companies. The great hope for our nation is to avoid those deep, deep divisions between workers and management that can paralyze action. (quoted in Rogers and Larsen 1984, 191)

This dim view of organized labour has persisted in the AI industry, often camouflaged in what Andrew Leonard (2014) calls "stealth libertarianism" by which anti-labour aims are concealed by progressive veneers. Less stealthily, in 2019, in the wake of a spate of employee activism, Google hired IRI Consultants, a company known for its successful campaigns to undermine attempts at unionization by healthcare workers (Scheiber and Wakabayashi 2019). Regardless, labour organizing is spreading to tech workers, aided by the efforts of grassroots organizations such as the New York City Democratic Socialists Tech Action Working Group, Tech Workers Coalition, and Tech Solidarity. Such groups organize education sessions and demonstrations and have also advised and aided tech workers in rare attempts at unionization.

In the Trump era, tech workers began to get visibly agitated, with many attending anti-Trump rallies (Buhr 2017; Coren 2017). Workers at both Microsoft and Amazon protested their employer's involvement with the US Immigration and Customs Enforcement (ICE) and its treatment of migrant families (Frenkel 2018; Shaban 2018). Google employees effectively protested their employer's secretive work with the Pentagon, causing the company to drop contracts (Harwell 2018). In addition, 20,000 Google employees staged a walkout after the company gave a $90 million severance package to a senior employee who was fired for sexual assault (Canon 2018).

The first instance of tech worker organizing occurred in 2018 when fourteen software engineers at the startup Lanetix (since rebranded as Winmore) attempted to join the union NewsGuild–Communications Workers of America (CWA). Shortly after receiving notice of this, management fired the involved employees. The retaliatory nature of the firings drew media attention and support from the Tech Workers Coalition, who joined employees at a protest outside Lanetix offices in San Francisco in March. The National Labour Relations Board ruled in the workers' favour and Lanetix paid them a $775,000 settlement (Perry 2018). While no union was formed, a precedent was set.

Another event occurred in February 2019, when web development tool company NPM laid off five workers who were talking to organizations, including the International Federation of Professional and Technical Engineers and the Tech Workers Coalition, about forming a union to combat degrading work conditions (Conger and Scheiber 2019). Once the issue was brought to the National Labour Relations Board, NPM paid a settlement to the workers, but once again no union was formed.

In January 2021, over two hundred tech workers at Google announced the formation of the Alphabet Workers Union (AWU). At the time of writing, the union's membership is over 800 and it is receiving support from the national Communication Workers of America (CWA). However, since the AWU is not yet a formally recognized bargaining unit, it cannot force Google management to engage in collective bargaining (Ghaffary 2021). While it is, of course, impossible to predict the future of tech work organization, some optimistic commentators descry a "budding socialist movement" in Silicon Valley (Spencer and Karlis 2019).

Conclusion

This chapter has surveyed the structure and dynamics of the contemporary AI industry; its highly concentrated oligopolistic capital side as well as its stratified, but newly politically active, labour force. AI is central to the hopes of contemporary cybernetic capital; it is the "next big thing" after the shift to mobile devices. Militaristic applications of AI and discriminatory workplace conditions have brought AI industry labourers into conflict with their employers. It is in this volatile context, where capital's technological impetus confronts an empowered labour, that AI is produced. The next chapter zooms into look more closely at this labour process.

Bibliography

ABC 7 News. 2018. Coolest Employee Perks at Silicon Valley Tech Companies. *ABC7 News*, July 24. https://abc7news.com/technology/coolest-employee-perks-at-silicon-valley-tech-companies/3816443/.

Aghabozorghi, Saeed, and Polong Lin. 2016. Data Scientist vs Data Engineer, What's the Difference? *Cognitiveclass.ai*, June 6. https://cognitiveclass.ai/blog/data-scientist-vs-data-engineer/.

Agrawal, Ajay, Joshua S. Gans, and Avi Goldfarb. 2018. *Prediction Machines: The Simple Economics of Artificial Intelligence*. Boston: Harvard Business Review Press.

AI Index. 2017. The AI Index 2017 Annual Report. https://www.aiindex.org/2017-report.pdf.

AI Now. n.d. Home Page. https://ainowinstitute.org/.

Allen, Gregory C. 2019. Understanding China's AI Strategy. *Center for a New American Security*, February 6. https://www.cnas.org/publications/reports/understanding-chinas-ai-strategy.

Amadeo, Ron. 2018. Google's Iron Grip on Android: Controlling Open Source by Any Means Necessary. *Ars Technica*, July 21. https://arstechnica.com/gadgets/2018/07/googles-iron-grip-on-android-controlling-open-source-by-any-means-necessary/.

Amodei, Dario and Danny Hernandez. 2018. "AI and Compute." *OpenAI Blog*, May 16. https://openai.com/blog/ai-and-compute/.

Anderson, Jess. 2018. Data Engineers vs Data Scientists. *O'Reilly*, April 11. https://www.oreilly.com/ideas/data-engineers-vs-data-scientists.

Bakunin, Mikhail. 1971 [1872]. On the International Workingman's Association and Karl Marx. In *Bakunin on Anarchy*, ed. Sam Dolgoff. New York: Vintage Books.

Benner, Katie. 2017. A Backlash Builds Against Sexual Harassment in Silicon Valley. *The New York Times*, July 3. https://www.nytimes.com/2017/07/03/technology/silicon-valley-sexual-harassment.html.

Berg, Janine, Marianne Furrer, Ellie Harmon, Uma Rani, and M. Six Silberman. 2018. Digital Labour Platforms and the Future of Work: Towards Decent Work in the Online World. *International Labour Organisation*. www.ilo.org/wcmsp5/groups/public/---dgreports/---dcomm/---publ/documents/publication/wcms_645337.pdf.

Bergen, Mark, and Kurt Wagner. 2015. Welcome to the AI Conspiracy: The 'Canadian Mafia' Behind Tech's Latest Craze. *Vox*. July 15. https://www.vox.com/2015/7/15/11614684/ai-conspiracy-the-scientists-behind-deep-learning.

Brockman, Greg. 2019. Microsoft Invest In and Partners with OpenAI to Support Us Building Beneficial AI. *OpenAI Blog*, July 22. https://openai.com/blog/microsoft/.

Brundage, Miles, Shahar Avin, Jack Clark, Helen Toner, Peter Eckersley, Ben Garfinkel, Allan Dafoe, Paul Scharre, Thomas Zeitzoff, Bobby Filar, Hyrum Anderson, Heather Roff, Gregory C. Allen, Jacob Steinhardt, Carrick Flynn, Seán Ó hÉigeartaigh, Simon Beard, Haydn Belfield, Sebastian Farquhar, Clare Lyle, Rebecca Crootof, Owain Evans, Michael Page, Joanna Bryson, Roman Yampolskiy, and Dario Amodei. 2018. *The Malicious Use of Artificial Intelligence: Forecasting, Prevention and Mitigation*. https://img1.wsimg.com/blobby/go/3d82daa4-97fe-4096-9c6b-376b92c619de/downloads/1c6q2kc4v_50335.pdf.

Brynjolfsson, Erik, and Andrew McAfee. 2017. The Business of Artificial Intelligence: What It Can—And Cannot—Do for Your Organization. *Harvard Business Review Digital Articles* 7: 3–11.

Buhr, Sarah. 2017. Tech Employees Protest in Front of Palantir HQ Over Fears It Will Build Trump's Muslim Registry. *TechCrunch*, January 18. https://techcrunch.com/2017/01/18/tech-employees-protest-in-front-of-palantir-hq-over-fears-it-will-build-trumps-muslim-registry/.

Canadian Federal Government. 2017. Building a Strong Middle Class (Budget 2017). https://www.budget.gc.ca/2017/docs/plan/budget-2017-en.pdf.

Canon, Gabrielle. 2018. Google Gave Top Executive $90m Payoff but Kept Sexual Misconduct Claim Quiet—Report. *The Guardian*, October 25. https://www.theguardian.com/technology/2018/oct/25/google-andy-rubin-android-creator-payoff-sexual-misconduct-report.

Cath, Corinne, Sandra Wachter, Brent Mittelstadt, Mariarosaria Taddeo, and Luciano Floridi. 2018. Artificial Intelligence and the 'Good Society': The US, EU, and UK Approach. *Science and Engineering Ethics* 24 (2): 505–528.

Chakraborty, Indranil. 2021. *Invisible Labour: Support Service Workers in India's Information Technology Industry*. London: Routledge.

Chang, Emily. 2019. *Brotopia: Breaking Up the Boys' Club of Silicon Valley*. New York: Portfolio/Penguin.

Chen, Angela. 2019. How to Regulate Big Tech Without Breaking It Up. *MIT Technology Review*, June 7. https://www.technologyreview.com/s/613640/big-tech-monopoly-breakup-amazon-apple-facebook-google-regulation-policy/.

China AI Development Report 2018. China Institute for Science and Technology Policy at Tsinghua University. http://www.sppm.tsinghua.edu.cn/eWebEditor/UploadFile/China_AI_development_report_2018.pdf.

Chinese State Council. 2017. China's New Generation of Artificial Intelligence Development Plan. State Council Document No. 35. Translated by Floria Sapio, Weiming Chen and Adrian Lo. https://flia.org/notice-state-council-issuing-new-generation-artificial-intelligence-development-plan/.

CIO DoD. 2018. Joint Artificial Intelligence Center. Chief Information Officer U.S. Department of Defense. https://dodcio.defense.gov/About-DoD-CIO/Organization/JAIC/.

Conger, Kate, and Noam Scheiber. 2019. Employee Activism Is Alive in Tech. It Stops Short of Organising Unions. *The New York Times*, July 8. https://www.nytimes.com/2019/07/08/technology/tech-companies-union-organizing.html.

Cook, James. 2018. Amazon Scraps 'Sexist AI' Recruiting Tool That Showed Bias Against Women. *The Telegraph*, October 10. https://www.telegraph.co.uk/technology/2018/10/10/amazon-scraps-sexist-ai-recruiting-tool-showed-bias-against/.

Cook, Tim. 2019. You Deserve Privacy Online: Here's How You Could Actually Get It. *Time*, January 16. https://time.com/collection-post/5502591/tim-cook-data-privacy/.

Coren, Michael J. 2017. Silicon Valley Workers Are Talking About Starting Their First Union in 2017 to Resist Trump. *Quartz*, March 24. https://qz.com/916534/silicon-valley-tech-workers-are-talking-about-starting-their-first-union-in-2017-to-resist-trump/. Accessed 28 June 2018.

Crawford, Kate. 2016. Artificial Intelligence's White Guy Problem. *The New York Times*, June 26. https://www.nytimes.com/2016/06/26/opinion/sunday/artificial-intelligences-white-guy-problem.html .

Cummings, M. L. 2018. Artificial Intelligence and the Future of Warfare. In *Artificial Intelligence and International Affairs: Disruption Anticipated*, 7–18. London: Chatham House.

Cummings, M. L., Heather M. Roff, Kenneth Cukier, Jacob Parakilas, and Hannah Bryce, eds. 2018. *Artificial Intelligence and International Affairs: Disruption Anticipated*. Chatham House. https://www.chathamhouse.org/sites/default/files/publications/research/2018-06-14-artificial-intelligence-international-affairs-cummings-roff-cukier-parakilas-bryce.pdf.

DeepMind. n.d. Home Page. https://deepmind.com/.

Dickson, Ben. 2018. Artificial Intelligence Has a Bias Problem, and It's Our Fault. *PC Magazine*, June 14. https://www.pcmag.com/article/361661/artificial-intelligence-has-a-bias-problem-and-its-our-fau.

Ding, Jeffrey. 2018. Deciphering China's AI Dream: The Context, Components, Capabilities and Consequences of China's Strategy to Lead the World in AI. *Future of Humanity Institute*. https://www.fhi.ox.ac.uk/deciphering-chinas-ai-dream/.

Doctorow, Cory. 2019. Regulating Big Tech Makes Them Stronger, So They Need Competition Instead. *The Economist*, June 6. https://www.economist.com/open-future/2019/06/06/regulating-big-tech-makes-them-stronger-so-they-need-competition-instead.

Dolata, Ulrich. 2018. Internet Companies: Market Concentration, Competition and Power. In *Collectivity and Power on the Internet: Sociological Perspective*, ed. Ulrich Dolata and Jan-Felix Schrape. Cham: Springer.

Dong, Catherine. 2017. The Evolution of Machine Learning. *TechCrunch*, August 18. https://techcrunch.com/2017/08/08/the-evolution-of-machine-learning/. Accessed 12 Sept 2018.

Dougherty, Conor. 2015. Astro Teller, Google's 'Captain of Moonshots,' on Making Profits at Google X. *The New York Times*, February 16. https://bits.blogs.nytimes.com/2015/02/16/googles-captain-of-moonshots-on-making-profits-at-google-x/.

Duke, Sue. 2018. Will AI Make the Gender Gap in the Workplace Harder to Close?" *World Economic Forum*, December 21. https://www.weforum.org/agenda/2018/12/artificial-intelligence-ai-gender-gap-workplace/.

Dutton, Tim, Brent Barron, and Gaga Boskovic. 2018. Building an AI World: Report on National and Regional AI Strategies. *CIFAR*. https://www.cifar.ca/docs/default-source/ai-society/buildinganaiworld_eng.pdf.

Ehrenkranz, Melanie. 2017. Google Employees Organize Their Own Study of Gender Pay Gap. *Gizmodo*, August 9. https://gizmodo.com/google-employees-organize-their-own-study-of-gender-pay-1802767010.

Ensmenger, Nathan L. 2012. *The Computer Boys Take Over: Computers, Programmers, and the Politics of Technical Expertise*. Cambridge: MIT Press.

Evans, Richard, and Jim Gao. 2016. DeepMind AI Reduces Google Data Centre Cooling Bill by 40%. *DeepMind Blog*, July 20. https://deepmind.com/blog/deepmind-ai-reduces-google-data-centre-cooling-bill-40/.

Executive Office of the President. 2016. Artificial Intelligence, Automation and the Economy. December. https://obamawhitehouse.archives.gov/sites/whitehouse.gov/files/documents/Artificial-Intelligence-Automation-Economy.pdf.

Fabian. 2018. Global Artificial Intelligence Landscape. *Medium*, May 22. https://medium.com/@bootstrappingme/global-artificial-intelligence-landscape-including-database-with-3-465-ai-companies-3bf01a175c5d.

Faggella, Daniel. 2019. Artificial Intelligence Industry—An Overview by Segment. *Emerj*. https://emerj.com/ai-sector-overviews/artificial-intelligence-industry-an-overview-by-segment/.

Faggella, Daniel. 2020. Artificial Intelligence in Insurance: Three Trends that Matter. *Emerj*. https://emerj.com/ai-sector-overviews/artificial-intelligence-in-insurance-trends/.

Fang, Lee. 2018. Leaked Emails Show Google Expected Lucrative Military Drone AI Work to Grow Exponentially. *The Intercept*, May 31. https://theintercept.com/2018/05/31/google-leaked-emails-drone-ai-pentagon-lucrative/.

Forbes, Jennifer. 2019. 'You're Good for a Girl'—Everyday Sexism in Tech. *CW Jobs*, August 5. https://www.cwjobs.co.uk/blog/everyday-sexism/.

Frenkel, Sheera. 2018. Microsoft Employees Protest Work with ICE, as Tech Industry Mobilizes Over Immigration. *The New York Times*, June 19. Retrieved from https://www.nytimes.com/2018/06/19/technology/tech-companies-immigration-border.html.

Fuchs, Christian. 2014. *Digital Labour and Karl Marx*. New York: Routledge.

Gallagher, Sean. 2017. Expensify Sent Images with Personal Data to Mechanical Turkers, Calls it a Feature. *Ars Technica*, November 27. https://arstechnica.com/information-technology/2017/11/expensify-acknowledges-potential-privacy-problem-by-calling-it-a-feature/.

Gao, Jack. 2017. China's Wage Growth: How Fast Is the Gain and What Does It Mean? *Institute for New Economic Thinking*, February 28. https://www.ineteconomics.org/perspectives/blog/chinas-wage-growth-how-fast-is-the-gain-and-what-does-it-mean.

Gershgorn, Dave. 2015. How Google Aims to Dominate Artificial Intelligence. *Popular Science*, November 9. https://www.popsci.com/google-ai.

Ghaffary, Shirin. 2021. Google's New Union, Briefly Explained. *Recode*, January 4. https://www.vox.com/recode/22213494/google-union-alphabet-workers-tech-organizing-activism-labor.

Gofman, Michael, and Jin, Zhao. 2020. Artificial Intelligence, Education, and Entrepreneurship. *SSRN*. https://ssrn.com/abstract=3449440.

Google. n.d.-a. AI and Machine Learning Products. https://cloud.google.com/products/ai/. Accessed 28 May 2018.

Google. n.d.-b. AI Solutions. https://cloud.google.com/solutions/ai/. Accessed 28 May 2018.

Gray, Mary L., and Siddharth Suri. 2019. *Ghost Work: How to Stop Silicon Valley from Building a New Global Underclass*. San Francisco, CA: HMH Books.

Haner, Justin, and Denise Garcia. 2019. The Artificial Intelligence Arms Race: Trends and World Leaders in Autonomous Weapons Development. *Global Policy* 10 (3): 331–337.

Harrison, Sara. 2019. Five Years of Tech Diversity Reports-and Little Progress. *Wired*, October 1. https://www.wired.com/story/five-years-tech-diversity-reports-little-progress/.

Harwell, Drew. 2018. Google to Drop Pentagon AI Contract After Employee Objections to the 'Business of War.' *The Washington Post*, June 1. https://www.washingtonpost.com/news/the-switch/wp/2018/06/01/google-to-drop-pentagon-ai-contract-after-employees-called-it-the-business-of-war/?utm_term=.f27036684980.

Hayes, James. 2020. Deep as Chips: The New Microprocessors Powering AI. *Engineering & Technology*, November 11. https://eandt.theiet.org/content/articles/2020/11/deep-as-chips-the-new-microprocessors-powering-ai/.

Hitlin, Paul. 2016. Research in the Crowd sourcing Age, a Case Study. *Pew Research Center*, July 11. https://www.pewinternet.org/2016/07/11/research-in-the-crowdsourcing-age-a-case-study/.

Hurst, Aaron. 2020. Google Revealed to Have Acquired the Most AI Startups Since 2009. *Information Age*, February 18. https://www.information-age.com/google-revealed-acquired-most-ai-startups-since-2009-123487752/.

Hyde, Alan. 2003. *Working in Silicon Valley: Economic and Legal Analysis of a High-Velocity Labor Market*. Armonk, NY: ME Sharpe.

Indeed.com. 2019a. Data Scientist Salaries. https://www.indeed.com/salaries/Data-Scientist-Salaries. Accessed 24 July 2019.

Indeed.com. 2019b. Data Engineer Salaries. https://www.indeed.com/salaries/Data-Engineer-Salaries. Accessed 24 July 2019.

Indeed.com. 2019c. Data Analyst Salaries. https://www.indeed.com/salaries/Data-Analyst-Salaries. Accessed 24 July 2019.

Intel Brandvoice. 2018. The Rise in Computing Power: Why Ubiquitous Artificial Intelligence Is Now a Reality. *Forbes*, July 17. https://www.forbes.com/sites/intelai/2018/07/17/the-rise-in-computing-power-why-ubiquitous-artificial-intelligence-is-now-a-reality/#246769ac1d3f.

International Data Corporation. 2018. Worldwide Spending on Cognitive and Artificial Intelligence Systems Will Grow to $19.1 Billion in 2018, According to New IDC Spending Guide, March 22. https://www.idc.com/getdoc.jsp?containerId=prUS43662418.

Kania, Elsa. 2017. AlphaGo and Beyond: The Chinese Military Looks to Future 'Intelligentized' Warfare. *Lawfare Blog*, June 5. https://www.lawfareblog.com/alphago-and-beyond-chinese-military-looks-future-intelligentized-warfare.

Karsten, Jack, and Darrell M. West. 2015. Rising Minimum Wages Make Automation More Cost-Effective. *Brookings Institute Blog*, September 30. https://www.brookings.edu/blog/techtank/2015/09/30/rising-minimum-wages-make-automation-more-cost-effective/.

Kaye, Kate. 2019. These Companies Claim to Provide 'Fair-Trade' Data Work. Do They? *MIT Technology Review*, August 7. https://www.technologyreview.com/s/614070/cloudfactory-ddd-samasource-imerit-impact-sourcing-companies-for-data-annotation/.

Kelly, Kevin. 2014. The Three Breakthroughs That Have Finally Unleashed AI on the World. *Wired*, October 27. https://www.wired.com/2014/10/future-of-artificial-intelligence/.

Kisner, James, David Wishnow, and Timur Ivannikov. 2017. IBM: Creating Shareholder Value with AI? Not so Elementary, My Dear Watson. *Jeffries*, July 12. https://javatar.bluematrix.com/pdf/fO5xcWjc.

Kolhatkar, Sheelah. 2017. The Tech Industry's Gender-Discrimination Problem. *The New Yorker*, November 13. https://www.newyorker.com/magazine/2017/11/20/the-tech-industrys-gender-discrimination-problem.

Langley, Hugh, and Jennifer Pattison Tuohy. 2019. Smart Home Privacy: What Amazon, Google and Apple Do with Your Data. *The Ambient*, November 8. https://www.the-ambient.com/features/how-amazon-google-apple-use-smart-speaker-data-338.

Lee, Kai-Fu. 2018. *AI Superpowers: China, Silicon Valley, and the New World Order*. New York: Houghton Mifflin Harcourt.

Leonard, Andrew. 2014. Tech's Toxic Political Culture: The Stealth Libertarianism of Silicon Valley Bigwigs. *Salon*, June 6. https://www.salon.com/2014/06/06/techs_toxic_political_culture_the_stealth_libertarianism_of_silicon_valley_bigwigs/.

Li, Fei-Fei. 2017. ImageNet: Where Have We Been? Where Are We Going? *ACM Webinar*. https://learning.acm.org/binaries/content/assets/leaning-center/webinar-slides/2017/imagenet_2017_acm_webinar_compressed.pdf.

Magoulas, Roger, and Steve Swoyer. 2020. AI Adoption in the Enterprise 2020. *O'Reilly*, March 18. https://www.oreilly.com/radar/ai-adoption-in-the-enterprise-2020/.

Markoff, John. 2012. How Many Computers to Identify a Cat? 16,000. *The New York Times*, June 25. https://www.nytimes.com/2012/06/26/technology/in-a-big-network-of-computers-evidence-of-machine-learning.html?pagewanted=all.

Metz, Cade. 2017. Tech Giants Are Paying Huge Salaries for Scarce A.I. Talent. *The New York Times*, October 22. https://www.nytimes.com/2017/10/22/technology/artificial-intelligence-experts-salaries.html.

Metz, Cade. 2018a. A.I. Researchers Are Making More Than $1 Million, Even at a Nonprofit. *The New York Times*, April 19. https://www.nytimes.com/2018/04/19/technology/artificial-intelligence-salaries-openai.html.

Metz, Cade. 2018b. Google Sells A.I. for Building A.I. (Novices Welcome). *The New York Times*, January 17. https://www.nytimes.com/2018/01/17/technology/google-sells-ai.html. Accessed 13 Sept 2018.

Microsoft. 2016. Democratizing AI: For Every Person and Every Organization. https://news.microsoft.com/features/democratizing-ai/.

Miller, Ron. 2017. AWS Continues to Rule the Cloud Infrastructure Market. *TechCrunch*, October 30. https://techcrunch.com/2017/10/30/aws-continues-to-rule-the-cloud-infrastructure-market/.

Milton, Laurie P. 2003. An Identity Perspective on the Propensity of High-Tech Talent to Unionize. *Journal of Labor Research* 24 (1): 31–53.

Murphy, Andrea, Jonathan Ponciano, Sarah Hansen, and Halah Touryalai. 2019. Global 2000: The World's Largest Public Companies: 2019 Ranking. *Forbes*, May 15.

Naimat, Aman. 2016. *The New Artificial Intelligence Market*. Sebastopol, CA: O'Reilly Media.

Nakashima, Ryan. 2018. AI's Dirty Little Secret: It's Powered by People. *Phys.org*, March 5. https://phys.org/news/2018-03-ai-dirty-secret-powered-people.html.

Oberhaus, Daniel. 2018. Military Contracts Are the Destiny of Every Major Technology Company. *Motherboard*, June 1. https://www.vice.com/en_us/article/pavzk7/military-contracts-are-the-destiny-of-every-major-technology-company.

Ochigame, Rodrigo. 2019. The Invention of 'Ethical AI': How Big Tech Manipulates Academia to Avoid Regulation. *The Intercept*, December 20. https://theintercept.com/2019/12/20/mit-ethical-ai-artificial-intelligence/.

OpenAI. 2019. OpenAI LP. *OpenAI Blog*, March 11. https://openai.com/blog/openai-lp/.

Partnership on AI. n.d. Home Page. https://www.partnershiponai.org.

Passieri, James. 2015. GE Expects Predix Software to Do for Factories What Apple's iOS Did for Cell Phones. *The Street*, June 3. https://www.thestreet.com/story/13174112/1/ge-expects-predix-software-to-do-for-factories-what-apples-ios-did-for-cell-phones.html.

Patel, Siddharth. 2017. Tech Workers: Friend or Foes? *Jacobin*, August 25. https://www.jacobinmag.com/2017/08/silicon-valley-gentrification-tech-sharing-economy.

Patrizio, Andy. 2018. Top 25 Artificial Intelligence Companies. *Datamation*, April 10. www.datamation.com/applications/top-25-artificial-intelligencecompanies.html.

Perez, Carlos E. 2017. Is Deep Learning Innovation Just Due to Brute Force? *Intuition Machine*, 23 September. https://medium.com/intuitionmachine/the-brute-force-method-of-deep-learning-innovation-58b497323ae5.

Perrault, Raymond, Yoav Shoham, Erik Brynjolfsson, Jack Clark, John Etchemendy, Barbara Grosz, Terah Lyons, James Manyika, Saurabh Mishra, and Juan Carlos Niebles. 2019. The AI Index 2019 Annual Report. AI Index Steering Committee, Human-Centered AI Institute, Stanford University, Stanford, CA.

Perry, Tekla. 2018. Startup Lanetix Pays US $775,000 to Software Engineers Fired for Union Organizing. *IEEE Spectrum*, November 12. https://spectrum.ieee.org/view-from-the-valley/at-work/tech-careers/startup-lanetix-pays-775000-to-software-engineers-fired-for-union-organizing.

Pham, Thuy T. 2017. 50 Companies Leading the AI Revolution, Detailed. *KDNuggets*, March 2017. https://www.kdnuggets.com/2017/03/50-companies-leading-ai-revolution-detailed.html.

Pichai, Sundar. 2015. TensorFlow: Smarter Machine Learning, for Everyone. *Google Blog*, November 5. https://googleblog.blogspot.com/2015/11/tensorflow-smarter-machine-learning-for.html.

Press, Gil. 2017. Equifax and SAS Leverage AI and Deep Learning to Improve Consumer Access to Credit. *Forbes*, February 20. https://www.forbes.com/sites/gilpress/2017/02/20/equifax-and-sas-leverage-ai-and-deep-learning-to-improve-consumer-access-to-credit/#584aee835a39.

Reed, Chris. 2018. How Should We Regulate Artificial Intelligence? *Philosophical Transactions of the Royal Society: Mathematical, Physical and Engineering Sciences* 376 (2128).

Revill, John. 2021. ABB's Robots to Meet Post Pandemic Demand for Workforce That Never Gets Sick. *Yahoo! Finance*, February 24. https://finance.yahoo.com/news/abbs-robots-meet-post-pandemic-122006775.html.

Roberts, Sarah T. 2014. *Behind the Screen: The Hidden Digital Labor of Commercial Content Moderation*. PhD dissertation, University of Illinois at Urbana-Champaign.

Rogers, Everett M., and Judith K. Larsen. 1984. *Silicon Valley Fever: Growth of High-Technology Culture*. New York: Basic Books.

Roth, Marcus. 2019. Artificial Intelligence at the Top 5 US Defense Contractors. *Emerj*, January 3. https://emerj.com/ai-sector-overviews/artificial-intelligence-at-the-top-5-us-defense-contractors/.

RT. 2017. 'Whoever Leads in AI Will Rule the World': Putin to Russian Children on Knowledge Day. *RT*, September 1. https://www.rt.com/news/401731-ai-rule-world-putin/.

Sadowski, Jathan. 2018. Potemkin AI. *Real Life Magazine*, August 6. https://reallifemag.com/potemkin-ai/.

Scharre, Paul. 2018. *Army of None: Autonomous Weapons and the Future of War*. New York and London: W.W. Norton.

Scheiber, Noam, and Daisuke Wakabayashi. 2019. Google Hires Firm Known For Anti-Union Efforts. *The New York Times*, November 20. https://www.nytimes.com/2019/11/20/technology/Google-union-consultant.html.

Schomer, Audrey. 2019. Google Ad Revenue Growth Is Slowing as Amazon Continues Eating into Its Share. *Business Insider*, May 1. https://www.businessinsider.com/google-ad-revenue-growth-slows-amazon-taking-share-2019-5.

Shaban, H. 2018. Amazon Employees Demand Company Cut Ties with ICE. *The Washington Post*, June 22. Retrieved from https://www.washingtonpost.com/news/the-switch/wp/2018/06/22/amazon-employees-demand-company-cut-ties-with-ice/?utm_term=.65c50c634d97.

Sheng, Ellen. 2018. The Shocking Truth: In Silicon Valley Wages Are Down for Everyone but the Top 10%. *Nightly Business Report*, December 3. http://nbr.com/2018/12/03/the-shocking-truth-in-silicon-valley-wages-are-down-for-everyone-but-the-top-10/.

Siemens. n.d. This Is Mindsphere! https://new.siemens.com/global/en/products/software/mindsphere.html.

Simonite, Tom. 2017. For Superpowers, Artificial Intelligence fuels New Global Arms Race. *Wired*. September 8. https://www.wired.com/story/for-superpowers-artificial-intelligence-fuels-new-global-arms-race/.

Snow, Jackie. 2018. We're in a Diversity Crisis: Cofounder of Black in AI on What's Poisoning Algorithms in Our Lives. *MIT Technology Review*, February 14. https://www.technologyreview.com/2018/02/14/145462/were-in-a-diversity-crisis-black-in-ais-founder-on-whats-poisoning-the-algorithms-in-our/.

South, Todd. 2018. DARPA to Use Artificial Intelligence to Help Commanders in Gray Zone Conflicts. *Army Times*, March 27. https://www.armytimes.com/news/your-army/2018/03/27/darpa-to-use-artificial-intelligence-to-help-commanders-in-gray-zone-conflicts/.

Spencer, Keith A., and Nicole Karlis. 2019. Silicon Valley, Once a Bastion of Libertarianism, Sees a Budding Socialist Movement. *Salon*, April 11. https://www.salon.com/2019/04/11/silicon-valley-once-a-bastion-of-libertarianism-sees-a-budding-socialist-movement/.

Sriraman, Anand, Jonathan Bragg, and Anand Kulkarni. 2017. Worker-Owned Cooperative Models for Training Artificial Intelligence. *Companion of the 2017 ACM Conference on Computer Supported Cooperative Work and Social Computing*, 311–314. New York: ACM.

Srnicek, Nick. 2017. *Platform Capitalism*. London: Polity.

Stackoverflow. 2018. Developer Survey Results 2018. https://insights.stackoverflow.com/survey/2018/#overview.

Statcounter. 2020. Search Engine Market Share China July 2019–July 2020. https://gs.statcounter.com/search-engine-market-share/all/china/.

Statista. 2020. Market Size and Revenue Comparison for Artificial Intelligence Worldwide from 2015 to 2025. https://www-statista-com.proxy1.lib.uwo.ca/statistics/941835/artificial-intelligence-market-size-revenue-comparisons/.

Surber, Regina. 2018. Artificial Intelligence: Autonomous Technology (AT), Lethal Autonomous Weapons Systems (LAWS) and Peace Time Threats, February 21. Zurich: ICT4Peace Foundation.

Symonds, Peter. 2019. Signs of Rising Levels of Workers' Struggles in China. *World Socialist Web Site*, February 18. https://www.wsws.org/en/articles/2019/02/18/chin-f18.html.

The Economist. 2016. The Rise of the Superstars, September 15. https://www.economist.com/special-report/2016/09/15/the-rise-of-the-superstars.

The Economist. 2017. Google Leads in the Race to Dominate Artificial Intelligence, December 7. https://www.economist.com/business/2017/12/07/google-leads-in-the-race-to-dominate-artificial-intelligence.

The Economist. 2019. Competition, not Break-up, Is the Cure for Tech Giants' Dominance, March 13. https://www.economist.com/business/2019/03/13/competition-not-break-up-is-the-cure-for-tech-giants-dominance.

Theuwissen, Martijn. 2015. The Different Data Science Roles in the Industry. *KDnuggets*, November 2015. https://www.kdnuggets.com/2015/11/different-data-science-roles-industry.html.

Think Tank Watch. 2018. *Think Tanks Getting Serious About AI. Think Tank Watch*. March 29. http://www.thinktankwatch.com/2018/03/think-tanks-getting-serious-about-ai.html.

Tractica. 2019. Revenues from the Artificial Intelligence (AI) Software Market Worldwide from 2018 to 2025 (in Billion U.S. Dollars). *Statista*. https://www.statista.com/statistics/607716/worldwide-artificial-intelligence-market-revenues/.

Trefis Team. 2019. Can Google Cloud Revenues Reach $20 Billion by 2020? *Forbes*, April 29. https://www.forbes.com/sites/greatspeculations/2019/04/29/why-cloud-could-be-a-game-changer-for-google/#2b13fef21694.

Turner, Matt. 2016. The CEO of United Technologies Just Let Slip an Unintended Consequence of the Trump-Carrier Jobs Deal. *Business Insider*, December 5. https://www.businessinsider.com/united-tech-ceo-says-trump-deal-will-lead-to-more-automation-fewer-jobs-2016-12.

U.S. Equal Employment Opportunity Commission. 2016. Diversity in High Tech. https://www.eeoc.gov/eeoc/statistics/reports/hightech/.

Vance, Ashlee. 2014. The Race to Buy the Human Brains Behind Deep Learning Machines. *Bloomberg*, January 27. https://www.bloomberg.com/news/articles/2014-01-27/the-race-to-buy-the-human-brains-behind-deep-learning-machines.

Vassallo, Trae, Ellen Levy, Michele Madansky, Hillary Mickell, Bennett Porter, Monica Leas, and Julie Oberweis. 2015. Elephant in the Valley. https://www.elephantinthevalley.com/.

Vincent, James. 2018. The World's Most Valuable AI Startup Is a Chinese Company Specializing in Real-Time Surveillance. *The Verge*, April 11. https://www.theverge.com/2018/4/11/17223504/ai-startup-sensetime-china-most-valuable-facial-recognition-surveillance.

Wakabayashi, Daisuke. 2017. Google Fires Engineer Who Wrote Memo Questioning Women in Tech. *The New York Times*, August 7. https://www.nytimes.com/2017/08/07/business/google-women-engineer-fired-memo.html.

Walker, Jon. 2019. Machine Learning in Manufacturing—Present and Future Use-Cases. *Emerj*, August 13. https://emerj.com/ai-sector-overviews/machine-learning-in-manufacturing/.

Warren, Elizabeth. 2019. Here's How We Can Break Up Big Tech. *Medium*, March 8. https://medium.com/@teamwarren/heres-how-we-can-break-up-big-tech-9ad9e0da324c.

West, Sarah Meyes, Meredith Whittaker, and Kate Crawford. 2019. Discriminating Systems: Gender, Race and Power in AI. *AI Now Institute*, April 2019. https://ainowinstitute.org/discriminatingsystems.html.

Working Partnerships USA. 2016. Tech's Invisible Workforce. https://www.wpusa.org/files/reports/TechsInvisibleWorkforce.pdf.

Yegulalp, Serdar. 2017. Google's Machine Learning Cloud Pipeline Explained. *Infoworld*, May 19. https://www.infoworld.com/article/3197405/tpus-googles-machine-learning-pipeline-explained.html.

Yu, Miaomiao. 2017. The Humans Behind Artificial Intelligence. *Synced*, April 30. https://syncedreview.com/2017/04/30/the-humans-behind-artificial-intelligence/.

Zilis, Shivon, and James Cham. 2016. The Current State of Machine Intelligence 3.0. *O'Reilly*, November 7. https://www.oreilly.com/ideas/the-current-state-of-machine-intelligence-3-0.

CHAPTER 6

A Dark Art: The Machine Learning Labour Process

Introduction

We have surveyed the history of the AI industry as well as its contemporary state. But how exactly are AI commodities produced therein? To answer this question, this chapter shifts from macro to micro scale, to look at the machine learning labour process. A labour process is the concrete series of actions that goes into creating any useful thing or service. Under capital, most things or services take the form of commodities; they are made to be sold to realize surplus-value. Therefore capital exercises control over labour processes and reconfigures them to maximize the harvest of surplus-value. Labour processes vary enormously from industry to industry and job to job, but they are alike insofar as they are all sites of direct confrontation between labour and capital.

Our analysis of the machine learning labour process occurs amid the intensifying industrialization of software work in general. While labour process studies discerned fragmentation and deskilling in software work decades ago (Kraft 1977, 1979; Kraft and Dubnoff 1986), now journalists and industry commentators report that the stereotypical image of the software producer as a "hoodied young Zuckerbergian" is being replaced by the "Blue-collar Coder" (Thompson 2019, 326; see also Dash 2012). At *MIT Technology Review*'s 2018 EmTech Digital AI industry conference, the entrepreneur and AI professor Oren Etzioni (2018) emphasized

J. Steinhoff, *Automation and Autonomy*, Marx, Engels, and Marxisms,
https://doi.org/10.1007/978-3-030-71689-9_6

that making AI requires "99 percent manual labor". While such formulations benefit from not imagining AI as an abstract or solely intellectual enterprise, they do not situate the labour of producing AI within an antagonistic relation to capital. That is the goal of this chapter. If AI work possesses the new autonomy attributed to immaterial labour, it should become visible in the labour process, where AI-producing labour confronts capital.

The first section looks at the three main stages of the ML labour process. Then I present four thematic discussions drawn from my interviews with people working in the AI industry. They are: the commodity form of AI, empirical control, AI as automation and the automation of AI work. All of these discussions impinge upon the purported new autonomy of immaterial labour posited by *post-operaismo*, as the next chapter elaborates. In general, the ML labour process is subject to familiar processes of fragmentation and automation, even if they are implemented in novel ways. I show this by exploring the technique for automating the production of ML called automated machine learning (AutoML). Finally, I interpret the significance of ML and AutoML as automation technologies via the concept of synthetic automation, a technique of automating labour processing without a previous capture of skill or knowledge from human labour.

The Machine Learning Labour Process

Any labour process is composed of individual days of work. Whether the process is begun anew each day, or whether the entire process takes several days, weeks or months to complete, depends on the job. When asked to describe a typical day at work in the AI industry, Arvin, a R&D programmer working at a startup, told me:

> You usually have some pending tasks from a previous project, or you have a new task from a new project … the CEO comes over to your desk and he starts talking about what exactly the vision is and what the project is about. He discusses certain algorithms and various concepts that need to be … fleshed out before it can be done in the code. There can be multiple people standing around a computer and talking about various … high level design principles. Then they can go to a white board and we can talk about … various little details … [but] most programming in any company is a solitary activity … that's the nature of programming.

My interviews revealed a rough consensus on this kind of workday breakdown—a coordinating meeting opening the day, followed by largely solitary work, interspersed with meetings. ML projects are not completed in a day, however, taking anywhere from weeks to months depending on the complexity and novelty of the task. But we can schematize the ML labour process, in general, as consisting of three stages: data processing, model building and deployment. In what follows I describe the essential moments of each stage.

Stage 1: Data Processing

The first stage is data processing or "cleaning and formatting vast amounts of data" (Dong 2017). Ready-to-use data is not simply found in the wild and a lot of work must be done to make data usable—if it can be found in the first place. Data processing is, in reality, a second step after data collection. While photos of cats may be abundant on the internet, in domains like medical image recognition, often "it is hard to obtain enough data or the quality of data is not good enough" (He et al. 2019, 2). One can get an idea of the importance of collecting and processing data by considering the results of one survey, which reports that data scientists spend 19% of their time at work collecting data sets, 60% preparing it and merely 7% building models (Crowdflower 2016, 6).

ML developer Jason Brownlee (2013) breaks data processing down into three sub-steps which are "likely to be iterative with many loops". First is selecting data. While, as a general rule, more data is better than less data, not all available data are going to be relevant to every problem. Important data may also be missing and may have to be simulated. On the other hand, datasets may need to be sampled, rather than used whole, to reduce computational load.

The second sub-step is preprocessing data, by formatting, labelling and cleaning it. This involves making the data usable by software, fixing errors or missing values and removing sensitive information. It is described as "frustrating manual labor" and "repetitive work" (Dong 2017). It is, however, very important. As Arvin told me, "[i]f you want to get very good results then you need to clean out the data a lot". Data also often need to be labelled. Labelling is repetitive labour that is often outsourced to ghost workers through platforms such as Amazon Mechanical Turk. AI companies have, however, developed creative methods to obtain labels without paying even miniscule ghost work wages. The reCAPTCHA system (acquired by Google in 2009), which prevents bots from accessing websites, asks users to prove their humanity by labelling objects, such as stop signs, in photos. The labels are then used to "solve hard AI problems" (Google, n.d.).

The third sub-step is "feature engineering" or transforming data so that important aspects of it are emphasized for algorithmic processing. Brownlee (2014) defines it as turning "raw data into features that better represent the underlying problem to the predictive models, resulting in improved model accuracy". It can involve combining, separating or relating data in different ways. Google (2019) describes it as "helping the model to understand the data set in the same way you do". This may involve drawing on specialized knowledge about a particular context or domain to determine which aspects of the data are useful. Sometimes such knowledge is obtained through collaboration with a domain expert, such as a physicist or biologist. Domain knowledge may also refer to common sense. For example, one might engineer a model to use the relative number of green and blue pixels in an image as a heuristic for whether the image contains a land or marine scene (Dettmers 2015). Useful features vary widely from problem to problem and "[m]uch of the success of machine learning is actually success in engineering features that a [learning algorithm] can understand" (Locklin 2014). Feature engineering is thus often described as an "art" requiring experience and a sense of intuition (Dettmers 2015; Brownlee 2014).

Stage 2: Model Building

In the second stage, the model is created. Processed data is input to a learning algorithm, which outputs a model. The model contains patterns or "relationships" learned from the input data (Brownlee 2015). The model can then be applied to analyze new data. Here it is useful to distinguish between the three primary types of machine learning—supervised, reinforcement and unsupervised learning—because each produces a model in a different way and requires different types of data and labour to do so.

The majority of commercial ML today is based on supervised learning. In supervised learning, the data from which the algorithm learns is categorized and labelled by humans (Sun 2014). The model learns the categories by discerning patterns across the labelled examples. The labelled data thus acts as a supervisor (Brownlee 2016). The "supervisor provides the correct values, and the parameters of a model are updated so that its output gets as close as possible to these desired outputs" (Alpaydin 2016, 111). Given enough labelled photos of red hexagonal signs with the word STOP on them, in various visibility conditions and from various angles, as well as examples of non-stop signs, a supervised learning system can discern relationships among the examples and form a "concept" (for lack of a better word) of *stop sign* and output the category "stop sign" whenever it is fed an image of a stop sign. Ideally, the concept of *stop sign* formed by the system will be robust enough for it to recognize stop signs in images not included in its training data.

Supervised learning continues to be successfully applied to new fields, but there are many fields in which large amounts of labelled data are not available, presenting the problem of a data "bottleneck" (Roh et al. 2019). The data bottleneck is simultaneously a labour bottleneck, because the manual labelling required for the vast quantities of data necessary for supervised learning can become expensive and sometimes requires specialized knowledge (Roh et al. 2019). The two other main types of machine learning may be understood as attempts to overcome the data/labour bottleneck.

One of these is unsupervised learning, where "there is no predefined output, and hence no supervisor ... only the input data" (Alpaydin 2016, 111). In unsupervised learning, data is unlabeled and thus "a lot easier and cheaper to find" (Alpaydin 2016, 117). Indeed, the internet is a vast trove of unlabeled data. The goal in unsupervised learning is to automatically "find structure in the data" (Alpaydin 2016, 117) which represents its "underlying factors and their interaction" (Alpaydin 2016, xi). Two prominent ways of doing so are "clustering", in which data points are grouped by some type of similarity, and "association" in which rules that describe correlations between data points are discovered (Brownlee 2016). Clustering may help support a theory about relationships between variables, but more interestingly, "there may be a cluster or clusters that no expert could have foreseen" (Alpaydin 2016, 115). Unsupervised learning may offer a way around the data bottleneck, and may actually be required for some applications. For instance, high definition video contains so much data that to analyze it with supervised learning would require "several orders of magnitude more labels" than doing the same for images, making it infeasibly labour-intensive (Luo et al. 2017, 2203).

The third main type of machine learning is reinforcement learning, which attempts to overcome the data bottleneck by generating data in the course of learning. The pioneers of this approach describe it as "learning what to do ... so as to maximize a numerical reward signal. The learner is not told which actions to take ... but instead must discover which actions yield the most reward by trying them" (Sutton and Barto 1998, 127). The numerical reward signal can be grasped via a hedonic analogy. There is "no external process that provides the training data" (Alpaydin 2016, 128). Instead, reinforcement learning aims to emulate the process of learning by experience, exploiting "pleasurable" results, avoiding "painful" ones and experimenting with new ones. Pleasurable results increase a reward score while painful ones subtract from it. A reinforcement learning algorithm thus "actively generates data by trying out actions in the environment and receiving feedback (or not) in the form of a reward" (Alpaydin 2016, 128). Since algorithms lack common sense, a lot of experimentation is required. Reinforcement learning has thus mainly been applied in artificial contexts where it is possible for an algorithm to be run iteratively at high speeds to accrue the requisite data (Knight 2017).[1] To this end, OpenAI has released Gym, a suite of tools for reinforcement learning in virtual environments. In the future, models trained via reinforcement learning within simulations may be transferable to the real world; at least, these are the hopes of the producers of autonomous vehicles, which can be dangerous to experiment with in the real world (Gray 2019).

Stage 3: Deployment

A trained ML model is deployed by integrating it "into an existing production environment in order to start using it to make practical business decisions based on data" (DataRobot, n.d.). Models may be embedded in websites, applications and incorporated into diverse commodities. Performance of models is typically tracked by monitoring real-time dashboards, or graphical representations of metrics of the model's functioning. Due to their accessibility, dashboards are also often used to present ML models to nontechnical stakeholders including management and customers.

One major hurdle to deployment is that there is often a discrepancy between the ML programming languages and other business software.

[1] For a startling video of reinforcement learning at work, see OpenAI (2019).

This entails either recoding the entire model or building an API (application programming interface), which translates between the two (Paul 2018). Further, if a model is to be deployed at scale, this presents its own hurdles, since diverse hardwares and clouds have to be made to function together; this can be "in some ways more complex than building the model in the first place" (Toews 2020). Deployment also involves maintenance. Models need to be updated on new data to reflect changes in their environment. It is common to "re-train production models on fresh data on a daily to monthly basis, depending on the application" (Dong 2017). The ML labour process does not terminate once the ML commodity has been produced.

These three stages sketch the ML labour process. It is now time to hear from those who work in the AI industry about what it is like to participate in this labour process. In the next sections, I present four thematic discussions drawn from my interviews. Each shows how the ML labour process is influenced by the valorization imperative.

The Commodity Form of AI

As should be evident by now, AI industry products are commodities. It should come as no surprise that the production of AI is structured for speed and efficiency in accord with the competitive dynamics of capitalist production. Juan, a startup CEO, told me that his near-term goal was to "knock down some more customers". Tolu, another CEO, described his company's goal as: "Make as much money as possible in as short a time as possible ... There's no such thing as enough ... honestly, we're making a magic factory ... What we're trying to do ... is that machine that shoots out baseballs and just throws strikes all day". In pursuit of profits, the AI industry requires the long workweeks familiar to software work in general.

Most of my interviewees reported working well over a typical 40 hour work week. As senior software engineer Albert put it, "if you want to work from 9 to 5, I mean it's fine, but don't expect that will be very competitive in the marketplace". Carlo, who was hired as an engineer at a company he had previously interned at, summed up his experience like this: "the CEO ... said 'the amount of hours [40] you're putting in were what we call, like, mediocre. You need to put more in if you come full time.' So he just made that known and I agreed to it ... I'd say maybe 50 to 60 hours, that's low". Chris, a startup CEO, told me that concerning his work week, "there's no fixed number to it, but it's definitely above … 80 hours a week". Tolu, also a CEO, described a downside of his startup's consulting business model:

> you know how they say that the sun never sets on the British empire? The same kind of deal. Because people are all in different time zones, it's really bad for my sleeping patterns … that's a major drawback of being a high availability consultant … it's not healthy for you. We're solving that with money. We got a cleaning lady who cleans the house. We've got a babysitter who watches the kids. So like, you know, a lot of things can be solved just with money.

In addition to generally long hours, AI work is subject to sporadic periods of intense, nearly non-stop work. So-called "death marches" have been an aspect of software production since the 1990s (Yourdon 2004). As Carlo told me, "when stuff broke or hit the fan or there was a deadline … it could easily go to 12 hours every single day. Including weekends. And there have been times as well when something breaks in the middle of the night. You get paged … You have to wake up and fix it".

The competitive nature of ML production also means that work is changing rapidly as new research is published and new tools are made available. Norms are subject to continual revision and workers must continually learn new skills. Martin told me that for a data scientist, work is:

> very fast paced and evolving every second … New articles, from even the most prominent researchers, are coming out twice a week … Or new applications that change the entire perspective of the field. So it's already very fast paced. So if … it's a data science job, it's an everyday story that the methods that you used previously are really not as good anymore … a lot of things are unknown. We don't know how to use all these potentials in the field … the thing that was state of the art two weeks ago is kind of taken for granted now.

Juan, a CEO, agreed and described the industry as having a "rate problem. It's not a fixed benchmark of what is enough, it's really how fast can you build. Because everything is changing. Nobody can predict in two years what the landscape is really going to look like". This compels many in the industry to augment their formal education with courses and certificates from platforms like Coursera and Udacity. Nikolas, a data scientist, told me he was "continuously improving" his skills on such sites, while Yimin, who reported spending around 50% of his time at work on research, said "I'm constantly trying to learn. New things are coming up. It's very difficult to keep up … with the new developments". According to Theuwissen (2015), most data scientists spend "between 25-75% of their time on R&D as opposed to production" (12).

Further instability is added by ML's reliance on data, which entails a suite of contingencies regarding quality and availability. According to CEO Tolu: "If you're too inflexible in data science you're setting yourself up to fail. Because the truth is, you don't know what's going to happen. You hope what's going to happen. You build a plan around it that makes a lot of sense, but oftentimes, weird things happen … you think you have the data and you don't have the data". One way companies attempt to control contingencies regarding data and other aspects of software production is a development practice called continuous integration.

Continuous integration means that "when someone checks his or her revised code into the repository, an automated system picks up the change, checks out the code, and runs a set of commands to verify that the change is good and didn't break any-thing" (Meyer 2014, 14). Many of my interviewees explicitly reported using continuous integration, and it is implicit in the Agile methods mentioned by others. Juan, a CEO, told me the general idea of continuous integration is: "you wanna be releasing as frequently as possible. So any time someone adds code to the code base that is polished and good it should go to production right away … that should all be done automatically. People shouldn't have to manually push code to the server. Which … is an error prone step … you wanna just have like an automatic flow". Arvin, the R&D programmer, explained to me that "when somebody finishes their code and pushes their code it'll automatically get built … They won't have to build it on their machine … It's very essential. Without continuous integration it's very difficult to get any work done". Juan reported doing continuous integration "at an unusual speed. So many companies have like a nightly build or a weekly build … We build … for every change somebody makes". Continuous integration aims to automate, and thus accelerate, testing for bugs. For one commentator this is necessary because, "[i]f tests run longer than 10 minutes, developer productivity drops, slowing down the process of shipping new features or bug fixes to the customer" (Meyer 2014, 14). The automatic checks of continuous integration allow AI commodities to be sent to market more quickly.

Intercapitalist competition drives long workweeks and a fast pace of work. But these are not the only ways the commodity form of AI influences the ML labour process. The commodity form also exerts influence through other stakeholders including customers, funders and management. The customer's influence on the labour process can be substantial since many AI companies offer a consulting service as part of their business model. Others must continually respond to changing customer demands throughout the development process. Yimin, a data scientist, reported spending 40% of his time at work "responding to … ad hoc requests coming from clients". Laslo, a CEO, told me that although he has a technical background, he spends a lot of time "going to conferences, going to events where we have to tell people how data science is different from BI [business intelligence] work. How data science is actually different … from any of the software-as-a-service solutions that they are using … You can call that business development or you can call that building up the client's knowledge base". He elaborated that his business model "requires immediate response to clients, immediate photo ops. Only then are you able to build a name big enough that you can … actually get word of mouth and clients start coming back to you. Rather than you going out and pitching to clients". Mahir, another CEO, noted that "the two things I spend most of my time on are pitching investors and sales". Tolu, also a CEO, even works as a chief technology officer for one of his largest clients as a way to, in his words, "offer something extra special".

Another possible vector of influence on the labour process comes from the potential for startups to be bought up. While none of my interviewees' companies were actively seeking acquisition, Mahir told me that:

> one of the things that I've heard other companies say is that they kind of realized that they couldn't get to the next phase on their own. So you know the cost of acquiring new customers or they didn't have the level of skill in their management to go after some big clients. That being part of a bigger company just helped them pursue their goal better … generally there's a strong desire for companies to exit, whether that means going public or becoming much, much bigger … being acquired.

Further influence comes from management, venture capital funders and incubator programs, to whom ML workers have to explain and justify their work. Nikolas, a data scientist, described how he presents his work to his managers:

> usually we sit in a conference room and we display the result on the projector. We zoom into the visualizations to see what is happening. I present to higher management and after the work is approved, we compile it into a report or dashboard and then the higher management goes to the user or the customer ... you have to do a number of iterations and then come up with some result and you have to convince your upper management that this is how I did it and this is the significance of that result.

Similar to Nikolas' explanatory and justificatory efforts were the experiences of Mahir, a CEO, in the context of an incubator program his company went through in its early days:

> every 8 weeks you meet a whole bunch of successful entrepreneurs, investors and they grill you. And if one or two is willing to spend 4 hours of their own time over the next eight weeks, then you can stay in the program. If no one wants to commit time to you, then you get kicked out. So ... obviously, it can be pretty anxiety provoking and stressful.

Such presentations to investors, advisors and management mean that there is a requirement for effective communication skills beyond the direct ML labour process. Yimin, a data scientist, told me: "My managers don't understand the complex mathematics ... I am the one who decodes all of this for them". According to one study, "the vast majority" of data scientists say their "key skills" are not their technical skills but rather their "abilities to learn on the fly and to communicate well in order to answer business questions, explaining complex results to nontechnical stakeholders ... and convincing decision makers of their results" (Bowne-Anderson 2018). All of these stakeholders have interests in the successful valorization of capital. Their influence derives from the commodity form of contemporary AI, which entails that its labour process be executed in accord with the exigencies of valorization.

In sum, the ML labour process involves long hours of work and a high speed of production. Workers must continually adapt both to rapid technological change in the field and to pressures, throughout the process, from stakeholders with an interest in commoditized AI.

Empirical Control

The ML labour process is structured for maximum control of an indirect, deterritorialized variety. This is visible in the development methodologies and software tools that are employed. Nearly all my interviewees reported that their workplace uses an Agile development methodology (with varying degrees of formality). A development methodology is simply a way of dividing software production into distinct phases with the goal of optimizing design, production and management. Agile is a methodology designed especially for managing immaterial labour (i.e. software production). Agile was preceded by the waterfall development model, which posits a process of production in which rigidly specified stages follow one another in a linear order (Fig. 6.1).

The waterfall methodology was used in manufacturing and was tried out in early software work. However, as early as 1970, it was deemed "risky and invit[ing] failure" for software production because testing only occurs at the very end of the process; failure is only discovered then and can thus require restarting the entire process (Royce 1970, 329). The notion is that software products, due to the likelihood of bugs in the code,

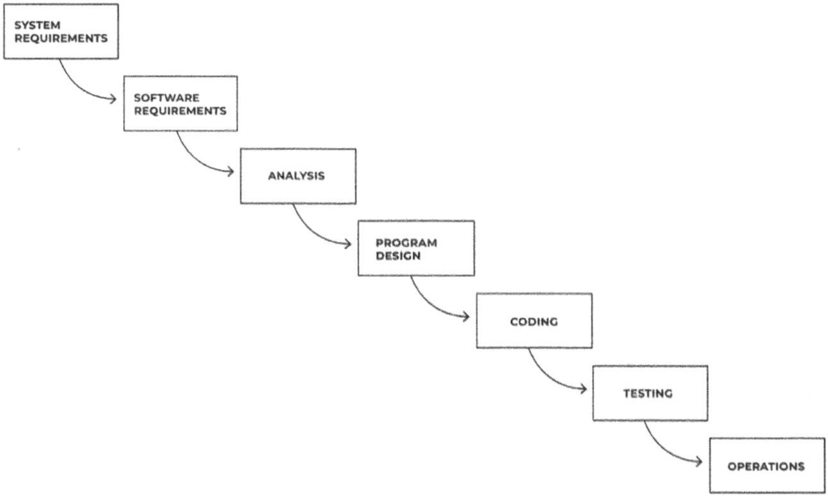

Fig. 6.1 Waterfall methodology (Adapted from Royce 1970)

cannot be specified in sufficient detail in advance, like a bridge or automobile can be. Agile was conceived to deal with this new degree of perceived contingency. While the waterfall method "assumes that variations are the result of errors", Agile expects that "external environmental changes cause critical variation", or in other words, that changes during development are inevitable (Highsmith and Cockburn 2001, 120). Proponents of Agile describe it as "the ability to create and respond to change. It is a way of dealing with, and ultimately succeeding in, an uncertain and turbulent environment" (Agile Alliance, n.d.). It is thus fitting for ML production which is "significantly … less predictable process than traditional software development since the models learn from data rather than specific human instruction" (Yao 2019). The "Manifesto for Agile Software Development" states the following principles:

> Individuals and interactions over processes and tools
> Working software over comprehensive documentation
> Customer collaboration over contract negotiation
> Responding to change over following a plan. (Beck et al. 2001)

The waterfall is a linear sequence that produces a complete product at its end. Agile, by contrast, functions incrementally, meaning that each step of the production process produces a new working part, and iteratively, recognizing the "impossibility (or at least improbability) of getting a feature right the first time" (Cohn 2010, 257). Agile development is thus organized into a series of loops called "sprints" which are usually between a week and a month long, at the end of which the workers are expected to deliver a working software component for integration into the larger project (Cohn 2010, 258). Dinesh, a senior software engineer, summed it up to me as "the idea of pushing something out early and iterating on it". A working prototype is produced as soon as possible and is progressively improved (Fig. 6.2).

There are dozens of approaches to software development that interpret and apply the principles of Agile in different ways. One that many of my interviewees mentioned (and perhaps the most popular overall) is Scrum (Denning 2015; Scrum Alliance 2018). Proponents of Scrum describe it as a "radically different approach" to software development which "reintroduces flexibility, adaptability, and productivity into systems development" (Schwaber and Beedle 2002, 1). It aims to increase the flexibility of Agile approaches by diffusing traditional management practices.

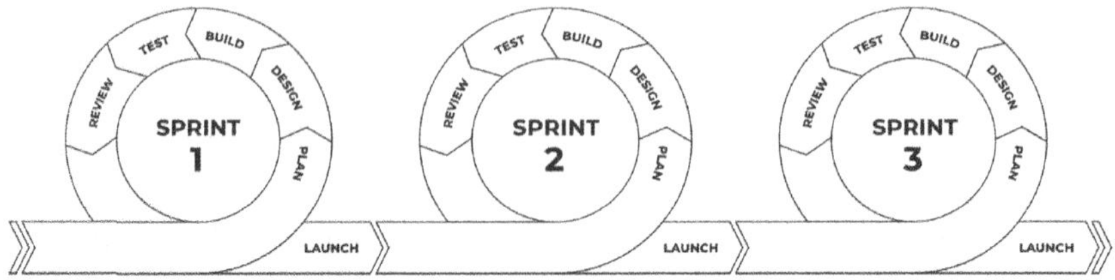

Fig. 6.2 Agile methodology (Adapted from Kuruppu 2019)

While Agile development in general may still be structured in a traditional hierarchical manner, in Scrum the workers, called the Scrum Team, are described as "self-organizing and fully autonomous. They are constrained only by the organization's standards and conventions, and by the Product Backlog that they have selected" (Schwaber and Beedle 2002, 9). The Product Backlog is a "prioritized list of project requirements" decided on by the Scrum Team, which is continually modified throughout production (Schwaber and Beedle 2002, 7). The items on the Product Backlog are dealt with through a system of commitment making. After deciding on a task and timeline, Carlo told me that management "treated it as a promise. Where if you missed it you'd have to give daily updates or hourly updates". He went on to elaborate how the commitment system is enforced through a peer accountability mechanism in which "there'd be someone else, another engineer, who'd co-sign with you. And they were also responsible for you finishing that task". With Scrum, a commitment to a peer takes the place of task delegation and specification by management (Fig. 6.3).

Since the Scrum Team determines how to complete its sprints autonomously, the function of management is redefined. Rather than direct and delegate, the manager's primary task is running the Daily Scrum. This is a fifteen-minute meeting, usually held in the morning, in which the Scrum Team assesses their progress, revises the Product Backlog and commits to their next tasks. People not in the Scrum Team may attend these meetings but may not speak or interfere in any way (Schwaber and Beedle 2002, 42). Outside the Daily Scrum, the manager interfaces with the rest of the company and beyond, to help the Scrum Team meet its commitments.

Proponents of Scrum argue that by "stripping away inappropriate and cumbersome management practices, Scrum leaves only the essence

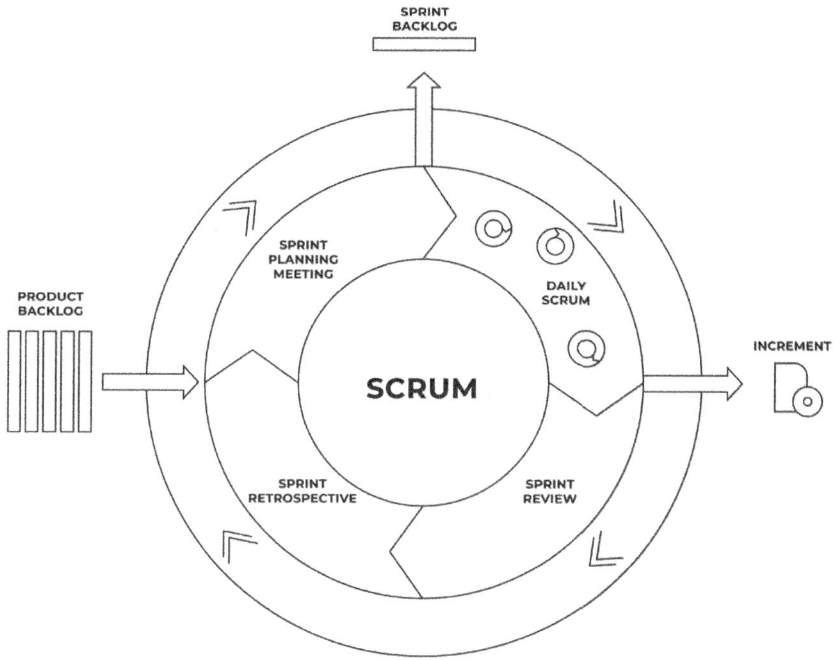

Fig. 6.3 Scrum methodology (Adapted from Weaver-Johnson 2017)

of work … Although the Scrum process seems simple and skeletal, it provides all the necessary management and controls to focus developers and quickly build quality products" (Schwaber and Beedle 2002, 10). My interviewees generally enjoyed the relative freedom provided by Scrum and Agile approaches. Chafic described the company he interned at as "very good about letting people manage their own time … They were pretty flexible. As long as your targets are being met. And you're making progress. I really liked that part. I didn't have to actually be at work. There would be days where I would just work from home". David, a lead scientist, expressed an interesting bipolarity of autonomy entailed by these development methods:

> On the one hand, what we are doing is decided … So on that level there is no autonomy because the projects are broadly set. But on the level of how exactly we're doing that I have complete autonomy. The absolute freedom

> to choose between techniques and approaches ... Or to do research into them if I feel it's necessary. That's one of the reasons I like working at a smaller place like this. I feel you get to set what the project is and you get to do what you're passionate about, what you like.

This agrees with Barrett's (2005) notion of "technical autonomy" in software work, as discussed in Chapter 2. However, while workers enjoy this sense of autonomy, Scrum remains a "management and control process" and a "kind of social engineering aiming to achieve the fulfillment of all by fostering cooperation", as its proponents put it (Schwaber and Beedle 2002, 1). And like other management techniques, Scrum has an interesting relationship to automation.

Scrum promoters Ken Schwaber and Mike Beedle distinguish between two kinds of production processes: defined and complex. Defined processes are "simple with unobtrusive noise", can be rigorously defined (like an algorithm) and can therefore be perfectly controlled or automated (Schwaber and Beedle 2002, 94). A process that cannot be rigorously defined is a complex process that must be controlled by what they call empirical means. The "empirical model of process control ... provides and exercises control through frequent inspection and adaptation for processes that are imperfectly defined and generate unpredictable and unrepeatable outputs" (Schwaber and Beedle 2002, 25). They offer this illustration:

> Chemical companies have advanced polymer plants that require empirical controls. Some chemical processes haven't been defined well enough for the plant to operate safely and repeatably using a defined process control model. Noise has rendered statistical controls ineffective. Frequent inspections and verification are required to successfully produce a batch. As chemical processes become better understood and the technology improves, the plants become more automated. However, assuming predictability too soon is the recipe for an industrial catastrophe. (Schwaber and Beedle 2002, 100–101)

Because the software labour process has only "partial and weak definitions", software development must likewise use empirical control (Schwaber and Beedle 2002, 95). Frequent surveillance is one function of the Daily Scrum. Rather than try to dictate step-by-step the work of expert software workers, Scrum management tracks their self-directed progress towards publicly agreed-upon commitments. The words of one

VP of engineering responding to a presentation on the Scrum methodology are instructive: "Fine … I'm willing to take the risk of giving the team autonomy for defined periods" (quoted in Schwaber and Beedle 2002, 82). Delimited autonomy is allowed because it enables workers to tackle problems that management does not know how to solve.

To better understand Scrum as a technique of empirical control, we can look at one of the software tools commonly used by its practitioners. Several of my interviewees reported using JIRA, a proprietary project management and bug tracking program. According to one commentator, "Agile methodology is built right into JIRA" (Nevogt 2019). JIRA allows centralized project management: "projects are logged into a central database and each one goes through a number of workflows (processes) … [which] control the status of the project as well as the rules by which it transitions to other statuses" (Nevogt 2019). A project is represented graphically as workflows consisting of issues represented as boxes (states) connected by arrows (transitions). This allows real-time collaboration and automatic generation of visualizations and reports tracking various aspects of the labour process. JIRA also functions as a surveillance system, including "feature-rich time tracking" and the option for automatic user screenshots, as frequently as every minute, so that management can "get accurate timesheets for [the] whole team" (Nevogt 2019). Advocates of Scrum are proud that there are "no mechanisms in Scrum for tracking the amount of time that a team works. Teams are measured by meeting goals, not by how many hours they take to meet the goal" (Schwaber and Beedle 2002, 73). JIRA, however, provides a technical way to inject time tracking and real-time surveillance into the ostensible freedom of the Scrum model. It provides fine-grained resolution for empirical control, the preferred management method for the ML labour process.

AI as Automation

AI is an automation technology and workers in the AI industry are its producers. It is true that many AI workers, as Siddharth Patel (2017) points out about tech workers generally, "are integral to the employing class's current efforts to flexibilize, speed up, or eliminate other people's work". Almost all of my interviewees recognized AI as an automation technology, although there was a range of evaluations as to its likely effects on employment and society.

Some interviewees held that eventually AI-based automation would entail a crisis of work (explored in the following section), while others expected that new jobs would appear to counterbalance those automated away. In both cases, they described automation in similar terms of desirable efficiency. Dinesh told me:

> people in the industry tend to think of ML, or AI … in terms of efficiency … We're discovering ways of making processes more efficient than they currently are … the way that technology contributes to the economy, it is in discovering new efficiencies … Uber is cool not because people are driving around or picking people up, but because it's more efficient than what the current system, or the preexisting system of getting rides was.

Dinesh went on to elaborate: "I definitely envision the work we're doing enabling automation in areas which are currently busywork … Should we pay someone four, five, six hundred thousand dollars a year just to say this is where the cancer is? That's a cost to our health system … In the long run, probably we shouldn't be paying that if we can automate that". This sentiment was echoed by David, a lead scientist, for whom "automation itself is about, broadly, timesaving" and by Tolu, a CEO, who said "It's about making processes more efficient. Which is what software is about in general … It's something people have to adopt to stay competitive … I sleep very well at night. I don't worry about … am I taking people's jobs away? Ask your blacksmith". David agreed that fears of technological unemployment are "always rooted in the lump of labour type fallacy where this certain demographic is going to be completely replaced and therefore those people will just lose their jobs … I think historically that hasn't really panned out".

The most popular opinion (even if it was not completely certain) was that AI-powered automation would ultimately produce a social benefit. Dinesh told me: "I am an optimist. I think if there are no sweatshops left, that would on the whole be a net good for humanity". Carlo similarly told me that he expects that the "overall impact on society … will be positive in the long run … I think it has potential to free up people's time so they can maybe do something else that's productive for the economy or their selves or whatever". David even evoked a Marxian spirit: "I would like to believe the early socialist and communist writers. That having that extra labour taken care of in the workforce will free people up for extra time. That your productivity will increase and therefore the time required for your work will decrease. That has never happened, but I would like to believe it".

The conversations I had with my interviewees about AI and automation were deep and nuanced, and a much longer discussion could be had here elaborating the similarities and differences of the different views expressed. However, the views of AI workers on the broadscale future social impacts of AI are not our primary concern here. Instead, I focus our analysis on how AI workers talked about AI work in particular. While discussing AI-powered automation and its prospects, my interviewees and I ended up talking about how their own labour was, and might be, affected by automation. What I learned surprised me and opened up an unexpected avenue for assessing the purported new autonomy of immaterial labour.

The Automation of AI Work

My interviewees told me that the production of ML is already being automated—via the recursive application of ML. Views on this were ambivalent; while some interviewees expressed concern for their jobs, others told me that they wanted more, not less, automation of their work. Those desiring more automation expressed their positive evaluation largely in terms of desirable efficiency, but also in terms of a unique necessity imposed by the nature of machine learning.

Carlo, an inference engineer, told me that while he thinks his job is safe for now, "something is going to automate it eventually ... But I'm not worried because I don't see any kind of general AI for decades, probably". Others saw more imminent threats. Nikolas, a data scientist, told me:

> if I want to secure my job in the future, maybe after five years, I need to learn new technologies. I need to step out of the typical ML models, move toward deep learning or move towards big data ... in my company, a few years before the data cleaning was performed using Excel. But now we have replaced all that with ... complex programs which take in the data and sort out all the anomalies and clean out the data.

Arvin, a R&D programmer, said:

> I think [the chance my work will be automated is] very high ... all work is possible to automate in my opinion ... the last few things to go will be very high end programming, that is, the part of my job that is the most creative and most intellectual ... But most of programming, let's say 70-80% of programming, is drudgery. It's a lot of ... moving around code ...

> doing all sorts of nonsense. All that is going to go away … the last things that will be to fall are other creative tasks, for instance, poetry and music. But even that, I hesitate to say because there are engines that can prepare … poetry now … Maybe mathematics … I need to start doing math … Too many people can do [programming]. And machines will soon be able to do it.

A comparable view was expressed by Yimin, a data scientist, who said "I think the next step for ML is to make it possible for anyone to run some pattern recognition or statistical task in little time, get the results for themselves". Chris, a startup CEO, discerned a similar threat:

> Machines will teach machines better. That's what's going to happen in the future … I think even ML jobs are going to be really, really replaced … most software related jobs are going to go eventually … in the next 20 years … People will just describe over voice commands – say 'OK, I want to build an Uber-like app that does X, Y, Z'. And then the computer will … simulate a couple of them … what you can build, as funny as it sounds, it's actually finite. It's very large, but it's finite. What's infinite is the design. But in terms of the core functionality what you're really doing is, you're inserting the data, you're applying some logic and you're storing the data. That's finite. What's infinite is 'OK, I want it to be this colour blue, I want the box here, I want this'. And we already have software solutions that do those kinds of approximations for us right now … people use Google Firebase, so I really see a lot of software jobs going in the future.

But not everyone was concerned. Some expressed the opposite opinion, calling automation desirable and even a necessity. Martin, a ML scientist, told me:

> for data scientists and ML scientists in general … I don't think the fact that it's being automated is a threat. It's sort of a convenience I would say, because then you can go and do more important stuff … higher level stuff. Things that actually matter … a few decades ago, you'd sit down and … use assembly, talking in 0s and 1s to the computer, which was really hard. And you wouldn't get too far. But now we have very high level languages … even the languages get updated and now the thing that was half a page of code is now just a couple of lines of code. So things go higher … You can go think about what matters.

Martin describes the automation of AI work as a convenience because it allows him to abstract from trivial details and work at a higher level of abstraction, getting more complex work done more easily. Yimin, a data scientist, was similarly enthusiastic about automation of his work and described it as a necessity in software production:

> I think if you work as a programmer, as a general rule, if you keep doing the same thing for six months you have to start to think of automating. It shouldn't take much longer than that. And if you keep doing the same routine job for a year, you're probably doing it wrong. There must be a higher level of abstraction ... make things easier for yourself ... you don't have the limitation of tools and material. A civil engineer needs all the steel, and all the workers, to build a thing he designed. But if you design something in the computer you can ... test it, tear it down and build something on top of it that operates it. We should always move towards automating. That's what I always ask everyone in our crew ... what is the routine and if we can automate it, let's do it.

For Yimin, software work has the advantage of occurring within the recursive environment of the computer. Since the material of software work is code, once a task becomes routinized, it can be easily automated by writing a suitable program; one does not have to build a specialized machine.

Yimin's desire for software work to always move towards automation appears to be shared by many workers in the AI industry. Automation is said to be appealing because data scientists "don't particularly love munging and cleaning data ... [they consider it a] waste of their skills to be polishing the materials they rely on" (Theuwissen 2015, 9). One industry commentator agrees that it "seems like a natural progression to automate what can be safely automated and preserve our time for the creative portions of data science" (Vorhies 2017b). Another even argues "automation is the *responsibility* of the seasoned practitioner" because it "ensures our work focuses solely on what is novel to the challenge" (McClure 2018, emphasis original). Efficient allocation of resources is not, however, the only reason for desiring more automation. Another reason derives from the unique nature of machine learning.

Dinesh, a senior software engineer, explained to me that the ML labour process requires a lot of guesswork and experimentation. This lack of knowledge, he held, was a primary motivation for automating ML work:

> there's a lot of dark art to the design and layout of a neural network. You're ... drawing a graph and ... you have this expectation that data is going to flow through this graph in some way and you're going to update these things and there's some relationship between the shape of the layout of this graph and the quality of the outputs that come through it. What is that relationship? ... nobody really has more than a cursory understanding ... Well, we know how to make it really, really bad. We know what not to do ... And if we wanna get better performance we can tweak it a little bit. But we don't actually have a firm model or theory behind it ... if you've got a model going, it's doing these predictions, you're sitting there and you're trying to tweak it to get a little more performance. And some of this tweaking is random and some of it is, like, enlightened randomness ... And we pay people quite a bit to be better than random at this. But at the end of the day, they're not experts at this. They don't have this deep understanding of how to make the perfect network that works as well as it possibly can ... In my mind, automating this process of exploring, trying different types of networks, that seems a very natural leap to me ... There are many aspects of ML where we actually use ML systems to try to tweak it in various ways. And this is just a growth of that into: can we try to use ML to learn all the parameters of a ML network itself? So it seems like an incremental development to me.

In Dinesh's formulation, it is the lack of knowledge about how to best create ML systems that drives the automation of their production. This position was not expressed by other interviewees, but its foundational point, that ML is an occult technology produced by occult means, is widely held. The occult nature of ML is connected to the nascence of the technology. An article in business magazine *Forbes* notes that a "mature ecosystem of machine learning developer tools simply does not exist [and] ML practitioners generally manage their workflows in ad hoc ways" (Toews 2020) and a survey of data scientists agrees that there "isn't a codified set of strategies" (Theuwissen 2015, 13). In the absence of a codified labour process, the production of ML relies on oblique means. Quoc Le, a Google machine-learning researcher, admits "We do it by intuition" (quoted in Simonite 2017b). AI entrepreneur Sean McClure (2018) argues that data science is an "art" because "knowing what knobs to turn, and by how much, cannot be codified. It involves experience, conversation with domain experts, and above-all trial and error".

Historically, as both Marx and Braverman argued, the automation of labour processes has been preceded by their analysis, fragmentation and codification. According to the above accounts, the ML labour process resists codification. The production of ML requires initiation into a "dark art" drawing on intuition, guesswork, aesthetic sense and experience. Despite this, it is being automated. Something would seem to be amiss with the Marxist understanding of automation; here automation is occurring without a preceding codification. Indeed, Dinesh's account suggests that the production of ML is being automated *precisely because* it has been resistant to codification. Can a Marxist perspective grasp this re-articulation of automation and codification? I believe so, and I believe this re-articulation provides a critical counterpoint to claims for the new autonomy of immaterial labour. Towards that end, the next section explicates the automation of the ML labour process in some detail.

Automated Machine Learning

The ML labour process is being automated with a growing collection of techniques known collectively as automated machine learning or AutoML. The mention, by one of my interviewees, of a particular technique called hyperparameter optimization put me on the trail of AutoML in general. AutoML uses ML to automate tasks in the ML labour process. Commenting on its recursive nature, Campbell (2020) compares AutoML to an "ouroboros eating its own tail". The roots of AutoML go back to the 1990s, but the term AutoML first appeared in 2014 when a workshop was devoted to it at the International Conference on Machine Learning. Its popularity increased thereafter, propelled by a series of contests (Guyon et al. 2015; Zöller and Huber 2019). In the handful of years since I conducted the interviews for this book in 2017–2018, AutoML has gone from an expensive experimental project for the tech giants to a practical automation technology. The creators of AutoML library TransmogrifAI (n.d.) boast that their product "achieves accuracies close to hand-tuned models with almost 100x reduction in time". AutoML is now the basis for open-source projects like Auto-sklearn and Auto-Keras as well as commodities from tech giants (Google Cloud AutoML, Baidu AutoDL, Amazon Sagemaker, Facebook FBNet, Microsoft Azure Automated ML) and startups (DataRobot, H2O Driverless AI, Big Squid).

AutoML can be applied in all three stages of the ML labour process. In the first stage, data processing, AutoML applications such as MLBox are available for automated cleaning and formatting of data. According to machine learning scientists Marc-André Zöller and Marco Huber (2019), "low quality data can be automatically detected and corrected" although "advanced and domain specific data cleaning is conferred to the user" (19–20). Feature engineering, which tends to require domain knowledge, as well as intuition and a lot of trial and error, is also being automated via "feature learning" networks which automatically generate and test possible features (Hardesty 2015; Koehrsehn 2018). Efforts to automate data labelling are also underway. Companies such as ClaySciences and DataLoop are producing "automatic annotation" AI systems, which make an initial pass at labelling datasets, so that ghost workers have only to provide corrections and supplementary information (Singer 2019; DataLoop, n.d.). While at the time of writing the worker remains essential, one machine learning expert predicts data labelling will be fully automated in five to ten years (Nakashima 2018).

AutoML is also being applied in the second stage of the ML labour process, model building, in at least two ways. The first is designing the architecture of artificial neural networks, a task which requires a "significant amount of time and experimentation by those with significant machine learning expertise" because "the search space of all possible models can be combinatorially large — a typical 10-layer network can have ~10^{10} candidate networks" (Zoph and Le 2017). It is often not possible to say in advance which architecture will work best for an unfamiliar problem. This task is automated with ML-powered "neural architecture search" which automatically designs and compares possible architectures (Elsken et al. 2019). Microsoft in particular has a technique called "human-assisted search" in which "researchers can identify a promising arrangement for massive neural networks, and then the system can cycle through a range of similar possibilities until it settles on this [sic] best one" (Metz 2016). AutoML can also be used to automate a second aspect of model building, the aforementioned hyperparameter optimization, which involves configuring the internal settings that govern the behaviour of a model to optimize specific metrics, such as training time and accuracy. It is automated in a way analogous to neural architecture search, via the automatic design and testing of many candidate configurations (Li and Talkwalkar 2018).

Finally, AutoML can also be used in the deployment stage. Companies such as Seldon automate the process of "wrapping" a ML model in a different programming language API while Microsoft Machine Learning Service automates the task of deploying a ML model as a web service, ready for embedding in applications (ThinkGradient 2019). Maintenance of deployed models can also be automated with applications such as DataRobot's MLOps.

The ML labour process is clearly automatable. Yet, as we have seen, it is resistant to codification. To grasp this situation, which seems to defy Marxist conceptualizations of automation, I propose the notion of synthetic automation.

Synthetic Automation

Marx (1993) aptly described the "road along which machinery, by and large, arose, and ... the road on which it progresses" as a process of "dissection" (704). Labour processes are fragmented through the division of labour, "which gradually transforms the workers' operations into more and more mechanical ones, so that at a certain point a mechanism can step into their places" (Marx 1993, 704). But Marx also suggested that once industry and technology are highly developed and "all the sciences have been pressed into the service of capital; and when ... the available machinery itself already provides great capabilities", new machines may be devised through the "analysis and application of mechanical and chemical laws, arising directly out of science" (Marx 1993, 704). Here it is possible to read Marx as suggesting that when technology is sufficiently advanced, automation becomes possible without the preceding capture and codification of a labour process. ML provides a concrete example of how this can occur.

Brynjolfsson and McAfee (2017) assert that, prior to ML, the "inability to articulate our own knowledge meant that we couldn't automate many tasks" (4). Indeed, during the first era of the AI industry, the capture of tacit knowledge via knowledge engineering was a recognized obstacle to making effective expert systems (Collins et al. 1986). However, because ML can extract models directly from data, it can be applied to automate labour processes for which "we do not have an algorithm" (Alpaydin 2014, 1). In other words, ML may be leveraged to automate labour processes, which have not been codified or broken down into precisely defined stages. The recursive production of algorithms with algorithms enables the automation of labour processes for which we do not have algorithms. With AutoML, another layer of recursion is added. The goal is not only to produce a model from data, but to produce a "machine learning model that can optimize the training of machine learning models" (Metz 2016).

I propose the term *synthetic automation* for the form of automation presented embryonically in ML and AutoML. Here I draw a comparison to Alfred Sohn-Rethel's (1978) notion of "synthetic timing" (155). In a meditation on the temporalities of capital, Sohn-Rethel (1978) describes how Taylorism progressed from simply studying how long a given task typically takes a worker (empirical timing) to specifying how long it ought to take (coercive timing) and eventually to synthetic timing, or construing a "time norm for a job … without consulting or watching the worker, even for new jobs which have never yet been practiced" (155). Synthetic timing norms are calculated on the basis of "technological categories" of time and motion derived from "no true terms of human labour at all … human labour is made into a technological entity" (Sohn-Rethel 1978, 155). Based on observation of task X and a particularly conception of the human body and its capacities, management projects the appropriate time norms for task Y before production ever begins. Synthetic automation represents an analogous shift from the empirical to the synthetic, but in the context of labour and its replacement by machines. Instead of automating by observing, fragmenting and codifying an existing labour process performed by workers and then engineering a machine replacement, synthetic automation aims to produce such replacements without regard for the precedents set by living labour. For another analogy, we can look to media theorist Vilém Flusser's distinction between traditional, technical and synthetic images.

For Flusser (2011), traditional images, such as paintings, which are produced by artists, are distinguished from technical images, which are produced automatically by machines such as the camera (36). Technical images are the results of mechanisms and chemical processes not under the direct control of an artist, but the indirect control of a user of a machine. Technical images, however, remain reflections of a pre-existing reality. This changes with the advent of "synthetically generated" models produced automatically from abstract specifications:

> The computer operator visualizes an airplane as one might be found in the outside world. Then he takes an apparatus in hand … to 'grasp' what he has visualized (through concepts such as 'aerodynamic equations' or 'production costs'). The apparatus calculates these concepts automatically … making a visualization of an airplane appear on the screen. (Flusser 2011, 42–43)

Synthetic automation likewise automates not by reflecting or capturing a pre-existing, codified labour process but by generating a model from data. An algorithm is produced without a labour process first being dissected.

Consider GOFAI or classical AI as automation. This is especially clear with the expert system, intended to eliminate the worker by capturing her knowledge and skills about how to solve a problem via knowledge engineering. ML is a different kind of automation. From a perspective concerned with labour, ML eliminates (in practice, imperfectly) the need for a worker who knows the solution to a problem by extracting a model from data. Consider DeepMind's go playing system AlphaGo Zero, which learned to defeat human masters of the game not by studying human game data, but by playing itself in simulations and refining a model via reinforcement learning (Silver et al. 2017). Could such an approach be applied to the automation of labour processes? This is what is suggested by ML, in which an algorithm produces an algorithm. One commentator thus describes ML as "automating automation" (Raschka 2016). However, as should be clear by now, ML is far from full automation; it requires skilled workers to collect and prepare data, build and tweak algorithms and architectures and train, deploy and maintain models. AutoML (again, imperfectly, in practice) aims to reduce the necessary human component, eliminating not only the need for a worker from whom knowledge of a labour process may be captured, but also the need for knowledge of the dark art of ML. It aims to replace the data scientist with brute force automated experimentation. AutoML has thus, prolixly, been called the "automation of automating automation" (Mayo 2016). I suggest that AutoML represents a possible technological trajectory for capital; a trajectory defined by the possibility of dispensing with labour in terms of both conceiving of the problem and a solution, as well as understanding and creating the means by which a solution might be produced automatically.

The ultimate recursive capacity of ML is imagined by Domingos (2015) as the "master algorithm" or a single algorithm that can "learn all that can be learned from data" (24). This is a hypothetical learning algorithm which, if given the appropriate data, "can approximate any function arbitrarily closely—which is math-speak for learning anything" (Domingos 2015, 24). In other words, the master algorithm can produce a model to solve any problem. Here Domingos gestures back to the Turing Machine's capacity for the universal simulation of other machines, but with a recursive enhancement. The master algorithm exceeds the

Turing Machine insofar as it not only simulates any other machine; it automatically produces any other machine. The master algorithm represents the ideal culmination of synthetic automation as an AGI devoted to the intensification of real subsumption. It is not difficult to imagine the enthusiasm capital would have for such a general means of automating labour processes.

It is no coincidence that AutoML is a primary component of the push for the so-called "democratization" of AI. This movement is motivated by the tech giants for whom it means making it possible for "the citizen data scientist (aka lesser or untrained amateurs) to build some [ML] models directly" (Vorhies 2017a). But this ostensibly benevolent gesture has as its other face the increasing organic composition of AI capital. Jeff Dean, head of Google Brain, asks: "[c]urrently the way you solve problems is you have expertise and data and computation … Can we eliminate the need for a lot of machine-learning expertise?" (Simonite 2017a). Towards this end, the tech giants have developed "one-click" and "end-to-end" AutoML packages which aim to streamline the entire ML labour process into a user-friendly app requiring little technical knowledge. Offerings include Uber Michelangelo ML, Baidu's EZDL and Facebook's FBLearner Flow, a "machine learning assembly line" (Metz 2016).

Existing end-to-end AutoML commodities are limited to producing simple models but experimental systems point to more complex possibilities (Toews 2020). In April 2019, Google's AI lab demonstrated a "full automation" AutoML system. The Google AutoML system was entered in a Kaggle Hackathon which challenged participants to produce a model for predicting manufacturing defects and took second place against grandmaster-level data science competition (Lu 2019). While precise details of the system have not been made available, according to the Google AI blog, "[d]ata and computation resources are the only inputs, while a servable TensorFlow model is the output. The whole process requires no human intervention" (Lu 2019).[2]

Despite this example, and the proliferation of AutoML commodities, one might reasonably argue that AutoML is merely the latest manifestation of the hype that has followed AI since its inception. AutoML

[2] An important qualification to note is that finding and collecting appropriate input data in the first place is a substantial task for which human intervention remains essential, so end-to-end is, in a sense, a misnomer until that too is automated.

techniques consume such large amounts of computational power (even by the high standards of ML) that critics argued in 2017 that it "that it's not yet practical to think about lightening the load, or partially replacing, machine-learning experts" with AutoML (Simonite 2017a; see also Simonite 2017b). However, only two years later in 2019 dozens of AutoML applications were finding customers via cloud platforms. That being said, there are good reasons not to expect the wholesale automation of AI work in the near future. Berthold (2019) argues that expert-level data science problems often involve answering "open-ended" or "research type" questions which are not amenable to the brute force methods of AutoML. Others argue that while AutoML has had some success in feature engineering, expert-level work on this task requires knowledge, extraneous to the data, of the domain being worked within. For this reason, data scientists often collaborate with domain experts, and this is a supposedly non-automatable phenomenon (Oliveira 2019). The future will tell. I will leave absolute statements about the capacities of AutoML to someone better qualified.

Other Forms of Automation in Machine Learning

According to data scientist Marcia Oliveira (2019), existing AutoML systems work only with supervised learning, for which data are labelled. AutoML works by automating the supervisory function, automatically adjusting a model until it achieves the desired output. Such an approach cannot be applied in unsupervised learning, where data is unlabelled and perhaps unstructured. If unsupervised learning is the future of ML, as some believe (LeCun et al. 2015), then AutoML may have a limited window of applicability. However, there are a variety of other attempts being made to automate unsupervised learning with ways other than AutoML. One of these is the use of evolutionary algorithms to evolve deep learning network architectures (Wistuba 2018). Another is meta-learning, which attempts to have a system learn its own learning algorithm (Finn 2017). Yet another is not typically described as automation, but could play a key role in overcoming the data/labour bottleneck.

Whether supervised or unsupervised, ML requires a lot of data. One recursive solution to this requirement is the production of synthetic data. ML is being applied to generate synthetic data which can then be used to train ML models which, according to one experiment, exhibit "no significant difference" in performance from models trained on real-world data (Patki et al. 2016, 1). Synthetic data can be created in several ways. One can use a generative adversarial network (GAN). GANs can generate very convincing photos of people and objects which have never existed in the real world by engaging in a metaphorical counterfeiting operation between two networks. One network tries to generate new images and pass them off as part of the original dataset while the other attempts to discern which ones the first has made (Goodfellow et al. 2014). Throughout this process, both networks improve at their respective tasks and can produce synthetic data indistinguishable from real. There are also less elaborate techniques for "data augmentation" which involve expanding existing datasets by automatically making small changes to the items therein (He et al. 2019, 3). In short, AutoML is only one way in which the production of ML is being automated.

Conclusion

This chapter has looked at the ML labour process. While workers are far from expendable in the contemporary AI industry, their labours are increasingly augmented with automation technologies. This is one way, I have argued, in which the ML labour process is evidently structured by the exigencies of valorization. The influence of the valorization process is also evident in the long working hours, frenetic pace of work, continuous influence of stakeholders and management practices of empirical control. I showed how, since the AI industry is a new industry, much of the ML labour process has yet to be codified, and even experts achieve results only by intuition, guesswork and sheer trial and error. Finally, I discussed how, despite a lack of codification, components of the ML labour process are being automated with the recursive application of ML. I suggested the notion of synthetic automation to describe this technique of automation. I also suggested that synthetic automation might represent a qualitatively novel type of automation and a future technological trajectory for capital. This possibility is elaborated further in the next chapter where I critique *post-operaismo*'s claim for a new autonomy of immaterial labour.

Bibliography

Agile Alliance. n.d. Agile 101. https://www.agilealliance.org/agile101/. Accessed 23 Aug 2019.

Alpaydin, Ethem. 2014. *Introduction to Machine Learning*. Cambridge: MIT Press.

Alpaydin, Ethem. 2016. *Machine Learning: The New AI*. Cambridge: MIT Press.

Barrett, Rowena. 2005. Managing the Software Development Labour Process: Direct Control, Time and Technical Autonomy. In *Management, Labour Process and Software Development: Reality Bites*, ed. Rowena Barrett. New York: Routledge.

Beck, Kent, Mike Beedle, Arie Van Bennekum, Alistair Cockburn, Ward Cunningham, Martin Fowler, James Grenning, Jim Highsmith, Andrew Hunt, Ron Jeffries, Jon Kern, Brian Marick, Robert C. Martin, Steve Mellor, Ken Schwaber, Jeff Sutherland, and Dave Thomas. 2001. Manifesto for Agile Software Development. http://agilemanifesto.org/.

Berthold, Michael R. 2019. What Does It Take to Be a Successful Data Scientist? *Harvard Data Science Review* 1 (2).

Bowne-Anderson, Huge. 2018. What Data Scientists Really Do, According to 35 Data Scientists. *Harvard Business Review*, August 15. https://hbr.org/2018/08/what-data-scientists-really-do-according-to-35-data-scientis=ts?referral=03758&cm_vc=rr_item_page.top_right.

Brownlee, Jason. 2013. How to Prepare Data for Machine Learning. *Machine Learning Mastery*, December 25. https://machinelearningmastery.com/how-to-prepare-data-for-machine-learning/.

Brownlee, Jason. 2014. Discover Feature Engineering, How to Engineer Features and How to Get Good at It. *Machine Learning Mastery*, September 26. https://machinelearningmastery.com/discover-feature-engineering-how-to-engineer-features-and-how-to-get-good-at-it/.

Brownlee, Jason. 2015. Gentle Introduction to Predictive Modeling. *Machine Learning Mastery*, September 20. https://machinelearningmastery.com/gentle-introduction-to-predictive-modeling/.

Brownlee, Jason. 2016. Supervised and Unsupervised Machine Learning Algorithms. *Machine Learning Mastery*, March 16. https://machinelearningmastery.com/supervised-and-unsupervised-machine-learning-algorithms/.

Brynjolfsson, Erik, and Andrew McAfee. 2017. The Business of Artificial Intelligence: What It Can–and Cannot–Do for Your Organization. *Harvard Business Review Digital Articles* 7: 3–11.

Campbell, Mark. 2020. Automated Coding: The Quest to Develop Programs That Develop Programs. *Computer* 53 (2, February).

Cohn, Mike. 2010. *Succeeding with Agile: Software Development Using Scrum*. Upper Saddle River, NJ: Pearson Education.

Collins, Harry M., Rodney H. Green, and Robert C. Draper. 1986. Where's the Expertise? Expert Systems as a Medium of Knowledge Transfer. In *Proceedings of the Fifth Technical Conference of the British Computer Society Specialist Group on Expert Systems on Expert Systems 85*, ed. M.J. Merry, 323–334. Cambridge: Cambridge University Press.

Crowdflower. 2016. 2016 Data Science Report. https://visit.figure-eight.com/rs/416-ZBE-142/images/CrowdFlower_DataScienceReport_2016.pdf.

Dash, Anil. 2012. The Blue Collar Coder. *Anil Dash's Blog*, October 5. https://anildash.com/2012/10/05/the_blue_collar_coder/.

DataLoop. n.d. Machine Learning Ready-to-Use Datasets. https://www.dataloop.ai/create-your-datasets#!!.

DataRobot. n.d. Machine Learning Model Deployment. https://www.datarobot.com/wiki/machine-learning-model-deployment/.

Denning, Steve. 2015. Agile: The World's Most Popular Innovation Engine. *Forbes*, July 23. https://www.forbes.com/sites/stevedenning/2015/07/23/the-worlds-most-popular-innovation-engine/#77ccfe27c769.

Dettmers, Tim. 2015. Deep Learning in a Nutshell: Core Concepts. *NVidia Developer Blog*, November 3. https://devblogs.nvidia.com/deep-learning-nutshell-core-concepts/. Accessed 5 Nov 2018.

Domingos, Pedro. 2015. *The Master Algorithm: How the Quest for the Ultimate Learning Machine Will Remake Our World*. New York: Basic Books.

Dong, Catherine. 2017. The Evolution of Machine Learning. *TechCrunch*, August 18. https://techcrunch.com/2017/08/08/the-evolution-of-machine-learning/. Accessed 12 Sept 2018.

Elsken, Thomas, Jan Hendrik Metzen, and Frank Hutter. 2019. Neural Architecture Search: A Survey. *Journal of Machine Learning Research* 20 (55): 1–21.

Etzioni, Oren. 2018. AI Advances Require 99 Percent Manual Labor. *MIT Technology Review*, March 26. https://www.technologyreview.com/video/610647/ai-advances-require-99-percent-manual-labor/.

Finn, Chelsea. 2017. Learning to Learn. *Berkeley Artificial Intelligence Research Blog*, July 18. https://bair.berkeley.edu/blog/2017/07/18/learning-to-learn/. Accessed 13 Sept 2018.

Flusser, Vilém. 2011. *Into the Universe of Technical Images*, trans. Nancy Ann Roth. Minneapolis/London: University of Minnesota Press.

Goodfellow, Ian, Jean Pouget-Abadie, Mehdi Mirza, Bing Xu, David Warde-Farley, Sherjil Ozair, Aaron Courville, and Yoshua Bengio. 2014. Generative Adversarial Nets. In *Advances in Neural Information Processing Systems* 27, ed. Z. Ghahramani, M. Welling, C. Cortes, N.D. Lawrence, and K.Q. Weinberger, 2672–2680.

Google. 2019. Data Preparation and Feature Engineering in ML. *Google Developers*. https://developers.google.com/machine-learning/data-prep.

Google. n.d. reCAPTCHA v3: The New Way to Stop Bots. https://www.google.com/recaptcha/intro/v3beta.html. Accessed 7 Nov 2018.

Gray, Drew. 2019. Introducing Voyage DeepDrive. *Voyage*. https://news.voyage.auto/introducing-voyage-deepdrive-69b3cf0f0be6.

Guyon, Isabelle, Kristin Bennett, Gavin Cawley, Hugo Jair Escalante, Sergio Escalera, Tin Kam Ho, Núria Macià et al. 2015. Design of the 2015 Chalearn Automl Challenge. In *2015 International Joint Conference on Neural Networks (IJCNN)*, 1–8. IEEE.

Hardesty, Larry. 2015. Automating Big-Data Analysis. *MIT News*, October 16. https://news.mit.edu/2015/automating-big-data-analysis-101.

He, Xin, Kaiyong Zhao, and Xiaowen Chu. 2019. AutoML: A Survey of the State-of-the-Art. arXiv preprint arXiv:1908.00709.

Highsmith, Jim, and Alistair Cockburn. 2001. Agile Software Development: The Business of Innovation. *Computer* 34 (9): 120–127.

Knight, Will. 2017. Reinforcement Learning. *MIT Technology Review*. https://www.technologyreview.com/s/603501/10-breakthrough-technologies-2017-reinforcement-learning/. Accessed 7 Nov 2018.

Koehrsen, William. 2018. Why Automated Feature Learning Will Change the Way You Do Machine Learning. *KDNuggets*. https://www.kdnuggets.com/2018/08/automated-feature-engineering-will-change-machine-learning.html.

Kraft, Philip. 1977. *Programmers and Managers: The Routinization of Computer Programming in the United States*. New York: Springer.

Kraft, Philip. 1979. The Industrialization of Computer Programming: From Programming to 'Software Production'. In *Case Studies on the Labor Process*, ed. Andrew S. Zimbalist. New York: Monthly Review Press.

Kraft, Philip, and Steven Dubnoff. 1986. Job Content, Fragmentation, and Control in Computer Software Work. *Industrial Relations: A Journal of Economy and Society* 25 (2): 184–196.

Kuruppu, Dasith. 2019. Agile Development from a Programmer's Perspective. *Level Up Coding*, January 2. https://levelup.gitconnected.com/agile-from-a-developers-perspective-27b23ea665f0.

LeCun, Yan, Yoshua Bengio, and Geoffrey Hinton. 2015. Deep Learning. *Nature* 521: 436–444.

Li, Liam, and Ameet Talkwalkar. 2018. What Is Neural Architecture Search? *O'Reilly*, December 20. https://www.oreilly.com/ideas/what-is-neural-architecture-search.

Locklin, Scott. 2014. Neglected Machine Learning Ideas. *Locklin on Science*, July 22. https://scottlocklin.wordpress.com/2014/07/22/neglected-machine-learning-ideas/.

Lu, Yifeng. 2019. An End-to-End AutoML Solution for Tabular Data at Kaggle-Days. *Google AI Blog*, May 9. https://ai.googleblog.com/2019/05/an-end-to-end-automl-solution-for.html.

Luo, Zelun, Boya Peng, De-An Huang, Alexandre Alahi, and Li Fei-Fei. 2017. *Unsupervised Learning of Long-Term Motion Dynamics for Videos*. arXiv preprint arXiv:1701.018212.

Marx, Karl. 1993. *Grundrisse*. New York: Penguin.

Mayo, Matthew. 2016. The Case for Machine Learning in Business. *LinkedIn*, October 3. https://www.linkedin.com/pulse/case-machine-learning-business-matthew-mayo/.

McClure, Sean. 2018. GUI-Fying the Machine Learning Workflow: Towards Rapid Discovery of Viable Pipelines. *Towards Data Science*, June 25. https://towardsdatascience.com/gui-fying-the-machine-learning-workflow-towards-rapid-discovery-of-viable-pipelines-cab2552c909f.

Metz, Cade. 2016. Building AI Is Hard—So Facebook Is Building AI That Builds AI. *Wired*, May 6. https://www.wired.com/2016/05/facebook-trying-create-ai-can-create-ai/.

Meyer, Mathias. 2014. Continuous Integration and Its Tools. *IEEE Software* 31 (3): 14–16.

Nakashima, Ryan. 2018. AI's Dirty Little Secret: It's Powered by People. *Phys.org*, March 5. https://phys.org/news/2018-03-ai-dirty-secret-powered-people.html.

Nevogt, Dave. 2019. JIRA Project Management: A How-to Guide for Beginners. *HubStaff*, May 16. https://blog.hubstaff.com/jira-project-management-guide-beginners/.

Oliveira, Marcia. 2019. 3 Reasons Why AutoML Won't Replace Data Scientists Yet. *KDnuggets*, March. https://www.kdnuggets.com/2019/03/why-automl-wont-replace-data-scientists.html.

OpenAI. 2019. Multi-Agent Hide and Seek. *YouTube*, September 17. https://www.youtube.com/watch?v=kopoLzvh5jY.

Patel, Siddharth. 2017. Tech Workers: Friend or Foes? *Jacobin*, August 25. https://www.jacobinmag.com/2017/08/silicon-valley-gentrification-tech-sharing-economy.

Patki, Neha, Roy Wedge, and Kalyan Veeramachaneni. 2016. The Synthetic Data Vault. In *2016 IEEE International Conference on Data Science and Advanced Analytics (DSAA)*, 399–410. IEEE.

Paul, Sayak. 2018. Turning Machine Learning Models into APIs in Python. *DataCamp*, October 25. https://www.datacamp.com/community/tutorials/machine-learning-models-api-python.

Raschka, Sebastian. 2016. How to Explain Machine Learning to a Software Engineer. *KDnuggets*, May. https://www.kdnuggets.com/2016/05/explain-machine-learning-software-engineer.html.

Roh, Yuji, Geon Heo, and Steven Euijong Whang. 2019. A Survey on Data Collection for Machine Learning: a Big Data-AI Integration Perspective. *IEEE Transactions on Knowledge and Data Engineering*. https://doi.org/10.1109/TKDE.2019.2946162.

Royce, Winston W. 1970. Managing the Development of Large Software Systems: Concepts and Techniques. In *Proceedings of the 9th International Conference on Software Engineering*, 328–338. Los Alamitos, CA: IEEE Computer Society Press.

Schwaber, Ken, and Mike Beedle. 2002. *Agile Software Development with Scrum*. Upper Saddle River: Prentice Hall.

Scrum Alliance. 2018. State of Scrum 2017–2018. https://www.scrumalliance.org/ScrumRedesignDEVSite/media/ScrumAllianceMedia/Files%20and%20PDFs/State%20of%20Scrum/2017-SoSR-Final-Version-(Pages).pdf.

Silver, David, Julian Schrittwieser, Karen Simonyan, Ioannis Antonoglou, Aja Huang, Arthur Guez, Thomas Hubert, Lucas Baker, Matthew Lai, Adrian Bolton, Yutian Chen, Timothy Lillicrap, Fan Hui, Laurent Sifre, George van den Driessche, Thore Graepel, and Demis Hassabis. 2017. Mastering the Game of Go Without Human Knowledge. *Nature* 550 (7676): 354.

Simonite, Tom. 2017a. AI Software Learns to Make AI Software. *MIT Technology Review*, January 18. https://www.technologyreview.com/s/603381/ai-software-learns-to-make-ai-software/.

Simonite, Tom. 2017b. Why Google's CEO Is Excited About Automating Artificial Intelligence. *MIT Technology Review*, May 17. https://www.technologyreview.com/s/607894/why-googles-ceo-is-excited-about-automating-artificial-intelligence/.

Singer, Daniel. 2019. This AI Startup Accelerates Machine Learning Model Creation. *StartupHub*, March 21. https://www.startuphub.ai/this-ai-startup-accelerates-machine-learning-model-creation/.

Sohn-Rethel, Alfred. 1978. *Intellectual and Manual Labour: A Critique of Epistemology*. London: Macmillan.

Sun, Ron. 2014. Connectionism and Neural Networks. In *The Cambridge Handbook of Artificial Intelligence*, ed. Keith Frankish and William M. Ramsey, 108–127. Cambridge: Cambridge University Press.

Sutton, Richard S., and Andrew G. Barto. 1998. *Reinforcement Learning: An Introduction*. Cambridge: MIT Press.

Theuwissen, Martijn. 2015. The Different Data Science Roles in the Industry. *KDnuggets*, November. https://www.kdnuggets.com/2015/11/different-data-science-roles-industry.html.

ThinkGradient. 2019. Automated Machine Learning—An Overview. *Medium*, January 20. https://medium.com/thinkgradient/automated-machine-learning-an-overview-5a3595d5c4b5.

Thompson, Clive. 2019. *Coders: The Making of a New Tribe and the Remaking of the World*. New York: Penguin.

Toews, Rob. 2020. A Massive Opportunity Exists to Build 'Picks and Shovels' for Machine Learning. *Forbes*, March 22. https://www.forbes.com/sites/robtoews/2020/03/22/a-massive-opportunity-exists-to-build-picks-and-shovels-for-machine-learning/#6b3f036a7ab3.

TransmogrifAI. n.d. About. https://transmogrif.ai/.

Vorhies, William. 2017a. Data Scientists Automated and Unemployed by 2025—Update! *Data Science Central*, July 17. https://www.datasciencecentral.com/profiles/blogs/data-scientists-automated-and-unemployed-by-2025-update.

Vorhies, William. 2017b. More on Fully Automated Machine Learning. *Data Science Central*, August 15. https://www.datasciencecentral.com/profiles/blogs/more-on-fully-automated-machine-learning.

Weaver-Johnson, Lonnie. 2017. What Is Scrum? *LWJ Solutions*. http://www.lwjsolutions.com/what-is-scrum/.

Wistuba, Martin. 2018. Using AI to Design Deep Learning Architectures. *IBM Research Blog*, September 4. https://www.ibm.com/blogs/research/2018/09/ai-design-deep-learning/.

Yao, Mariya. 2019. A Quick Overview of Enterprise AutoML Solutions. *Topbots*, March 31. https://www.topbots.com/automl-solutions-overview/.

Yourdon, Edward. 2004. *Death March*. Englewood Cliffs, NJ: Prentice Hall.

Zöller, Marc-André, and Marco F. Huber. 2019. Survey on Automated Machine Learning. arXiv preprint arXiv:1904.12054.

Zoph, Barret, and Quoc V. Le. 2017. Neural Architecture Search with Reinforcement Learning. Under Review as Conference Paper at ICLR 2017. https://arxiv.org/pdf/1611.01578.pdf.

CHAPTER 7

New Autonomy and Work in the AI Industry

Introduction

After an excursion into the AI industry, we now return to the realm of Marxist theory, and in particular, to *post-operaismo*'s claim for a new autonomy of immaterial labour. In Chapter 3, I reconstructed the technological argument for new autonomy as a process consisting of three cyclically occurring stages: human–machine hybridization, abstract cooperation and new autonomy. To recap: the proliferation of information technologies and technical skills enables a hybridization of immaterial labour with machines. Technologically prostheticized immaterial labour develops social and creative capacities that cannot be implemented in machines and thus captured by capital. Human–machine hybridization thereby enables for labour a new capacity for abstract cooperation, by which labour produces value outside the circuits of capital. Traditional forms of control and exploitation cannot be applied to labour organized in this abstract mode and capital is reduced to a parasite, at best appropriating, after the fact, the products of an increasingly autonomous labour. The argument for new autonomy can be summed up by Hardt and Negri's (2009) proclamation that the "powers of the new technical composition of labor-power cannot be contained by the capitalist modes of control" (143). Information technology inclines labour towards communism and capital towards dissolution.

J. Steinhoff, *Automation and Autonomy*, Marx, Engels, and Marxisms,
https://doi.org/10.1007/978-3-030-71689-9_7

We have seen that work in the AI industry, particularly that performed by data scientists and machine learning engineers, is undoubtedly a type of what *post-operaismo* refers to as immaterial labour. Yet, as I argue in this chapter, work in the AI industry does not appear to possess the qualities that *post-operaismo* attributes to immaterial labour. Work in the AI industry does not demonstrate human–machine hybridization, abstract cooperation or an emergent autonomy for labour. Each of these three stages of the technological argument is undermined by capital's continued control over high-technology work and appropriation of computational capacities for recursion. Work in the AI industry is subject to familiar processes of control, fragmentation and automation by capital, although they sometimes appear in new technological and organizational guises, like AutoML and Scrum. Automation is here reconfigured, as the necessity of codification based on the captured knowledge and skill is mitigated by the recursive application of ML to the production of ML. I conclude that *post-operaismo*'s theorization of immaterial labour does not adequately reflect contemporary high-technology work in the AI industry.

One might, however, argue that discourse about the new autonomy of immaterial labour describes a tendency or potentiality and that I am demanding too much of the theory of immaterial labour by assuming its full manifestation in the present. In response to such an objection, I set out a countervailing tendency. If ultimately the argument for new autonomy is about a tendency, then one may also consider counteracting tendencies. I develop the idea that ML and AutoML represent, in nascent form, a new kind of automation—synthetic automation—that might indicate a new technological trajectory for capital to overcome its reliance on the capture of living labour. Capital might gain a new autonomy from labour, rather than the other way around. If there is a visible tendency in AI work, it is towards the continued annexation of novel productive capacities of labour by capital.

AI Work and Human–Machine Hybridization

The theory of immaterial labour is founded upon the becoming-machine of labour. Hardt and Negri (2000) assert that with the proliferation of information technologies, the "hybridization of humans and machines is no longer defined by the linear path it followed throughout the modern period" and labour develops the "capacity to take control of the processes of machinic metamorphosis" (367). Immaterial labour wrests control over machinery from capital, uses it for its own ends and merges with it, creating a “machinic humanity” (Hardt and Negri 2017, 114). Capital’s affinity with machines is nullified and reversed and the “very existence” of humans who are “absorbed in machinic assemblages” becomes “resistance” (Hardt and Negri 2017, 123). However, human–machine hybridization does not seem to be occurring in any meaningful sense in work in the AI industry.

It is hard to imagine how labour could be merging with AI or the means of its production, in some way separated from capital, when the research and production of AI are dominated by an oligopoly of large capitalist firms (*The Economist* 2017; Lee 2018; Agrawal et al. 2018) for which academic AI researchers are leaving universities at an increasing rate (Gofman and Jin 2020) and even national governments lack the resources to compete with (Cummings 2018). Further, the AI industry is largely oriented around the production of fixed capital; it is focused on the production of an automation technology which capitals can integrate into their production processes in the hopes of minimizing living labour (Statista 2019). The AI industry is not only capitalist, but directly serves the immanent drive of capital towards an increasingly machinic state. If something is merging with AI, it would seem to be capital, rather than labour.

Post-operaismo asserts that with the proliferation of information technology there occurs a dramatic reversal in class control over technology. Fixed capital is “reappropriated” by labour and “integrated into the machinic assemblages, as a constituent of subjectivity” (Hardt and Negri 2017, 122). Rather than a new cyborg subjectivity, AI work evinces a new wave of the same processes of deskilling, fragmentation and automation that Marx noted in industrial labour, Braverman (1998) later noted in both industrial and clerical labour and Kraft (1977, 1979) noted in early software work. AI work is already being automated piecemeal, suggesting the continued operation of capital’s “immanent drive, and … constant tendency, towards increasing the productivity of labour, in order to cheapen commodities and, by cheapening commodities, to cheapen the worker himself” (Marx 1990, 436–437). From the high-skill work of data scientists and machine learning engineers to the digital manual labour of the ghost workers who label training data, the organic composition of the AI industry is increasing, but without augmenting the powers of labour to resist capital. AI work does not evince a “silent revolution” in which “[w]aged labor and direct subjugation (to organization) no longer constitute the principal form of the contractual relationship between capitalist and worker" (Lazzarato 1996, 140). The production of AI remains strictly dominated by capital, even if capital deploys more deterritorialized, empirical forms of control.

Empirical control, however, is applied to labour processes which resist codification, such as the ML labour process, so one might argue that it is true that immaterial labour's "intimate and internal knowledge of machines" means that now "worker appropriation of knowledge can become decisive" (Hardt and Negri 2017, 119). While the dark art of making ML does appear to resist codification, this has resulted in quite the opposite of an empowered cyborg labour, as automation techniques based on ML have presented the option of skipping the previously necessary steps of capture and of codification. AutoML and particularly, the possibility of end-to-end AutoML, with its aim to reduce the technical knowledge required for machine learning production to near zero, point towards a possible future in which algorithms produce algorithms and automated machines produce automated machines. Even if it is not completely realized, such a prospect suggests an increasingly literal rereading of Marx's description of the products of labour confronting the worker as "something alien, as a power independent of the producer" (Marx and Engels 1988, 71). A user may click buttons in an end-to-end AutoML program and witness the automatic generation of a functional ML model, but this is far from merging with the machine.

But perhaps I am not paying attention to the right developments. One might argue that the proliferation of open-source AI tools signifies a more important phenomenon of human–machine hybridization because it indicates that the production of AI is spreading beyond industry, into the broader "multitude" (Hardt and Negri 2000, 82). Both the contemporary AI industry and *post-operaismo* are united in their enthusiasm for open-source software (Hardt and Negri 2005, 339–240; Moulier-Boutang 2012, 79–83; Simonite 2015). However, as we saw in Chapter 5, AI capitals are using the open-source model as a means to achieve market domination (Gershgorn 2015). Indeed, the notion that open-source software is developed by independent users might be wholly overturned as oligopolistic tech rivalry escalates. The recent development of Linux open-source operating systems is instructive. The 2017 Linux kernel report reckons that only 8.2% of contributions came from unpaid developers, down from 14.6% in 2012, while over 85% of contributions came from "developers being paid for their work" (Corbet and Kroah-Hartman 2018, 15). A survey of open-source AI projects concludes that "most popular projects are heavily influenced by a single large entity such as Google, Facebook, IBM, etc." (Haddad 2018, 98). According to Rowley (2017), in the past decade, open-source software has become a "surprisingly lucrative industry" in which companies "more often than not … offer their underlying software for free but charge hefty premiums for custom configurations and implementation consulting services". Free AI tools offer an analogous way for capitals to recruit users and free workers into their valorization circuits.

To get to the root of human–machine hybridization, we need to consider its foundational belief that certain social and creative capacities of technologically prostheticized humans simply cannot be implemented in machines, and that therefore immaterial labour is safe from wide-scale automation. Virno (2003) asserts that in post-Fordism, the most important means of production are "not reducible to machines" and are "inseparable from living labor" (61). Moulier-Boutang (2012) likewise highlights the centrality of "implicit knowledge that is irreducible to machinism" (54). Hardt and Negri (2017) thus regard with little concern the prospect of a new "Digital Taylorism" (131). This belief about the irreducible humanity of immaterial labour aligns *post-operaismo* with capitalist centaur theorists, as discussed in Chapter 3, for whom AI will perform routine work while humans devote their labour to creative tasks or those requiring judgement (Agrawal et al. 2018; Daugherty and Wilson 2018). But the belief in irreducible human capacities which AI cannot implement stands on an unsteady foundation, as Brynjolfsson and McAfee's revision to their centaur theory, published only three years after the original, demonstrates.

Brynjolfsson and McAfee (2014) originally reserved creative thinking or "idea creation" for the human component of centaurs (192). But in light of advances in deep learning ML, they admit that "machines are getting quite good at coming up with powerful new ideas on their own" (McAfee and Brynjolfsson 2017, 111). They therefore imagine a new division of labour:

> the ability to work effectively with people's emotional states and social drives will remain a deeply human skill for some time to come. This implies a novel way to combine minds and machines as we move deeper into the second machine age: let the computers take the lead on making decisions (or judgments, predictions, diagnoses, and so on), then let people take the lead if others need to be convinced or persuaded to go along with these decisions. (McAfee and Brynjolfsson 2017, 123)

Their new conclusion is that human workers should specialize in affective labour, working with emotions and social interactions too complex for machines to adequately emulate. In the healthcare context, for instance, "most patients ... don't want to get their diagnosis from a machine", but from a "compassionate person who can help them understand and accept often difficult news" (McAfee and Brynjolfsson 2017, 123). This specific task of acting as an interpreter and perhaps lobbyist for the output of AI systems does not seem to be automatable yet, but it would seem to be a rather limited growth industry, and probably not the most satisfying line of work. As it is for *post-operaismo*, the idea in the world of business-oriented literature on AI seems to be that communicative and affective capacities, which are not automatable, will allow humans to thrive amid a new centaur economy. As another business-oriented analysis of AI-powered automation puts it: "the parts of our jobs we'll keep are just the parts that can't be codified" (Davenport and Kirby 2016, 14).

The obvious problem here is that, in a capitalist world, what can or cannot be codified remains a perpetually open question since capital is driven to continually expand its technological capacities. The line between what machines can and cannot do does not remain fixed for long. And if advances in synthetic automation provide the possibility of automation without a preceding codification, such a distinction will become even more tenuous. A brief look at the history of technology shows that declarations drawing an eternal divide between what machines can and cannot do tend not to pan out in the long run. AI's encounters with language translation, Chess and Go provide easy examples. Research into manipulating and emulating affect with AI is underway (McStay 2018). Already AI is applied to generate all kinds of convincing linguistic output, from news stories to interactive virtual customer assistants (Faggella 2018, 2020). OpenAI's GPT-3 (Generative Pre-trained Transformer 3), released in mid-2020, quickly made the automation of sophisticated linguistic and communicative capacities even more plausible. GPT-3 is a deep learning model trained on an unprecedentedly massive dataset (the approximately 6 million articles that make up English Wikipedia account for only 0.6% of its training data) from all corners of the internet. The model extracted from this data can string together words, purely based on statistical patterns, to produce output, which is sometimes startlingly coherent. GPT-3 is very far from AGI and, as Vincent (2020) points out, is better understood as a very sophisticated autocomplete function. But it is not implausible that future versions of large language models will perform quite adequately at explaining a patient's diagnosis in an ostensibly cogent and apparently compassionate manner.

Quite the opposite to a cyborg becoming of labour seems to be happening in the AI industry. Instead, capital, in the form of machinery, is taking on more and more capacities previously reserved for humans as technical AI knowledge and skills are baked into automated AI tools. Some labour process theory thinkers have held that software production is resistant to deskilling and automation because to "fully standardize computer programming ... would require the seemingly omniscient knowledge of both the emergent problems and the associated solutions" (Andrews et al. 2005, 67). But we have seen how AI work is already being automated without such omniscient knowledge, and how with AutoML the need for both knowledge of a solution and the skills to implement that solution are, at least ideally, dissolved into a process of automated brute force iterative experimentation. AI work thus evinces the "development of the means of labour into machinery ... the historical reshaping of the traditional, inherited means of labour into a form adequate to capital" (Marx 1993, 694). Tiziana Terranova (2004), who endorses a version of immaterial labour theory, supports *post-operaismo*'s humanist reconfiguration of the general intellect as the creative and communicative capacities of immaterial labourers because otherwise the "Marxian monster of metal and flesh would just be updated to that of a world-spanning network, where computers use human beings as a way to allow the system of machinery (and therefore capitalist production) to function" (87). I suggest that Terranova's monstrous image, rather than *post-operaismo*'s humanist reconfiguration of the general intellect as the "linguistic reiteration of living labour" (Virno 2003, 106), seems quite adequate to the contemporary situation in the AI industry, where arrays of computational fixed capital in vast data centers run increasingly dense recursive operations aimed at minimizing the human component necessary for AI production.

AI Work and Abstract Cooperation

The second stage of the technological argument is "abstract cooperation", a novel, more intensely social, manner of cooperation (Hardt and Negri 2000, 296) which is "immediately collective" (Lazzarato 1996). Self-organized workers connected by digital technologies are spatially dispersed and thus immaterial labour "exists only in the form of networks and flows" (Lazzarato 1996, 154). Immaterial labour takes diverse forms and occurs in places beyond the traditional workplace; the "new productive forces have no place … because they occupy all places" (Hardt and Negri 2000, 210). Because of this diffusion, capital cannot control and exploit immaterial labour by Fordist and Talyorist means.

AI work is characterized by labour processes which are resistant to codification such that traditional methods of management control do not work well. AI workers do have choices in how to accomplish their assigned goals in the limited sense of what Barrett (2005) calls "technical autonomy" (82) and they often direct their own day-to-day work activities under Agile development methodologies. However, we have seen that capital retains control over AI work through decentralized, empirical control practices such as the Scrum development methodology and software like JIRA. These technologies and techniques are new ways of organizing immaterial labour by surveilling and measuring its productivity, and devolving managerial functions to peers via peer-accountability mechanisms. To borrow from Pitts (2018), practices like Scrum, along with related technologies, "serve the same role as the conveyor belt in structuring labour within commensurable limits" (42). Sohn-Rethel (1978) described the management practice of "synthetic timing" in which the "time norm for a job is construed without consulting or watching the worker, even for new jobs which have never yet been practised" (155). The time norm is instead extrapolated from what capital already knows about other labour processes. Empirical control further abstracts the timing of labour through frequent or continuous surveillance into something closer to a constant "modulation" (Deleuze 1992, 4). The importance of time for empirical control suggests that AI work remains structured by the value-form, even as it appears organizationally decentralized. Capital's ability to mutate over time and from place to place is based precisely on the fungibility of the value-form, which can "persist regardless of whether a worker uses a keyboard or a hammer, ideas or nuts and bolts" (Pitts 2018, 187). If this is taken into account, it is thus difficult to discern abstract cooperation in the AI industry. Instead of the abstraction of the cooperation of labour, AI work evinces abstracted methods of capitalist control. Just because management cannot dictate precisely how to do AI work does not mean it cannot control it. The decentralization of control is still control (Galloway 2004). In the context of the AI industry, cooperation is still directed by capital.

AI Work and New Autonomy

On the basis of human–machine hybridization and abstract cooperation, *post-operaismo* attributes to immaterial labour "real (and increasing) productive powers and capacities for autonomy" (Hardt and Negri 2017, 77). Having "incorporated the tools of production" and having "been metamorphosed anthropologically", immaterial labourers "act and produce machinically, separately and autonomously from capital" (Hardt and Negri 2017, 133). Immaterial labour escapes the yoke of capital valorization and instead engages in "self-valorization" or the autonomous expansion of its own capacities (Hardt and Negri 2017, 119). In sum, the "powers of the new technical composition of labor-power cannot be contained by the capitalist modes of control" (Hardt and Negri 2009, 143).

I argue that work in the AI industry does not demonstrate any sense of new autonomy. Instead, this sector of high-tech labour reveals the same dynamics towards the increasing machinic state of capital which Marx discerned over one hundred and fifty years ago. Labour continues to be subjugated to the valorization of capital amid the proliferation of AI. Recognizing the continuity of the contemporary capitalist technological milieu with those of the past is an essential condition for critical thought and practice. Hardt and Negri (2017) suggest:

> Today we can really begin to think of a reappropriation of fixed capital by the workers and the integration of intelligent machines under autonomous social control into their lives, a process, for example, of the construction of algorithms disposed to the self-valorization of cooperative social production and reproduction in all of their articulations. (119)

We certainly should think about the possibility of such things. The algorithmic enhancement of productive and reproductive activities is desirable, and increasingly, technologically feasible. The digital infrastructure of data, platforms and algorithms created by capital allows for fruitful reconsideration of socialist possibilities, such as a planned economy (Morozov 2019). However, an essential precondition for the reappropriation of algorithmic technologies, such as AI, is the recognition that such technology remains, by and large, under the control of capital. In the context of AI, the kind of autonomous production imagined by *post-operaismo* only occurs in minute quantities and appears to be becoming increasingly unlikely due to ballooning computational hardware requirements for AI production.

In Chapter 5, I discussed how in 2019 the non-profit research lab OpenAI converted to a limited-profit model in partnership with Microsoft, which provided it with $1 billion in funding. OpenAI justified this change by stating that cutting-edge AI work "requires a lot of capital for computational power" (Brockman 2019). OpenAI now runs a supercomputer hosted on Microsoft's Azure cloud platform. In return, Microsoft will be the primary beneficiary of OpenAI's research and has already secured exclusive rights to commercializing its large language model GPT-3 (Langston 2020; Scott 2020). Even with substantial philanthropic endowments, cutting-edge AI research cannot subsist for long outside the circuits of capital.

Even national governments may not be able to contest capital's domination of AI. One report on the military prospects of AI and autonomous weapon systems worries that the "large disparity in commercial versus military autonomous R&D spending could have a cascading effect on the types and quality of autonomy that are eventually incorporated into military systems" (Cummings 2018, 16). This could lead, the report speculates, to "critical AI services" being "leased" by governments from AI capital (Cummings 2018, 17). If neither states nor think tanks funded by the philanthropy of billionaires can manage to produce AI outside of the circuits of capital, the multitude may have difficulties obtaining the requisite resources for autonomous AI production.

The AI industry thus does not appear as a context ripe for an epochal break in labour-capital relations on technological grounds. How then should the rupture of new autonomy posited by *post-operaismo* be evaluated today? Is it simply a hangover from the techno-optimism surrounding the novelty of digital networks in the late 1990s and early 2000s when Hardt and Negri's *Empire* was first published? That is, no doubt, a contributing factor, but it is not the whole story. Another contributing factor is theoretical. The notion of a new autonomy of immaterial labour also derives from *post-operaismo's* particular triangulation of labour, capital and machines, which contains a fundamental category error in terms of value, as several critics have pointed out (Thoburn 2001; Camfield 2007; Rigi 2015; Pitts 2017). Value, in Marx's schema, is a historically specific phenomenon of capital, distinguished from use-value, which describes any useful thing or process. A value-form perspective emphasizes how this ontological duality obtains widely in life under capital. Use-value is one instance of the "natural form" of something while value is its "social form" which is a product of its location within the social totality of capitalism (Heinrich 2012, 40).

The contribution of machines to the self-valorization of capital is not comparable to the contribution of machines to what *post-operaismo* calls the self-valorization of immaterial labour. In the first case, the primary purpose of machines is to increase the productivity of labour and thereby to increase capital's harvest of relative surplus-value. In the second case, machines function solely as use-values, enabling new modes of communication and other capacities for immaterial labour. As *post-operaismo* sees it, these new use-values entail a radical technological break with capital's totality, supposedly propelling labour beyond the reach of capital and the imposition of its form of value. However, concrete changes in labour processes, such as the introduction of information technologies, do not necessarily entail changes to the operations of real abstractions like value. According to *post-operaismo*, the valorization process can no longer be mapped on to the labour process when information technology explodes labour processes beyond the workplace and makes all kinds of work increasingly dependent on the new communicative and creative capacities developed by technologically prostheticized labour. However, information technology could only cause such a rupture in the real abstraction of value if it somehow disintegrated the underlying social relations which the real abstraction of value consists of. That does not seem to be the case in the AI industry, which is a thriving sector of capital in which capital's immanent drive towards an increasingly machinic state remains evident. Here, the increasingly computational nature of labour is not in conflict with capital's valorization imperative. Indeed, the continued operation of capital's drive towards an increasingly machinic state is revealed in the emerging automation of the ML labour process. The valorization imperative continues to determine the labour process, contrary to *post-operaismo* assertions that the purported immateriality of computational labour processes render valorization impossible. Capital continues, in the AI industry, to remodel the concrete world "in the image of the value-form" (Pitts 2018, 188). *Post-operaismo* underestimates the malleability of the value-form and the impetus of capital to conscript new technologies into the service of valorization.

Autonomy for What?

Despite the critique I have presented, and despite the frequent statements of *post-operaismo* writers in which immaterial labour theory is described as empirically founded, one might still argue that the technological argument for a new autonomy best describes a tendency or potentiality, something yet to come. While this book will not delve into how to debate the existence of tendencies and potentialities (see Nunes 2007), it can at least explore one counteracting tendency.

In an essay originally published in 1990, Caffentzis described recursive applications of information technology such as "computers … used to produce computers" as the "automatization of automation" (2013, 129). Nearly three decades later, AutoML has added a few more layers of recursion, earning itself the moniker the "automation of automating automation" (Mayo 2016). I have suggested that in AutoML we might be seeing a primitive instance of a more general technique of synthetic automation, or the automation of labour processes without their prior codification, which is itself premised on their prior capture from living labour. Historically, capital's autonomy has been limited by its necessary supervenience on human actors. As a "higher-order alien power" (Smith 2009, 123) composed of the social relations of humans, capital takes concrete form when it can capture and objectify the capacities of labour, forming its technological armamentarium, the general intellect. Capital is not a malicious machine system wholly distinct from humans, like the Terminator franchise's Skynet, but a meta-entity, which exists as a complex of human products and human social relations. Synthetic automation is a technique for augmenting the general intellect without first capturing knowledge or skills from human labour. If the technique of synthetic automation becomes widely applicable to all kinds of labour processes, then the AI industry would be the birthplace not of newly autonomous immaterial labour, but of a technology by which capital could approach its dream of the "complete dissociation of living labour … from the production process" (Ramtin 1991, 58).

We saw earlier that the notion of fully automated production was considered as early as the nineteenth century by the political economist David Ricardo who reasoned that if "machinery could do all the work that labour now does, there would be no demand for labour. Nobody would be entitled to consume any thing who was not a capitalist, and who could not buy or hire a machine" (1951–1973, VIII: 399–400, cited in Kurz 2010, 1195). In Ricardo's scenario, we see a capitalism in which all workers have been replaced with machines owned by human capitalists who continue to direct their operations and reap the spoils of machine labour.[1] But what if capital's machinic tendency extended to the capitalists as well? Would this then be a capital which truly constitutes an autonomous entity, distinct from humans? This scenario is most notably explored by the neoreactionary philosopher Nick Land, who champions a theory of "capital autonomization" (Vast Abrupt 2018).[2]

Land, for whom Marx is an essential, if scorned,[3] theoretical reference, follows Deleuze and Guattari in suggesting that human labour is implicated so deeply in machines that there is no point drawing a boundary between the two: "[a]nthropormorphic surplus-value is not analytically extricable from transhuman machineries" (Land 2012, 347).Land recognizes capital's inherent drive to an increasingly machinic state but does not see it as posing an existential threat to capital, since surplus-value does not depend on the exploitation of only living labour. Rather than collapsing due to a hypertrophic organic composition, capital only truly becomes capital when it disposes of its human element: "Capital only retains anthropological characteristics as a symptom of underdevelopment ... Man is something for it to overcome" (Land 2012, 446). Capital's means of escape from its reliance on living labour is AI,[4] which replaces human cognition, porting the program of capital from running on the hardware of biological brains and bodies to silicon-based machinery: "Just as the capitalist urbanization of labour abstracted it in a parallel escalation with technical machines, so will intelligence be transplanted into the

[1] One might object that such a machine economy would not constitute capitalism. Since machines in production function as fixed capital and do not produce surplus-value, such an economy devoid of human labour would not be capitalism. Ricardo's scenario, or an economy based on production by AI, would be more accurately compared to a slave economy, since slaves function formally in a manner identical to fixed capital (Roberts 2018). Marx (1993) asserts that in the "slave relation the worker is nothing but a living labour-machine" (465). However, Marx also described nineteenth century slavery as capitalistic, asserting that on plantations the "capitalist mode of production exists" (Marx 1968, 303). There are good reasons, both historical and theoretical, for not drawing hard lines between capitalism and slave-based production (Robinson 2000; Banaji 2010; Clegg 2020).

[2] By citing Land in no way do I endorse his neo-reactionary and alt-right politics. I am interested here solely in his theorization of cybernetic capital.

[3] See "Critique of Transcendental Miserablism" in Land (2012).

[4] Land's vision of autonomous machine capital more recently includes blockchain technology (Land 2018).

purring data zones of new software worlds in order to be abstracted from an increasingly obsolescent anthropoid particularity" (Land 2012, 293). The capacities for recursive technological autonomy presented by AI embody, for Land, the ideal functioning of the market; more perfect information can be circulated faster among superintelligent artificial agents exchanging increasingly abstract commodities on digital markets immanent in diverse and minute facets of the world: all social reproduction is "progressively subordinat[ed]" to "techno-commercial replication" (Land 2012, 340). AI is the perfect entity to inhabit this world in which nothing exists outside the market. Land (2014) thus posits a "teleological identity of capitalism and artificial intelligence". The notion is that ultimately, AI will provide a more adequate means of valorizing capital than the human being; capital and AI will fuse into a "technomic automatism" (Land 2012, 407).

Primož Krašovec (2018) has elaborated the tendency plotted by Land with the notion of the "real autonomy" of capital, in which recursion plays a pivotal role. Krašovec (2018) argues that "autonomous machines and artificial intelligence" are instituting an "ever greater independence of capital from humanity" via an "autonomisation that simultaneously denotes self-referentiality". Recursion, he suspects, could allow capital to develop new capacities without first capturing them from labour; "we might be entering an era where … technologies of design, production and multiplication of technological innovation are immanent to capital itself (and are not borrowed from humanity)" (Krašovec 2018). When labour and valorization processes can be planned, executed and completed, and their results integrated back into capital without the input of living labour, Krašovec suggests that we can speak of a capital that is non-metaphorically autonomous.[5]

I contend that synthetic automation renders such speculations (slightly) more plausible. It provides a technical means for extrapolating capital's drive towards an increasingly machinic state into the future. It allows one to imagine more easily the generalized capitalist production and circulation of machines by machines. This possibility presents interesting avenues for the ramification of Marxist theory. If synthetic

[5] Ian Wright (2020) is developing interesting work on the autonomy of capital from an occult perspective, inspired by Marx's mention of capital as a "real God" (Marx 1975 [1844]).

automation can indeed automate labour processes in all kinds of fields without prior capture and codification from human workers, then labour could be displaced as the motive force in capitalism, throwing into question the long-term viability of the Marxist dictum that there are "no powers of capital that are not ultimately the collective social powers of labour (or the powers of nature, machinery and science mobilized by collective social labour)" (Smith 2009, 124). How many generations of machines produced by machines does it take before the residual contributions of labour are negligible? The media theorist Marshall McLuhan (1994) described humans as the "sex organs of the machine world ... enabling it to fecundate and evolve ever new forms" (46). If it becomes possible for a machine to design and produce a machine without human intervention, then one can imagine a further diminished role for McLuhanian sex organs.

An obvious Marxist objection to autonomous capital scenarios is that, as Marx insisted, machines cannot be exploited and thus cannot generate surplus-value; the machine "creates no new value but yields up its own value to the product it serves to beget" (Marx 1990, 509; see also Caffentzis 1997). The program of capital cannot be run on wholly machine hardware for it would starve itself of essential surplus-value. The human component remains essential if capital is to persist. However, a speculative perspective on increasingly autonomous capitalist machinery allows one to entertain the heretical possibility of the proletarianization of machines. While there is not adequate space to explore the notion of proletarianized machines here, from a formal perspective, it is at least possible to imagine sufficiently advanced AI which is made "free in the double sense"; legally free insofar as it could dispose of its own labour-power and is responsible for its subsistence and free from ownership of the means of production, thus forcing it into the wage relation (Marx 1990, 272). Under the right conditions, of which being free in the double sense is only one, it is possible that a sufficiently advanced machine could create surplus-value (Dyer-Witheford et al. 2019, 135–138).

Admittedly, this is highly speculative territory that goes far beyond this book's focus on actually existing AI. My goal in entertaining such speculations here is merely to sketch a counteracting tendency to a tendential reading of immaterial labour theory. It is true that it is impossible to predict exactly how far automation can and will go. Yet, on the other hand, capital remains driven by the same historical imperative to increase. As new means to achieve that imperative appear, capital will investigate them and attempt to utilize them. We should not underestimate capital's nihilistic onslaught on barriers to valorization nor its ability to impose the value-form on diverse concrete situations. If there is a tendency towards increasing autonomy for labour amid the proliferation of information technologies, it is likely to run up against a countervailing tendency for capital to appropriate those same technologies and apply them in the interests of unceasing valorization.

Conclusion

In this chapter, I argued that the study of the AI industry renders dubious all three stages of the technological argument for the new autonomy of immaterial labour. Rather than human–machine hybridization, in the AI industry, we find a mysterious labour process, which even experts do not understand the precise nature of and a burgeoning spate of automated tools for the unskilled production of ML models. Capital, rather than labour, seems to be increasingly infused with AI. Rather than abstract cooperation, work in the AI industry is characterized by management practices of surveillance-intensive empirical control. In sum, there is little evidence for new autonomy in AI work. The case of OpenAI and contemporary concerns of governments about their inability to contest capital's control over AI demonstrate how difficult it is to make cutting-edge AI outside the circuits of capital. Further, synthetic automation can be interpreted as a means by which capital, rather than labour, might increase its autonomy.

Bibliography

Agrawal, Ajay, Joshua S. Gans, and Avi Goldfarb. 2018. *Prediction Machines: The Simple Economics of Artificial Intelligence*. Boston: Harvard Business Review Press.

Andrews, Chris K., Craig D. Lair and Bart Landry. 2005. The Labor Process in Software Startups: Production on a Virtual Assembly Line? In *Management, Labour Process and Software Development: Reality Bites*, ed. Rowena Barret. New York: Routledge.

Banaji, Jairus. 2010. *Theory as History: Essays on Modes of Production and Exploitation*. Leiden/Boston: Brill.

Barrett, Rowena. 2005. Managing the Software Development Labour Process: Direct Control, Time and Technical Autonomy. In *Management, Labour Process and Software Development: Reality Bites*, ed. Rowena Barrett. New York: Routledge.

Braverman, Harry. 1998. *Labor and Monopoly Capital: The Degradation of Work in the Twentieth Century*. New York: New York University Press.

Brockman, Greg. 2019. Microsoft Invest in and Partners With OpenAI to Support us Building Beneficial AI. *OpenAI Blog*, July 22. https://openai.com/blog/microsoft/.

Brynjolfsson, Erik, and Andrew McAfee. 2014. *The Second Machine Age: Work, Progress, and Prosperity in a Time of Brilliant Technologies*. New York and London: W.W. Norton & Company.

Caffentzis, George. 1997. Why Machines cannot Create Value: Marx's Theory of Machines. In *Cutting Edge: Technology, Information Capitalism and Social Revolution*, ed. Jim Davis, Thomas Hirschl and Michael Stack. London: Verso.

Caffentzis, George. 2013. *In Letters of Blood and Fire: Work, Machines, and the Crisis of Capitalism*. Oakland, CA: PM Press.

Camfield, David. 2007. The Multitude and the Kangaroo: A Critique of Hardt and Negri's Theory of Immaterial Labour. *Historical Materialism* 15 (2): 21–52.

Clegg, John. 2020. A Theory of Capitalist Slavery. *Journal of Historical Sociology* 33 (1): 74–98.

Corbet, Jonathan and Greg Kroah-Hartman. 2018. "2017 Linux Kernel Development Report." *Linux Foundation*. https://www.linuxfoundation.org/2017-linux-kernel-report-landing-page/.

Cummings, M.L. 2018. Artificial Intelligence and the Future of Warfare. In *Artificial Intelligence and International Affairs: Disruption Anticipated*, 7–18. London: Chatham House.

Daugherty, Paul R., and H. James Wilson. 2018. *Human+Machine: Reimagining Work in the Age of AI*. Boston: Harvard Business Press.

Davenport, Thomas H., and Julia Kirby. 2016. *Only Humans Need Apply: Winners and Losers in the Age of Smart Machines*. New York: Harper Business.

Deleuze, Gilles. 1992. Postscript on the Societies of Control. *October* 59: 3–7.

Dyer-Witheford, Nick, Atle Mikkola Kjøsen, and James Steinhoff. 2019. *Inhuman Power: Artificial Intelligence and the Future of Capitalism*. London: Pluto Press.

Faggella, Daniel. 2018. News Organization Leverages AI to Generate Automated Narratives from Big Data. *Emerj*, December 7, 2020. https://emerj.com/ai-case-studies/news-organization-leverages-ai-generate-automated-narratives-big-data/.

Faggella, Daniel. 2020. Natural Language Processing Use-Cases Primer—Chatbots, Search, Voice and More. *Emerj*, January 4, 2020. https://emerj.com/ai-sector-overviews/natural-language-processing-use-cases-primer/.

Galloway, Alexander R. 2004. *Protocol: How Control Exists After Decentralization*. Cambridge: MIT Press.

Gershgorn, Dave. 2015. How Google Aims to Dominate Artificial Intelligence. *Popular Science*, November 9, 2015. https://www.popsci.com/google-ai.

Gofman, Michael and Jin, Zhao. 2020. Artificial Intelligence, Education, and Entrepreneurship. Working Paper. *SSRN*. https://ssrn.com/abstract=3449440.

Haddad, Ibrahim. 2018. Open Source AI: Projects, Insights and Trends. *The Linux Foundation*. https://www.linuxfoundation.org/publications/2018/05/open-source-ai-projects-insights-and-trends/.

Hardt, Michael, and Antonio Negri. 2000. *Empire*. Cambridge, MA: Harvard University Press.

Hardt, Michael, and Antonio Negri. 2005. *Multitude: War and Democracy in the Age of Empire*. London: Penguin.

Hardt, Michael, and Antonio Negri. 2009. *Commonwealth*. Cambridge, MA: Harvard University Press.

Hardt, Michael, and Antonio Negri. 2017. *Assembly*. Oxford: Oxford University Press.

Heinrich, Michael. 2012. *An Introduction to the Three Volumes of Karl Marx's Capital*. New York: Monthly Review Press.

Kraft, Philip. 1977. *Programmers and Managers: The Routinization of Computer Programming in the United States*. New York: Springer.

Kraft, Philip. 1979. The Industrialization of Computer Programming: From Programming to 'Software Production.' In *Case Studies on the Labor Process*, ed. Andrew S. Zimbalist. New York: Monthly Review Press.

Krašovec, Primož. 2018. The Alien Capital. *Vast Abrupt*. https://vastabrupt.com/2018/07/11/alien-capital/.

Kurz, Heinz D. 2010. Technical Progress, Capital Accumulation and Income Distribution in Classical Economics: Adam Smith, David Ricardo and Karl Marx. *The European Journal of the History of Economic Thought* 17 (5): 1183–1222.

Land, Nick. 2012. *Fanged Noumena: Collected Writings 1987–2007*. Falmouth: Urbanomic.

Land, Nick. 2014. *The Teleological Identity of Capitalism and Artificial Intelligence*. Remarks to the Participants of the Incredible Machines 2014 Conference, March 8, 2014. Transcription by Jason Adams.

Land, Nick. 2018. Crypto-Current, An Introduction to Bitcoin and Philosophy. *Šum* 10 (2). http://sumrevija.si/en/sum10-2-nick-land-crypto-current-an-introduction-to-bitcoin-and-philosophy/.

Langston, Jennifer. 2020. Microsoft Announces New Supercomputer, Lays Out Vision for Future AI work. *Microsoft AI Blog*, May 19. https://blogs.microsoft.com/ai/openai-azure-supercomputer/.

Lazzarato, Maurizio. 1996. Immaterial Labor. In *Radical Thought in Italy: A Potential Politics*, ed. Paulo Virno and Michael Hardt, 133–147. Minneapolis: University of Minnesota Press.

Lee, Kai-Fu. 2018. *AI Superpowers: China, Silicon Valley, and the New World Order*. New York: Houghton Mifflin Harcourt.

Marx, Karl, and Frederick Engels. 1988. *Philosophic Manuscripts of 1844 and The Communist Manifesto*. Amherst, NY: Prometheus Books.

Marx, Karl. 1968. *Theories of Surplus-Value*. Moscow: Progress Publishers.

Marx, Karl. 1975 [1844]. Comments on James Mill. In *Marx and Engels Collected Works*, vol. 3. New York: International Publishers.

Marx, Karl. 1990. *Capital*, vol. 1. New York: Penguin.

Marx, Karl. 1993. *Grundrisse*. New York: Penguin.

Mayo, Matthew. 2016. The Case for Machine Learning in Business. *LinkedIn*, October 3, 2016. https://www.linkedin.com/pulse/case-machine-learning-business-matthew-mayo/.

McAfee, Andrew, and Erik Brynjolfsson. 2017. *Machine, Platform, Crowd: Harnessing Our Digital Future*. New York and London: W.W. Norton & Company.

McLuhan, Marshall. 1994. *Understanding Media: The Extensions of Man*. Cambridge: MIT Press.

McStay, Andrew. 2018. *Emotional AI: The Rise of Empathic Media*. London: Sage.

Morozov, Evgeny. 2019. Digital Socialism? The Calculation Debate in the Age of Big Data. *New Left Review* 116/117. https://newleftreview.org/issues/II116/articles/evgeny-morozov-digital-socialism.pdf.

Moulier-Boutang, Yann. 2012. *Cognitive Capitalism*. Cambridge: Polity.

Nunes, Rodrigo. 2007. Forward How? Forward Where? I: (Post-)*Operaismo* Beyond the Immaterial Labour Thesis. *Ephemera: Theory and Politics in Organisation* 7 (1): 178–202.

Pitts, Frederick Harry. 2017. Beyond the Fragment: Postoperaismo, Postcapitalism and Marx's 'Notes on Machines', 45 Years on. *Economy and Society* 46 (3–4): 324–345.

Pitts, Frederick Harry. 2018. *Critiquing Capitalism Today: New Ways to Read Marx*. London: Palgrave Macmillan.

Ramtin, Ramin. 1991. *Capitalism and Automation: Revolution in Technology and Capitalist Breakdown*. London: Pluto Press.

Ricardo, David. 1951–1973. *The Works and Correspondence of David Ricardo*, vol. 11, ed. Piero Sraffa with collaboration of Maurice H. Dobb. Cambridge: Cambridge University Press.

Rigi, Jakob. 2015. The Demise of the Marxian Law of Value? A Critique of Michael Hardt and Antonio Negri. In *Reconsidering Value and Labour in the Digital Age*, ed. Christian Fuchs and Eran Fisher, 188–204. London: Palgrave Macmillan.

Roberts, Michael. 2018. UNAM 3—The Robotic Future. *Michael Roberts Blog*, March 9. https://thenextrecession.wordpress.com/2018/03/09/unam-3-the-robotic-future/.

Robinson, Cedric J. 2000. *Black Marxism: The Making of the Black Radical Tradition*. Chapel Hill: University of North Carolina Press.

Rowley, Jason D. 2017. Open Source Software is Big Business With Big Funding. *Crunchbase News*, April 17. https://news.crunchbase.com/news/open-source-software-big-business-big-funding/.

Scott, Kevin. 2020. Microsoft Teams up with OpenAI to exclusively license GPT-3 Language Model. *Official Microsoft Blog*, September 22, 2020. https://blogs.microsoft.com/blog/2020/09/22/microsoft-teams-up-with-openai-to-exclusively-license-gpt-3-language-model/.

Simonite, Tom. 2015. Facebook Joins Stampede of Tech Giants Giving away Artificial Intelligence Technology. *MIT Technology Review*, December 10, 2015. https://www.technologyreview.com/2015/12/10/164605/facebook-joins-stampede-of-tech-giants-giving-away-artificial-intelligence-technology/.

Smith, Tony. 2009. The Chapters on Machinery in the 1861–63 Manuscripts. In *Re-reading Marx: New Perspectives After the*, Critical, ed. Riccardo Bellofiore and Robert Fineschi, 112–127. London: Palgrave Macmillan.

Sohn-Rethel, Alfred. 1978. *Intellectual and Manual Labour: A Critique of Epistemology*. London: MacMillan.

Statista. 2019. In-depth: Artificial Intelligence 2019. Statista Digital Market Outlook. *Statista*.

Terranova, Tiziana. 2004. *Network Culture: Politics for the Information Age*. London: Pluto Press.

The Economist. 2017. Google Leads in the Race to Dominate Artificial Intelligence. December 7, 2017. https://www.economist.com/business/2017/12/07/google-leads-in-the-race-to-dominate-artificial-intelligence

Thoburn, Nicholas. 2001. Autonomous Production? On Negri's New Synthesis. *Theory, Culture & Society* 18 (5): 75–96.

Vast Abrupt. 2018. Ideology, Intelligence, and Capital: An Interview with Nick Land. *Vast Abrupt*, August 15. https://vastabrupt.com/2018/08/15/ideology-intelligence-and-capital-nick-land/.

Vincent, James. 2020. OpenAI's Latest Breakthrough is Astonishingly Powerful but Still Fighting its Flaws. *The Verge*, July 30. https://www.theverge.com/21346343/gpt-3-explainer-openai-examples-errors-agi-potential.

Virno, Paolo. 2003. *A Grammar of the Multitude*. Los Angeles: Semiotext(e).

Wright, Ian. 2020. Marx on Capital as a Real God. *Dark Marxism*, September 20. https://ianwrightsite.wordpress.com/2020/09/03/marx-on-capital-as-a-real-god-2/

CHAPTER 8

Conclusion: Harry Braverman Overdrive

Introduction

Let us return to where we began, namely, the memetic visit from the Time Travelling Terminator of Full Automation. This Terminator symbolizes automation, capital's favoured tactic for the domination of labour, being turned against capital and disintegrating the conditions for its existence, the exploitation of labour and the harvest of surplus-value. We have followed the analogous narrative promulgated by *post-operaismo* to explain changes in the technological milieu of post-Fordism, wherein information technologies are said to flip the balance of power between capital and labour, producing a newly autonomous immaterial labour and an emaciated, parasitic capital. This book has argued that work in the artificial intelligence industry provides little support for this claim for new autonomy. The Terminator has not turned on its machinic kin.

Since the advent of the computer, capital's machine component has attained increasing capacities for technological recursion which allow the dissection and automation of all kinds of labour, including, quite recently, the labour that goes into producing AI. I have argued that such AI work is characterized by capitalist influence and control in ways familiar to previous industries going back to industrial manufacturing in Marx's time. As we have seen, the ML labour process is structured in accord with the exigencies of commodity production and is subject to empirical control by management via development methodologies such as Agile and Scrum.

J. Steinhoff, *Automation and Autonomy*, Marx, Engels, and Marxisms,
https://doi.org/10.1007/978-3-030-71689-9_8

Based on these attributes alone, it is fair to say that AI work does not evince an emergent autonomy from capital. But I have also pushed the argument one speculative step further. Considering machine learning and recently developed techniques for its automation, I argued that we may be witnessing the appearance of a nascent form of synthetic automation. Represented by AutoML, this is a form of automation that dispenses with both the need for a codified labour process prior to its automation, as well as skilled workers who can build and apply machine learning tools to extract solutions from data automatically. I have suggested that synthetic automation could be a technological trajectory that capital will pursue in the future as a means to overcome its reliance on living labour. Of course, this is not meant to be a prophecy. Future research will be required to determine whether synthetic automation is a trajectory which might be generally applied by capital.

Theoretical Synthesis

In the course of critiquing *post-operaismo*, I have drawn, in addition to my own reading of Marx, on labour process theory (LPT) and value-form Marxism, particularly the New Reading of Marx (NRM). Yet, *post-operaismo*, NRM and LPT are not necessarily incompatible with one another. While considerably beyond the scope of this book, pursuing a thorough synthesis of all three approaches would be a worthwhile task. I will briefly indicate why.

NRM is valuable because it insists on the continuing relevance of Marx's formal conception of value and capital's capacity to exert influence on the concrete world via "economic form-determination" (Heinrich 2012, 40). However, as it tracks the protean manifestations of value, it sometimes portrays labour as wholly enthralled to an omnipotent capital. Insofar as it is fixated on the permutations of value, NRM tends to pay little attention to the particular concrete technologies and forms of labour which comprise the production processes on which valorization supervenes. Overstating the revolutionary significance of new technologies should be avoided but neither should the salient novelties of these technologies be overlooked. NRM also tends to focus little on broader social dynamics beyond the circuits of capital. As Werner Bonefeld (2014) argues, NRM has largely "kept at arms' length the political form of capitalist society, that is, the state, and in particular the class antagonism and class struggle" (6). This lack is mirrored and inverted in *post-operaismo* as one of its strengths.

Post-operaismo places the class antagonism front and centre, taking up *operaismo*'s claim that labour is the active force in the struggle at the centre of value creation, always pushing forward against an essentially reactive capital. *Post-operaismo* admirably focuses on the emergence of new technological milieus and theorizes the new social capacities they impart to labour. But in doing so, it tends to pay little attention to the concrete deployment of those technologies (such as AI) in particular contexts and instead tends to draw epochal conclusions about the mutations of global capital. For *post-operaismo*, value in Marx's sense (as the social form imposed on the world by capital), is replaced by the self-valorization of labour, labour's integration of technology by which it generates its autonomy. Herein lies its downside. While *post-operaismo* conceives of labour's technological capacities as necessarily tied to class struggle, it conceives of that struggle as already taking place outside the value-form. In a partial but significant sense, the revolution has already occurred. An enfeebled capital is no longer able to control networked immaterial labour and seems to be already withering away. Capital produces new technologies but it can no longer use them to extract value from labour. The technological future thus seems already in the hands of labour, even if capital lingers on in its diminished state. This optimism does not seem justified based on what we have seen of the AI industry.

A useful synthesis of these two approaches would combine the technological fixation and the broader perspective of social struggle of *post-operaismo* with NRM's formal perspective, insisting on the dual ontological nature of the capitalist world with the immaterial form of value structuring the concrete processes on which it supervenes. The former tracks the changing technological capacities of labour. The latter grasps how capital can perpetually mutate and subsume new technologies and social relations while still remaining capital.

Automation on Steroids

The importance of the third line of thought I have drawn on, labour process theory, can be best grasped by redoubling a point made throughout this book. This is the importance of considering AI as a technology for the fragmentation and automation of labour. In an impressively painstaking archaeology of machine learning, Adrian Mackenzie (2017) recognizes ML as a form of control, but is "less certain about treating

[it] as automation" because "[l]earning from data … often sidesteps and substitutes for existing ways of acting, and practices of control, and it thereby reconfigures human-machine differences" (8). He elaborates that machine learning is "not simply automating existing economic relations or even data practices" but instead is reconfiguring objects and populations into statistical projections in an operation he calls "probabilization" (Mackenzie 2017, 13). Mackenzie thus argues that ML should be understood on an epistemological, rather than political economic, level: "[t]o qualify or specify how machine learners exist in their generality, we would need to specify their operations at a level of abstraction that neither attributes a mathematical or algorithmic ideality to them nor frames them as yet another means of production of relative surplus value" (2017, 17). One of the many virtues of Mackenzie's book is its intense scrutiny of the technical details of ML, but not once does it suggest that it might be important that ML sits at the centre of a burgeoning industry.

If nothing else, I hope this book demonstrates that whatever ML's epistemological properties might be, it is indisputably also deployed as fixed capital in diverse sectors of industry, including the production of ML. This need not be posed as an either/or problem. My argument is precisely that ML might be *both* automation—"yet another means of production of relative surplus value" (Mackenzie 2017, 17)—and, with its ability to generate algorithms from data, a novel way of sidestepping or substituting for "existing ways of acting, and practices of control" (Mackenzie 2017, 8). The notion of synthetic automation refers precisely to the possibility of automating *by* sidestepping the capture of human skills and knowledge. The situation is not one of either/or if automation may be applied to labour processes that have not already been codified. If this is so, then more, rather than less, attention to conceptualizing AI as automation ought to be paid because the practice of automation may be changing at a fundamental level. LPT's stubborn insistence on discerning processes of automation and the fragmentation and deskilling of labour might seem boring to some commentators, but the Bravermanian perspective remains relevant because the valorization of capital, with its tendency towards an increasingly machinic state, continues to be an organizing principle of the world.

While it is important to reckon with epistemological shifts that might be wrought by ML (and there are also good reasons to speculate on possibilities of proletarianized, superintelligent and/or sentient AI), I tend to agree with Andrew Ng (2017) that if you are trying to understand actually existing AI and its near future, think "automation on steroids". Under capital, hypertrophic capacities for technological recursion entail new means of fragmenting and automating labour processes, to pun on the title of one of William Gibson's great cyberpunk novels: *Harry Braverman Overdrive*. To repeat, I am not predicting an imminent jobs apocalypse, nor am I saying that there are no countervailing tendencies to capital's drive towards an increasingly machinic state. Rather, I am pointing to how some historical tendencies of capital continue, even as new technologies change diverse aspects of our lives.

It does not require a study of AI to come to similar conclusions. The collective *Endnotes* ends up with a comparable assessment based on a reading of Marx's discussion of surplus populations. Marx (1990) suggested that one result of capital's tendency towards an increasingly machinic state is the production of a "redundant working population… which is superfluous to capital's average requirements for its own valorization" (782). This "surplus population" is a cyclical by-product of industrial production, a sort of pressure-release valve for capital by which it keeps the cost of labour from rising too high (Marx 1990, 517). *Endnotes* suggests that the long-term dynamics of capital's increasing organic composition tend towards a secular increase in surplus populations, not merely cyclical periods of blowing off steam. This is because often, machines do not only replace living labour for a particular task or job, but become widely distributed across different sectors of capital: "*labour-saving technologies tend to generalise, both within and across* [production] *lines*, leading to a relative decline in the demand for labour" (Endnotes 2010, emphasis original). This relative decline was counteracted throughout the twentieth century by countervailing forces, such as the shift from collectively consumed services like telegraphy and train rides to individual commodities like telephones and automobiles. Such changes propelled mass consumerism and demanded large amounts of labour and capital, as well as the accumulation of surplus capital which could be leveraged to provide more and more consumer debt. However, *Endnotes* suggests, ultimately the trend is towards an absolute decrease in necessary labour:

> Marx … notes that the higher the organic composition of capital, the more rapidly must accumulation proceed to maintain employment, 'but this more rapid progress itself becomes the source of new technical changes

> which further reduce the relative demand for labour.' This is more than just a feature of specific highly concentrated industries. As accumulation proceeds, a growing 'superabundance' of goods lowers the rate of profit and heightens competition across lines, compelling all capitalists to 'economise on labour'. Productivity gains are thus 'concentrated under this great pressure; they are incorporated in technical changes which revolutionise the composition of capital in all branches surrounding the great spheres of production. (Endnotes 2010)

The recursive process of valorization entails the recursive application of technology to the production of technology itself. Competition between individual capitals entails the generalization of automation technologies which reduce the need for living labour in existing sectors. The only countervailing factor here is the opening of new sectors. Otherwise the "relatively redundant population ... tends to become a consolidated surplus population, absolutely redundant to the needs of capital" (Endnotes 2010). Today, as swaths of desperate migrants throw themselves against hostile borders, as conventional labour diminishes while precarious platform labour and ghost work proliferate, and as new applications of automation continue to appear, it is difficult to deny this analysis some plausibility.

To make general claims about the economic effects of automation is not, however, my ambition here. Such claims, as the Introduction pointed out, are highly disputed, and regardless, need to be based on empirical research of a different kind than I have conducted. What is certain is that, despite the centrality I have given to it here, automation should not be taken as the sole phenomenon determining future relations between capital and labour, nor should its social effects be imagined as limited to destroying jobs. Aaron Benanav (2019a) argues that automation is of secondary importance after overcapacity for production or the "global redundancy of technological capacities" (27). Benanav also makes the important point that automation does not currently seem to be annihilating jobs on a wide scale. Rather than unemployment, he argues that the major result of automation today is under-employment or people being "forced to work for lower than normal wages, and in worse than normal working conditions" (Benanav 2019b, 125). Benanav's point is well taken. Overly simplistic notions of automation and its effects should be avoided. The automation-centric analysis presented in this book should not be taken as the whole story of cybernetic capitalism.

That being said, I expect that automation will remain a significant factor for any study of work or capital in the near future. Special significance may be imparted to automation by the COVID-19 pandemic, still unfolding at the time of writing in early 2021. While the long-term effects of the pandemic, and its interactions with pre-existing economic conditions, remain to be seen, a global recession has already manifested which is, according to some measures, the worst since the Great Depression of the 1930s (Lu 2020). Automation tends to be deployed more during recessions (Blit 2020) and there is no reason to expect the 2020–2021 pandemic-recession will be different in this respect. Economist David Autor calls the COVID-19 recession an "automation-forcing event" (Leeson 2020). Already reports are being drawn up evaluating which essential jobs might be fully automated, such as grocery cashiers, which jobs, like educators, are "remoteable" but non-automatable and which non-remotable jobs, such as nurses, can be augmented with support from "AI and automation technologies" (MIT Technology Review Insights 2020). ML-powered techniques of synthetic automation, purveyed by the AI giants, may find fertile ground amid companies seeking new automated solutions to their valorization woes.

The AI tech giants are some of the best faring capitals during the pandemic so far. In the first half of 2020, Amazon's profits, driven by stay at home purchases, doubled from the previous year to $5.2 billion and Facebook reported a 98% increase in profits, also racking up $5.2 billion (Wakabayashi, Weise, Nicas and Isaac 2020). Google had its first-ever quarterly decline in early 2020, but by the end of September, it reported $11.2 billion in profits, a 59% increase from the previous year (CBS News 2020). Facebook has also taken the opportunity to invest in international markets, investing $5.7 billion in Reliance Jio, an Indian telecom company and millions in building a nearly 23,000-mile fibre-optic cable around Africa (Isaac 2020). It seems plausible that these companies will emerge thriving from the current recession like Microsoft did from the 1990s dot com crash. But enough about the pandemic.

Optimism and Agency

Someone might object that this book attributes too much agency to capital, which is, after all, composed of the social relations of humans. I describe capital in this way as a counterpoint to the optimism of *post-operaismo,* as well as left accelerationism, which I hold both attribute too much agency to labour. To attribute agency to capital is, I suggest, one way to come to terms with the dire social-technological milieu of the present. Like Marx's references to capital as a subject, attributing agency to capital highlights the essential weirdness or horror of capitalism, in which real abstractions rule over human life. Referring to capital's agency thus aims to help generate what Pitts (2018) calls the "requisite pessimism" for grasping the depth of capital's subsumption of the contemporary world (259). I have focused on *post-operaismo* throughout this book, but I want to briefly indicate how the argument I have mounted also applies to left accelerationism.

Left accelerationists argue correctly that under capital, technology is constrained and directed "towards needlessly narrow ends" and that it can and should be appropriated: "existing infrastructure is not a capitalist stage to be smashed, but a springboard to launch towards post-capitalism" (Williams and Srnicek 2014, 355). They advocate the use of artificial intelligence, and other new technologies, to contribute to full automation, such that machines can eventually "liberate humanity from the drudgery of work while simultaneously producing increasing amounts of wealth" (Srnicek and Williams 2015, 109). While left accelerationism does not endorse the same sense of irreducible humanity held by *post-operaismo*, it does evince a comparable unbridled technological optimism, unhindered by a recognition of capital's diverse apparatuses of capture via the value-form. Srnicek and Williams (2015) note that not every capitalist technology can be appropriated by labour since "power relationships are embedded within technologies" and they "cannot therefore be infinitely bent towards purposes that oppose their very functioning" (151). However, as Nathan Brown (2016) points out, considering the use-values of particular technologies is not the same as considering how those technologies are implicated in the "immaterial process of valorisation requisite for the *reproduction* of the technological process of production" (169). In other words, like *post-operaismo*, left accelerationists focus on the possibilities of particular technologies without considering their actual and possible implications within value, formally conceived. Left accelerationist appraisals of AI and other emerging technologies thus echo *post-operaismo* enthusiasm for the internet and open-source software and similarly downplay the control capital retains over technology and labour. The technological augmentation of labour is supposed to increase labour's autonomy, but as Michael Gardiner (2016) puts it, "no tangible force exists to propel us to an 'outside' purged of the capitalist value-form.

Acceleration per se therefore only augments the power and dynamism of capital" including "its seemingly limitless power to reinvent itself" (31). The emphasis in left accelerationism is, as it is in *post-operaismo*, placed too heavily on the technological capacities of labour, to the detriment of a clear-eyed understanding of the technological capacities of capital.

By dwelling on the notion of synthetic automation at the end of this book, I have aimed to switch focus in the analysis of cybernetic capitalism, from the new capacities provided to labour by information technologies, to the new capacities such technologies supply to capital. This switch has also entailed a reconsideration of autonomy in cybernetic capitalism. Synthetic automation, I have suggested, may provide a new way for capital to decrease its reliance on living labour. Capital is always searching for ways to overcome barriers to valorization. The circulation of money, for instance, allows capital to overcome the temporal and spatial barriers inherent in direct exchange (Marx 1990, 209). Automation, or what Marx (1990) called the "automatic mechanism" enables the overcoming of a different barrier; it helps "reduce to a minimum the resistance offered by man, that obstinate yet elastic natural barrier" (527). Even if we do not go so far as to consider the possibility of a capitalism without humans, the notion of synthetic automation should remind us that capital is not "exclusively a reorganisation of human production" but also a trajectory towards a "radically new, alien way of production" (Krašovec 2018). The needs of capital are alien to humans and only coincide with them accidentally. In a striking and horrific passage, Tony Smith (2009) puts it admirably: capital is a "higher-order alien power operating at the level of society as a whole. It systematically selects for human ends compatible with its end, 'the self-valorization of value', and systematically represses all human ends that are not compatible with this non-human end" (123). At this point, we can only speculate on what new operations of selection and repression might be provided to capital by more mature forms of synthetic automation.

Conclusion

The goal throughout this book has been to determine how well theory maps onto the real world. I was tempted to dub my approach something admirably promethean like "communist realism", but that term has already been used by Jimmy Wu (2019) to refer to a future hegemonic order for scientific research in a communist society, a successor to the myopia of contemporary "capitalist realism" (Fisher 2009). I think it more appropriate that the argument advanced in this book be taken as something more like a communist pessimism. While Wu's realism imagines a set of constraints on science, directing it towards socially and planetarily beneficial ends, communist pessimism seeks to uncover contemporary constraints on elaborating the communist prospect. It is thus arrayed against the resolute optimism of *post-operaismo*, for which most or all constraints on the communist prospect are now immanent to the multitude itself and can therefore be eliminated if only a sufficient level of self-valorization can be achieved. That being said, this book is not intended to argue for the technologically determined destiny of humanity as subjugation to cybernetic capital; it is not fatalism. But it refuses any interpretations of the technological milieu of contemporary capital which attribute too little power to capital and too much to labour.

AI professor and entrepreneur Kai-Fu Lee (2018) asserts that "if left unchecked, AI will throw gasoline on the socioeconomic fires" (161). I agree. But, as the reader might have already noticed, this book has not discussed at all how AI might be, as Lee puts it, "checked". On such grounds, this book might be accused of lacking in constructive content by which critical research and activism concerning AI might proceed. That is intentional. Somehow "checking" AI means very little if it does not include recognition of how AI is fundamentally tied up with the recursive technological process that is capital. In other words, "checking" AI in any substantial sense means no less than confronting capital's nihilistic drive to valorization. How to do so is a project certainly beyond the means of one volume, or one person. This book is merely intended to provide a sober sketch of the contemporary technological milieu while assessing a popular theoretical framework. Yet, as this book wraps up, it is worth looking briefly at a few ways in which AI capital might be confronted by labour.

Data scientists and machine learning engineers working in the AI industry occupy positions of considerable power within cybernetic capitalism. If they follow up on the early stirrings of labour activism and organizing in tech work discussed in Chapter 5, it is impossible to predict what might happen. Indeed, it might be argued that those agitations are signs of the new autonomy which I have argued against in this book. Let us hope so. If AI becomes a ubiquitous technology, then the positions occupied by AI workers within capital could become even more powerful. Workers who service and control infrastructure can wield considerable social power by obstructing key moments of the valorization process (Bernes 2013; Frase 2015). If AI takes on infrastructural ubiquity, then AI workers could hold the controls to key functions and sites of the cybernetic value chain (at least until such work is automated).

Another possibility for checking the advance of AI capital is suggested by Gray and Suri's paradox of automation's last mile or "the ever-moving frontier between what machines can and can't solve" (2019, 206). Ghost workers are employed to complete key tasks in AI production that machines, for the moment, cannot. When someone figures out how to automate the tasks they are set to, they are shuttled on to the next currently un-automatable task. However, during that window, before they are replaced, ghost workers are critical to the functioning of AI systems and are therefore essential to the valorization processes of the capitals that employ them. Although their leverage is mitigated by their precarious, platformized employment situation, as long as AI production relies on them, ghost workers will also occupy a potentially strategic position in the AI industry (again, until such work is automated). However, one might reasonably argue that expecting only workers in the AI industry to contest the capitalist use of AI is misguided. One might further insist that what is needed is an active relationship to AI capital by labour as such. In the last words of this book, I want to consider this by returning, perhaps unexpectedly, to the eminent *post-operaismo* thinker Negri.

Specifically, I want to consider a concept I have critiqued throughout this book, the self-valorization of labour. More accurately, I want to consider the dark inverse of self-valorization which *post-operaismo* tends not to refer to. Before the emergence of *post-operaismo*, the young Negri described self-valorization as the positive aspect of a negative power he called sabotage. While self-valorization refers to labour's ability to technologically bootstrap new capacities, sabotage refers to its ability to "destructure capital" (Negri 1979). Every moment of self-valorization is simultaneously an act of sabotage and vice-versa. Sabotage, in this sense, means not only throwing a wrench in the gears. It refers more generally to "confront[ing]—in a destructive manner—capital's powers of stabilization" (Negri 1979). All new capacities developed by labour are immediately offensive acts of sabotage.

This formulation has a wonderful symmetry, but Negri's proposed identity between self-valorization and sabotage can only obtain if self-valorization generates capacities, which capital in fact cannot subsume under the value-form, and which, by exceeding capital's constraints, in fact constitute a destabilizing force. If the value-form is mutable and applicable to highly variable circumstances, including new technological capacities of labour, this identity cannot be assumed to hold generally. I have held that it does not hold in the particular context of the AI industry, at least. But even if the identity of the two concepts does not hold, the concept of sabotage remains a valuable one. Divorced from its positive double self-valorization and autonomous cyborg immaterial labour, this solitary conception of sabotage is perhaps more vulgar and perhaps more akin to simply throwing a wrench in the gears. But even this vulgar notion of sabotage still requires delineating capital's contemporary mechanisms for stabilization, which include the technologies underpinning new waves of subsumption. In Matteo Pasquinelli's (2010) words, one needs to learn anew for each concrete situation the "grammar of sabotage" (679). The proliferation of machine learning entails a new reliance of capital on big data and its requisite computational infrastructure. What might sabotage mean in this context? Some ideas are provided by technical problems discussed in AI research. Such problems point out areas of instability within the technology and thus also for applications built on its basis. As AI is increasingly integrated into business processes, technical problems become points of weakness for capital. We can consider just one.

Law scholar Jonathan Zittrain (2019) asserts that the use of ML incurs "intellectual debt" because "most machine-learning models cannot offer reasons for their ongoing judgments [and] there is no way to tell when they've misfired if one doesn't already have an independent judgment about the answers they provide". If ML is used to produce models automatically, perhaps with end-to-end AutoML tools, such intellectual debt will presumably balloon. Zittrain (2019) warns that widespread use of ML will result in a "world of knowledge without understanding … a world without discernible cause and effect" in which humans rely on machines to interpret and guide them through an incomprehensible world. In this scenario, users will be subject to intellectual debt. But so will the companies who produce AI; perhaps they will bear the brunt of it. They may not care as long as valorization continues apace. But as capital reconfigures itself around occult machine logics, it inadvertently assembles a new grammar of sabotage. As Zittrain (2019) notes, ML models can be intentionally deceived in a multitude of ways "by someone who knows just what kind of data to feed into that system" (Zittrain 2019). If immaterial labour theory and the notion of the self-valorization of labour do not provide us with leverage on contemporary cybernetic capital, let us endeavour to know how a capital increasingly reliant on the automation of automation might be practically destructured.

Bibliography

Benanav, Aaron. 2019a. Automation and the Future of Work—I. *New Left Review* 119 (September–October), 5–38.

Benanav, Aaron. 2019b. Automation and the Future of Work—II. *New Left Review* 120 (November–December), 117–146.

Bernes, Jasper. 2013. Logistics, Counterlogistics and the Communist Prospect. *Endnotes* 3. https://endnotes.org.uk/issues/3/en/jasper-bernes-logisticscounterlogistics-and-the-communist-prospect.

Blit, Joel. 2020. Automation and Reallocation: Will COVID-19 Usher in the Future of Work? *Canadian Public Policy* 46 (S2): S192–S202.

Bonefeld, Werner. 2014. *Critical Theory and the Critique of Political Economy: On Subversion and Negative Reason*. New York: Bloomsbury.

Brown, Nathan. 2016. Avoiding Communism: A Critique of Nick Srnicek and Alex Williams' Inventing the Future (Verso, 2015). *Parrhesia* 25: 155–171.

CBS News. 2020. Big Tech Companies Fully Recovered from Pandemic, Report Record Earnings. https://www.cbsnews.com/news/google-apple-amazon-facebook-twitter-big-tech-record-earnings-q3-2020/.

Endnotes. 2010. Misery and Debt: On the Logic and History of Surplus Populations and Surplus Capital. *Endnotes* 2. https://endnotes.org.uk/issues/2/en/endnotes-misery-and-debt.

Fisher, Mark. 2009. *Capitalist Realism: Is There no Alternative?* London: Zero Books.

Frase, Peter. 2015. Ours to Master. *Jacobin*. https://jacobinmag.com/2015/03/automation-frase-robots.

Gardiner, Michael. 2016. Critique of Accelerationism. *Theory, Culture & Society* 34 (1): 29–52.

Gray, Mary L., and Siddharth Suri. 2019. *Ghost Work: How to Stop Silicon Valley from Building a New Global Underclass*. San Francisco, CA: HMH Books.

Heinrich, Michael. 2012. *An Introduction to the Three Volumes of Karl Marx's Capital*. New York: Monthly Review Press.

Isaac, Mike. 2020. The Economy is Reeling. The Tech Giants Spy Opportunity. *The New York Times*, June 13. https://www.nytimes.com/2020/06/13/technology/facebook-amazon-apple-google-microsoft-tech-pandemic-opportunity.html?fbclid=IwAR22gRDDh8jdvRB_zX05UGZ3l1AMOoBSYzunaFLWnPfyMcZ9fNa36m0iw0Q.

Krašovec, Primož. 2018. The Alien Capital. *Vast Abrupt*. https://vastabrupt.com/2018/07/11/alien-capital/.

Lee, Kai-Fu. 2018. *AI Superpowers: China, Silicon Valley, and the New World Order*. New York: Houghton Mifflin Harcourt.

Leeson, Sarah. 2020. The Economics of a Global Emergency. *WGBH*, April 17. https://www.wgbh.org/news/national-news/2020/04/17/the-economics-of-a-global-emergency.

Lu, Joanne. 2020. World Bank: Recession is the Deepest in Decades. *NPR*, June 12. https://www.npr.org/sections/goatsandsoda/2020/06/12/873065968/world-bank-recession-is-the-deepest-in-decades.

Mackenzie, Adrian. 2017. *Machine Learners: Archaeology of a Data Practice*. Cambridge: MIT Press.

Marx, Karl. 1990. *Capital*, vol. 1. New York: Penguin.

MIT Technology Review Insights. 2020. Covid-19 and the Workforce. *MIT Technology Review*.

Negri, Antonio. 1979. Capitalist Domination and Working-Class Sabotage. Online at: https://antonionegriinenglish.files.wordpress.com/2010/08/capitalist-domination-and-working-class-sabotage.pdf.

Ng, Andrew. 2017. *Twitter Post*, May 1. https://twitter.com/AndrewYNg/status/859106360662806529.

Pasquinelli, Matteo. 2010. The Ideology of Free Culture and the Grammar of Sabotage. *Policy Futures in Education* 8 (6): 671–682.

Pitts, Frederick Harry. 2018. *Critiquing Capitalism Today: New Ways to Read Marx*. London: Palgrave Macmillan.

Smith, Tony. 2009. The Chapters on Machinery in the 1861–63 Manuscripts. In *Re-reading Marx: New Perspectives After the, Critical*, ed. Riccardo Bellofiore and Robert Fineschi, 112–127. London: Palgrave Macmillan.

Srnicek, Nick, and Alex Williams. 2015. *Inventing the Future: Postcapitalism and a World Without Work*. London: Verso.

Timpanaro, Sebastiano. 1975. *On Materialism*. London: NLB.

Traverso, Enzo. 2017. *Left-Wing Melancholia: Marxism, History, and Memory*. New York: Columbia University Press.

Wakabayashi, Daisuke, Karen Weise, Jack Nicas and Mike Isaac. 2020. The Economy is in Record Decline, but not for the Tech Giants. *The New York Times*, July 30. https://www.nytimes.com/2020/07/30/technology/tech-company-earnings-amazon-apple-facebook-google.html. Columbia University Press.

Williams, Alex, and Nick Srnicek. 2014. "#accelerate: Manifesto for an Accelerationist Politics. In *#accelerate: The Accelerationist Reader*, ed. Robin Mackay and Arven Avanessian. Falmouth: Urbanomic.

Wu, Jimmy. 2019. Optimize What? *Commune*, March 15, 2019. https://communemag.com/optimize-what/. Columbia University Press.

Zittrain, Jonathan. 2019. The Hidden Costs of Automated Thinking. *The New Yorker*, July 23. https://www.newyorker.com/tech/annals-of-technology/the-hidden-costs-of-automated-thinking.

Index

J. Steinhoff, *Automation and Autonomy*, Marx, Engels, and Marxisms, https://doi.org/10.1007/978-3-030-71689-9

W

The manufacturer's authorised representative in the EU is Springer Nature Customer Service Centre GmbH, Europaplatz 3, 69115 Heidelberg, Germany. If you have any concerns regarding our products, please contact ProductSafety@springernature.com

Printed and bound by CPI Group (UK) Ltd, Croydon, CR0 4YY
30/09/2026
02225311-0009